Living Liberia:
Laughter, Love & Folly

Living Liberia

Laughter, Love & Folly

BY ROBERT CHERRY

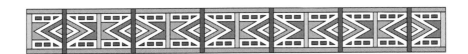

Living Liberia: Laughter, Love & Folly

Front cover (from the top): Rebecca Bormentar, Mary Pratt, Arthur Wonyou, Kamah Fendahn; and unknown dancers

Copyright © 2017 by Robert Cherry

ISBN: 978-0-9913864-5-1

Book Design by Cheryl Mirkin, CM Design
Photos © by Robert Cherry

First edition printed in the USA, 2017
Also available in Ebook

robertcherry2@aol.com
www.robertcherry.org

For Tado Jackson, my Liberian buddy;
and Bill Fickling, my American buddy.

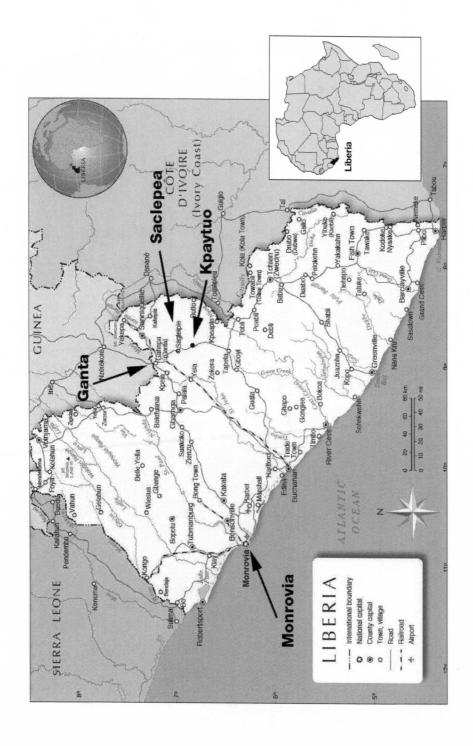

Contents

List of Characters and Their Ages in 1982 ◆ viii

Prologue ◆ xiii

Kpaytuo (chapters 1–8) ◆ 1

Saclepea (chapter 9) ◆ 73

Monrovia (chapters 10–17) ◆ 89

Kpaytuo (chapters 18–26) ◆ 129

Ganta (chapters 27–30) ◆ 195

Monrovia (chapters 31–39) ◆ 227

Kpaytuo (chapters 40–43) ◆ 275

Epilogue ◆ 294

Afterword ◆ 295

Acknowledgements ◆ 311

List of Characters
and Their Ages in 1982

1. **David and Maud Carson**: Missionaries in Saclepea, residents of Liberia for more than thirty-five years. He was seventy-one, she was sixty-nine.

2. **The Coopers**: A wealthy and powerful Americo-Liberian family who owned the sawmill outside of Kpaytuo in 1966. I knew three of the Coopers—Samuel B., the father, who was about sixty; and Ben and John, two of his sons, who were in their late-thirties.

3. **Alhagy Mansano Dabo**: A diamond and gold merchant from The Gambia in his mid-fifties, who didn't have a penny to his name.

4. **Samuel Z. Dahngbae**: Usually called Sammy: my houseboy and "Man Friday" during my Peace Corps years in Kpaytuo; after the coup of 1980, he enlisted in the Liberian Armed Forces for five years. He was approximately twenty-eight.

5. **Samuel K. Doe**: A twenty-eight-year-old master sergeant in the Liberian Armed Forces when he and sixteen other noncommissioned officers overthrew William R. Tolbert's government on April 12, 1980. A man of obvious talents, Doe became a Five-Star General and was awarded a doctorate within two years. Dr. Doe headed the People's Redemption Council, Liberia's ruling body.

6. **Kamah Fendahn**: My cook in Kpaytuo; by 1982, a resident of Monrovia, where, at age twenty-eight, she cleaned house for a well-off Liberian couple. She was the mother of three, with one on the way.

7. **Tado Jackson**: A member of the Inland Church of Liberia, he was my dearest friend in Kpaytuo. I rented Tado's home during my Peace Corps years—while he was away upgrading his education—and stayed with him and his family during my return trip. He was a forty-six-year-old farmer.

8. **Mary Jackson**: Tado's second wife and the mother of their four children. She was about thirty.

9. **Thomas Karngbeae**: One of my former students, himself later a teacher in Zuatuo, a village near Kpaytuo. He was about twenty-eight.

10. **Betty Leeleh**: The favorite of my former students; in 1982, in her late-twenties, she was a tenth grade student in Ganta. When she was fifteen, her father, desperate for money, had married her off to a much older man from whom she ran away.

11. **Scott Lewis**: The twenty-two-year-old Peace Corps Volunteer in Ganta with whom I stayed.

12. **Zoelay Retty Sonkarlay**: My girlfriend during part of the time I lived in Kpaytuo. In 1982 she was around thirty-six.

13. **Paul Steinwachs**: The Ganta Peace Corps Volunteer who guided me around the Ganta leprosarium. He was in his early-twenties.

14. **William R. Tolbert**: Was Liberia's president from 1971 until 1980, when he was murdered in a coup, age sixty-six.

15. **Paul Tuazama**: A major in the Liberian National Police Force. In conventional terms, he was the most successful of my former students. He was in his late-twenties.

16. **Old Man Tuazama**: Paul's father, an ornery town elder and an influential member of Kpaytuo's tiny Christian community. He was in his late-thirties when I was in the Peace Corps, so in his early-fifties by 1982.

17. **Otto "Arthur" Whern**: In 1966–67 the principal and a teacher at the Kpaytuo Elementary School, where I also taught. He was a rascal—a charming but worthless rascal.

18. **Arthur Wonyou**: Known as "Dr. Wonyou" since he became affiliated with the new clinic in Kpaytuo. He was one of only about 12 of my 120 former students residing in Kpaytuo in 1982.

19. **Sammy Wowah**: Owned the clinic in Kpaytuo, which Arthur Wonyou operated. In his mid-twenties, he lived and worked in Monrovia.

A Kpaytuo girl in 1982 carrying wood for her family's fire—alas the first of many such trips to and from the bush she (and her male and female counterparts) would make that day for wood and water.

"Why did I come to Africa? thought I.
Why! Who would not come to its twin brother
Hell itself
for all the beauty and charm of it!"

Mary Kingsley
Travels in West Africa, 1897

Walking down Kpaytuo's main—and only—road is Josiah Peye, my contemporary and friend, on his way to hunt game, circa 1967.

Prologue

Africa has a special place in my heart, for it was there, in the rain forest of Liberia, in a village called Kpaytuo, I spent my twenty-second and twenty-third years.

Liberia lies on the bulge of Africa's West Coast, slightly above the equator in the region once called, in a more Eurocentric age, "the white man's graveyard." Founded by former American slaves and free-born blacks in 1847, "the great object for forming these colonies being to provide a home for the dispersed and oppressed children of Africa," Liberia has always had a unique relationship with the United States: indeed, its capital, Monrovia, is named after President James Monroe.

When I lived there, Liberia was, in many respects, two countries: one was composed of the descendants of the approximately twenty thousand former American slaves and free-born blacks repatriated to Liberia from the United States in the nineteenth century. Known as America-Liberians, they dominated the political, social and cultural life of the country, even though they made up only about three to five percent of the population of one and a half million. The "other" Liberia—the one in which I lived and functioned—was made up of the indigenous tribal people, sixteen groups in all, speaking eleven dialects in a country the size of Tennessee.

From February 1966 to late December 1967 I lived in Kpaytuo, pronounced by most Westerners who can't duplicate the "kp" sound of the Gio dialect as "PAY-too-oh." I was the second non-African to call it home. The first was a Lebanese merchant who left when he realized he was not going to make his fortune selling onions, salt and bouillon cubes to the seven hundred barely literate residents of the village. Kpaytuo had no electricity or running water, no indoor toilets, no medical clinic, never mind a nurse or a doctor; and very little of anything else, except the cone-shaped mud and thatched huts in which people lived, six to ten to a hut.

Like the other villages in the country's interior, Kpaytuo had been carved and hacked out of the rain forest, the most dense and imposing in Africa, save possibly the great jungle in Zaire. In these remote hamlets and villages Liberia's indigenous tribal people practiced back-breaking subsistence agriculture, barely raising enough rice by this primitive and inefficient method to feed their large, extended families. Theirs was a conservative, communal life regulated by powerful secret societies, the *Poro* for the men, the *Sande* for the women—the violation of whose taboos, not that many years before I arrived, meant death. They worshipped their ancestors, whose spirits were reputed to reside in rocks and trees. They believed in the efficacy of witchcraft, permitted a man as many wives as he could afford, and were by Western standards promiscuous—although I was happy to overlook their trespasses, especially those committed by unattached tribal women, whom I found beautiful and alluring.

When I think of Liberia and Kpaytuo, the person who first comes to mind is my houseboy, Samuel Dahngbae. (I'm aware that the term "houseboy" smacks of nineteenth or mid-twentieth century colonialism, but in 1967 that was the name all of us, including Liberians, used to describe the position.)

Sammy was around thirteen years old when we met (and I was twenty-two). I estimate his age, for birth and death records were not kept in a village like Kpaytuo nor by the central government. Samuel is hardly a Gio name—Gio being a dialect *and* the name of a tribe. Gaylah, which means "the man who lives on the hill," or Sueme, which means "son of the best hunter," are Gio names. But like most young Liberians of his generation, when he entered school Sammy selected a Western or *kwi* name, this to appear modern. (*Kwi* is the term the Gio people use to signify an educated person or the modern world and its practitioners. It comes from *kwipoo*, the Gio word for a white person.)

It was not uncommon for Liberian schoolchildren to change their Western names frequently, and for a few weeks Sammy announced that his name was Augustus. I was grateful he didn't call himself "Pencil" or "Saturday," the names chosen by two of his friends. All the children in Kpaytuo had tribal names, but most of the children also selected Western names: the most popular being the Biblical names Mary, Esther and

Rebecca among the girls, and Peter, Joshua, Paul and Samuel among the boys.

Sammy was short, wiry, muscular and pitch black. Although he was around thirteen, he was in the second grade. That had nothing to do with brains, for he was clever. In the mid-1960s, all too many of Africa's children entered school around age twelve, if not later. (Sadly, this is still the pattern for many in the twenty-first century.) Tribal Liberian parents, subsistence farmers who managed to get through life without this new thing called "book," saw no urgency for their children, who were needed to perform domestic chores in the village proper and on the families' nearby small farms, to attend school. Consequently many parents refused to allow their children, especially their daughters, to attend school until age eleven to thirteen (when their young siblings took over their responsibilities on the farm).

Sammy's official job was fetching water for me from the well in our quarter of the village. Four or five times a day during the dry season, which lasts roughly from December to March, he walked to the well and returned thirty minutes later with a bucket full of water expertly balanced on his head. Aside from enabling the Liberians to carry loads of up to fifty pounds as adults, balancing endless buckets of water and bundles of firewood on their heads as children gives them stately bearing, perfect posture, and for the women, a sensual gait. I paid Sammy $5 a month for his labors, a princely sum for a boy his age in a country where the annual average per capita income was about $300.

Helping Sammy run my household was Kamah Fendahn, a shy, sweet-tempered girl of about fourteen who cooked for me. She chose the *kwi* name Anna, but since her country name was so lovely, I always called her Kamah. The third member of the household staff was Peter Menlae, a fifteen-year-old student who, after school once a week or thereabout, washed my clothes in a nearby stream. Once they were dry, Peter pressed them exquisitely with an iron filled with hot charcoal. But it was Sammy, younger than Peter and about the same age as Kamah, who ran the show.

Sammy was with me from 6:30 A.M., when with a soft tap on my bedroom door and the phrase "Teacher, it can be time" he woke me, until 8:00 in the evening, when he (and Kamah) returned to their families' huts for the night. I taught him during the morning. After school, and after he had returned from fetching water, he helped me dispense medicine, an antiseptic powder to treat foot and ankle infections, to which the tribal children were prone from often going shoeless—usually the poorest or the youngest—or wearing only cheap, flimsy, plastic flip-flops. Eventually I taught him how to clean and dress wounds and infections, and he and a friend, Samuel Gweh, relieved me, except in the most serious cases, of this task.

Liberia's official language was English, the mother tongue of the Americo-Liberians, who would not be caught dead speaking one of the tribal dialects. English is the language of government and commerce and is also used for situations as commonplace as arguing over a bus seat in Monrovia. Most of the tribal people, aside from their native

The author, 23, and my household staff, Kamah Fendahn, about 14, and Sammy Dahngbae, about 13, circa 1967. Kamah cooked and Sammy fetched water from the well.

dialect, spoke a lilting, colorful Pidgin English often adding the sound of "oh" to the last word in a sentence.

"Teacher Cherry, the sun, he coming to sleep soon-oh" was the poetic way Sammy described the setting sun. "A fork is a spoon with teeth," he once explained to me. He called my kerosene-powered refrigerator "the machine that cooks ice." And like all the children in Kpaytuo, he called the eraser on a pencil the "pencil's nose" and described a flat tire as "the car's foot is broken."

It was Sammy who was always vigilant in spotting a freshly killed antelope, a hindquarter of which I would buy from a hunter, once I—with Sammy interpreting—had negotiated the price. (Though I picked up a smattering of words, I did not speak Gio.) Sammy cut the meat into chunks, which we stored in the freezer of my kerosene refrigerator, and each night Sammy, Kamah and I ate rice and meat for dinner.

Day and night tribal children—many of them Sammy's age—congregated in the front room of my house, which Liberians called "the piazza." They joked or sang or silently sat on the floor (there were never enough chairs) and looked at the pictures in American magazines, the photographs in which astounded and fascinated them. When I was not present, everyone knew Sammy was in charge.

Sammy, like most Liberians, believed in the supernatural, and in the power of totems, incantations, witches, and most of all in the medicine man, called in Liberia a *Zo*. There was a little man named Duna who lived in our village, and as a result of an illness or injury, he waddled like a duck. Sammy spoke of Duna with reverence and used to tell me, "When that old man dies, we all die."

"How do you know Duna can be a powerful medicine man?" I would ask Sammy.

"Look at the fine, young wives that ugly, old man has," Sammy answered. "Look at his fine clothes and so-so big farm." How but through "medicine," Sammy contended, had Duna acquired these luxuries? And how could I, who knew "American book," be so dense as to fail to see the obvious?

While I doubted Duna's powers, the Liberians did not. People in Kpaytuo and from nearby villages and towns flocked to Duna's hut. A young man wishing to win a young woman's fancy asked Duna to concoct a potion for the young man to rub on his body, presumably making him irresistible to the young woman; someone setting off to prospect for diamonds in the Nimba mountains paid Duna for "medicine" to increase his chances of striking it rich; and if you wanted to bewitch a greedy relative, Duna was the man to see.

Sammy was well versed in tribal lore. He liked to display his knowledge and I drew upon it to my delight and edification. His mother had not been able to conceive, hence the *Zo* ordered the family to refrain from eating bullfrogs. They did. Sure enough, Sammy's mother conceived soon thereafter. Thus he and the rest of his family, out of respect, were forbidden from eating bullfrogs (not that I was ever thinking of asking Kamah to prepare any for our dinner). Sammy's family also was forbidden from eating snails. His grandfather's sister died while she was away from the village, in the bush. That same day a line of snails materialized, leading from the village into the bush. The villagers, ever alert to such phenomena, followed the line of snails, which led them to the dead woman's body. To honor the snails for leading them to the body—which otherwise they might never have discovered—Sammy's family did not eat them.

One day an old man, in tattered clothes and obviously down on his luck, came to my house to ask for a favor. As was the tribal custom in such situations, the supplicant brought a gift, in this instance a mangy, unhealthy looking chicken. The old man stated his case, which Sammy translated; but while the man spoke Sammy and I avoided making eye contact, lest we burst out in laughter over the man's well-intentioned but pitiful offering. I'm sure I granted the man's wish—exactly what it was I don't remember. Yes, Sammy and I were disrespectful, but it was a funny moment, one of many he and I shared.

Sammy had a devilish sense of humor and a cackling, infectious laugh. Everyone, regardless of age or position, took to him. He considered himself a Christian, although he had never been baptized. He liked to listen to the Western-born missionaries from a nearby town and their Liberian converts recite Biblical tales, and he loved to look at illustrated Biblical storybooks; the depiction of the bearded patriarchs from the Old Testament, with their colorful robes, fascinated him, reminding him of powerful old tribal chiefs.

Liberians eat rice every meal, hot or cold, day or night, laced with enough pepper in the sauce to blow the top off of a volcano. Here are four Kpaytuo girls, circa 1967, beating rice stalks in mortars fashioned from a tree trunk.

Sammy and Kamah ate dinner with me almost every night. Sammy said a Christian prayer before the meal, while Kamah and I abstained. One evening as Sammy prayed, his eyes closed and head bowed, Kamah reached across the table, took Sammy's plate of rice, and hid it on her lap. When Sammy opened his eyes, momentarily stunned to find his plate gone, he said to Kamah, who was on the verge of bursting out laughing, "You will not be smiling so when Jesus reaches Lowyee." Lowyee was the village before Kpaytuo on the road from the capital into the interior. Sammy envisioned Jesus bringing salvation to each village in Liberia, beginning, of course, in Monrovia, the head and heart of the country, and traveling up the only road into the interior. No doubt he expected Jesus to do likewise in neighboring Sierra Leone and the Ivory Coast, and in Mali, Ghana, Nigeria et al., and once finished with every hamlet, village, town and city in Africa, moving on to the rest of the world, of whose existence he had only the foggiest notion, save for that magical land America, from which rich white people, who knew book, came.

❖   ❖   ❖

At twenty-one I sought to right the world's wrongs. I also, not incidentally, wanted to see foreign shores and to experience foreign cultures, so I joined the Peace Corps. Why were young, liberal arts graduates from American colleges, most of us, like myself, without teaching degrees, sent to Liberia to teach? Because the Liberian government had requested us, as there were insufficient numbers of qualified Liberians to do the job. Most Liberian teachers, especially in the interior, had the equivalent of about a ninth-grade American education, if that. And teachers were desperately needed: ninety percent of the tribal population was illiterate.

When I arrived in Kpaytuo from Philadelphia in February 1966 as a freshly-minted Peace Corps Volunteer (PCV)—after a two-month crash course in teaching—I found the school had no chairs or desks, few books (those we had were outdated American textbooks with bucolic scenes of Vermont), no blackboard, until we fashioned one by painting a piece of insulating cardboard black; and no paper, chalk, pens or pencils. We collected 5¢ from each student and commissioned the village carpenter to build benches, as otherwise the students would have had no place to sit. In the time I lived and taught in Kpaytuo, the village received nothing from the Liberian Department of Education, except the principal—who also taught—and another teacher, both, in my opinion, dubious contributions to the educational program.

Although we were supposed to hold school five days a week, I was happy if we managed to get in four: no country in the world, I would wager, has more national holidays than Liberia. And when there wasn't a legitimate holiday, the principal, a cad named Otto Whern, thought nothing of making one up. Then there were the numerous days when either the principal or the other teacher was absent, often to defend himself in an adultery suit; or they had traveled to the county head-

The author making a point to one of my students, Peter Lankah, a gentle and sweet-natured young man. He was the goalie on the village's soccer team.

quarters, there to seek, mostly without success, that month's or the previous month's pay. Their salaries on such occasions had been embezzled by one of their superiors; if not that, then the government had been unable to make its payroll.

Besides these man-made disasters, there were natural impediments: we couldn't hold school regularly during the rainy season, roughly from April to November, because of copious rain—about 120 inches a year—and no one could walk to school without being soaked.

On the mornings when school was in session, it began around 7:30 A.M. I say "around," for I was the only person in the village with a working timepiece, and after six months in Liberia's humidity and heat, my watch, like everything else in the country, worked irregularly. (The principal owned a battery-operated radio, which broadcast the hour, but he was no stickler for starting on time.) We all stood at attention in the dirt compound in front of the school, and the hundred and twenty or so students pledged allegiance to the Liberian flag. God help the poor villager, on his way to his farm, who, on a few occasions, failed to stop walking and stand at attention during flag raising. The principal and a few of the more obnoxious older schoolchildren considered this a serious affront to the national honor. The principal seized on the moment for a demagogic sermon on the importance of national pride, and if he needed money for palm wine, often fined the farmer.

Every day after the flag was raised, the principal turned to me and sighed, "Ah, Life, Mr. Cherry. Ah, Life."

I taught 30 first and second graders, who ranged in age from eight to sixteen, from 8:00 A.M. to 10:00 A.M. in one small room, following which we had recess until 10:30 A.M. Then I taught for one hour each the third and fourth graders, ages around ten to twenty. By 12:30 P.M. the tropical sun was too strong to endure, especially under an uninsulated corrugated metal roof, and the school day ended. The students dispersed, usually to help their families around the home or farm.

I instructed my students, whose mother tongue was the Gio dialect, how to read, print, write and speak English better. Most were the first members of their families to attend school. An American friend of mine marvels that there are men and women in Liberia who may pronounce some words in English—like "water," "gasoline" and "no"—with a Philadelphia accent. (Whether he thinks this is good or bad he has never said.)

As is true for other teachers in any place or circumstance, on many days for me teaching in Liberia was beyond the scope of the most dedicated and talented educator—not that I placed myself in that category. But then there were the frequent days when I saw my students' desire, against steep odds, to learn; and the days when they "got" my point; and the days when they were exposed to a story for the first time and enjoyed it. On those days, teaching was the most wonderful job in the world.

There were also moments of unforgettable pathos. I remember one story we read from an American textbook in which the protagonists were two sisters who slept in bunkbeds in their own room. It was inconceivable to my students that children could live so well, having their own beds and a room. For in the homes of my students, children slept on the ground and adults on a mound of hardened dirt, in both cases on mats woven from palm fronds for a "mattress," six to ten people to a smoky one-room hut. There was also the day in my fourth grade class when we were reading a story from another old American textbook about a boy and his horse. The horse lived in a big, clean, white barn, overflowing with bales of neatly-stacked hay. There was a picture of the horse asleep, covered by a pretty red blanket. After looking at the barn and the horse and the pretty red blanket, one of my students said, without rancor, "Horses in America live better than Africans."

And then there was the school's principal, Otto Whern, who had few administrative duties, so his main job was teaching. He and the other Liberian teacher worked in a recently built rectangular shed, sixty feet long and thirty feet wide, adjacent to the main "school"—the principal at one end of the mud-walled room, his Liberian colleague at the other. One taught kindergarten, the other history, science and mathematics to grades one through four. They often switched or combined their classes. We had no history, science or mathematics books, and the principal and the other teacher knew little about the subjects, so theirs was a formidable task. Making matters worse, both were ill trained, poorly motivated, lazy and venal. On the rare occasions when they were actually present and conducting classes (one act did not necessarily follow the other), they taught and required the students to sing hymns; not that the teachers were pious: it was the easiest way to pass the time.

◆ ◆ ◆

Liberia was the first sovereign black republic in Africa, and after Haiti, the second in the world. When the European powers divvied up Africa in the nineteenth century, the heyday of European colonialism, both Britain and France desired, and eventually secured, small parts of Liberia. But somehow the tiny, weak, isolated and impoverished black republic survived, an accomplishment for which the Americo-Liberians deserve credit. However, Liberia's indigenous people paid a price for Liberia's survival as an independent country. The ruling Americo-Liberians cut off the hinterlands from European commercial, missionary and other influences during much of the nineteenth century,

That quintessential scene of Liberian life circa 1967: females, young or old, cooking rice—in this case my students after school, with their million-dollar smiles.

limiting foreign commerce to the coastal ports, where the freed slaves had settled and their descendants lived and ruled. No surprise that in 1906 the Africanist Sir Harry Hamilton Johnston called the interior of Liberia "the least known part of Africa."

By the late 1960s, about twenty Americo-Liberian families ruled Liberia, and through intermarriage perpetuated their reign. Well into the 1970s there were two sets of laws in the country, one for the approximately thirty thousand Americo-Liberians, who were referred to in court and law as "civilized"; and one for the million-plus indigenous tribal population, who were referred to as "aborigines."

What the Americo-Liberians did not control was the economic life of the country. That was controlled by Europeans and Americans who ran the few big corporations in Liberia (such as Firestone rubber and several mining companies that extracted iron ore); and at the wholesale and retail level by a few thousand Lebanese businessmen; and finally on the lowest rungs of the commercial ladder, by a smattering of Africans, ironically most of whom were not even Liberians, but members of the Mandingo tribe from nearby West African countries.

◆   ◆   ◆

The day arrived when my assignment was over and, sadly to be sure, I left Liberia. I corresponded with Sammy, telling him about my life: that I had become, in turn, a teacher in Philadelphia, my hometown, and then a journalist in Phoenix and New York City. He reported on events in Kpaytuo: who was attending school and who was not (as the years passed, more of the latter than the former); which of my former female students were pregnant or mothers (within a few years, literally every one); about the progress of the new school being constructed in Kpaytuo; and, best of all, which of my friends in Kpaytuo sent their regards.

Given the nature of the Liberian postal system—dreadful in the capital city, nonexistent at that time in the interior—and the nature of life in Liberia, getting letters to and receiving letters from the interior was difficult. (Forget about a package; about 30 percent got through.) It was common knowledge that postal employees, who might not have been paid for months, opened letters and packages from the United States, and sometimes stole the contents. So I was not surprised when, five years after my departure, I lost touch with Sammy and the few other Liberians with whom I had been corresponding.

But a few years later I met an ex-Liberian Peace Corps Volunteer who knew one Volunteer still in the country. That Volunteer was stationed in a village five miles from Kpaytuo. I wrote Sammy a letter, in care of the Volunteer, telling Sammy, among other things, that I hoped one day to return to Liberia.

My letter was delivered, for in August 1977 I received a response from him, an excerpt from which, with the punctuation intact, follows:

Father, please make your coming formal. I mean the actual date, time, month and year. I want to inform everybody so that we can all await your arrival. It would be a swell party. I beg you—please make it formal. Also, please tell me the type of soup [sauce] you want to eat that day. Maybe an African soup like cassava leaf, palm butter or potato green. Which one is good for you?

Everybody here is alright. Only that some of the people you ask for have drop from school because of hardship. Some moved to other places to obtain living. The hard cost of living here in Liberia cannot allow poor people to learn. I'm not even ready to tell you about myself. For example, the following persons are not going to school again. Andrew, Kamah, Peter Lankah, Moses Grant, etc. They all left school because there is no body to help them. For the girls, some are living with boy-friends and consider themselves married women. (smile)

Father, I have really been trying to talk to you through letter, but have always been a failure. I've been out of school for two years. I tried all my best without help (except from you) and stopped as far as the 10th grade. I did not spend the whole year in school that year. I was able to stay for only half semester. It was not easy then. I would have gone through high school and even to college by now, but poverty was another big trouble behind me. He would kill me if I didn't leave.

I wrote back, suggesting he attend the Booker Washington Institute, one of the two trade schools in Liberia and sent him some money. He responded in October 1977 with another letter, part of which follows:

Father, it was very nice again receiving your nice and encouraging letter. At this time I felt as if I had entered heaven. Not because I received money from you, but that you are too concern about my learning. You don't want me to suffer. You want me to become somebody in life. This is why I felt as if I had entered the kingdom of heaven.

I would prefer agriculture and electricity at the Booker Washington Institute. My first choice is electricity. This is what I'm doing presently. I am an electrician helper at my part-time job. I could stay to complete the job with my boss, but the job is not a permanent one and also my boss is a French man. Sometimes we talk through sign. So it is not easy for me to learn this job well. However, I have an idea about light. This is why I chose electricity. This is one idea.

Another idea is that if there is any way for me to come over, I will be happy. Maybe I can work with your father and learn business or go to any trade school in America. I am happy to learn in America.

xxvi

Usually when people leave Liberia and go to the United States to learn trade, when they come back, they can make heavy money. The respect is too great. They can assign car to you right away. This is why Liberian boys want to learn at the U.S. Maybe I will be one of those boys. (smile)

My mother extend her warmest greeting to the family. She says that if there was any way she would send some new rice. I say hello to your family too. I've stopped seeing you for a long time. So I would like for you to send me a picture. If mine is ready, I will send it.

I answered his letter and sent him a bank draft for $400, more than enough for one year's tuition at the Booker Washington Institute. No other letters arrived from him. I never knew if he received my letter or what had happened to him or my money.

Scant was the news—public or private—from Liberia over those years. Nevertheless, I followed keenly whatever was reported in newspapers and magazines. President William Vacanarat Shadrach Tubman, after twenty-eight years in power, died at seventy-five. He was succeeded by his vice president of nineteen years, William Tolbert, both of course Americo-Liberians. Then in 1980 the shock: President Tolbert was murdered in a coup. The world awoke to the news that the Americo-Liberians, creators of the first, and the oldest, one-party state in Africa, rulers of Liberia for *a hundred and thirty years*, had been toppled in hours. Liberia was now in the hands of young, noncommissioned tribal officers, few of whom had graduated from high school. Liberia's new masters called themselves the People's Redemption Council. Their leader was Samuel K. Doe, a twenty-eight-year-old master sergeant whose name and politics were unknown to his countrymen, let alone the world.

Nineteen eighty-one was the bleak year in which I lost my father— a good, kind, wise and gentle man. Soon afterwards, with expenses up and revenues down, I closed the weekly newspaper I had founded two years before in Philadelphia. Emotionally and physically drained, I needed change and rejuvenation. I knew just where to seek it.

But what would it be like returning to Liberia, especially when the country was ruled for the first time in its history by a military government, one that had come to power in a bloody coup? Fourteen years had elapsed since my departure from Kpaytuo. What was Kpaytuo like since the coup? My students were no longer twelve and eighteen years old, but men and women in their twenties and thirties, undoubtedly with families of their own. What kinds of adults had they become? I was no longer twenty-two years old, fresh from the university, come to Liberia to save its people. (Given the situation, God Himself wouldn't have set such an ambitious goal; nor did I after a few months in Liberia.) What kind of adult, at age thirty-nine, had *I* become? What were Sammy, my houseboy, and Kamah, my cook, up to and like as adults? And what about my favorite student, Betty Leeleh, whose father, desperate for money, had married her off at fifteen? Was my good friend Tado Jackson—along with my houseboy Sammy the Kpaytuo resident with whom I corresponded most frequently, if irregularly—still eking out a living growing peppers and cucumbers? Did Andrew Karma still smile all the time? And was Zoelay Retty Sonkarlay, my lover, still beautiful? Would I even find them? Which of my ex-students and friends still lived in Kpaytuo? Which of them were alive, never mind where?

On a clear day in February of 1982, I boarded a jet in New York bound for Liberia to find out.

KPAYTUO

A young girl returning from the well, the first of many 30-minute round-trips she and her counterparts, which included young boys, made daily. Balancing endless buckets of water on their heads as children gives Liberians as adults a stately bearing and perfect posture.

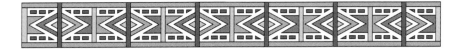

Chapter 1

I woke up excited if slightly anxious. Small wonder, for I was in Monrovia, the capital of Liberia, and on this day, after fourteen years, I was returning to Kpaytuo.

Upon my arrival back in the country, I inquired about Kpaytuo at the Peace Corps office in Monrovia. No one knew anything about it, except that no Peace Corps Volunteers were currently stationed there. Since I didn't know if Kpaytuo had become electrified in the intervening years, I wanted to start early in order to arrive before dark, the better to see and be seen by my friends. When I lived there, returning to

Tado Jackson's house, which the Peace Corps rented for me while he was away from the village upgrading his education. Cows, of which there were not many in Kpaytuo—too expensive for almost everyone—roamed freely.

3

the village in the dark had been a hassle: I was forced to stumble around my house looking for a flashlight or fishing about for matches to light the lanterns, which always seemed to need kerosene at these inopportune times; it was difficult to find anything to eat; and I was wary of entering my outhouse, being more likely in the night to disturb or even step on a cockroach, frog, spider or snake.

Knowing I'd always be welcomed to stay with his family and him, about five months before by letter I had informed Tado Jackson, my dearest Kpaytuo friend, that I planned on returning around Christmas. I ended up postponing my departure until mid-February. In any case, I never received a response from Tado and couldn't be sure he had received my letter. Thus I did not know where I was going to stay in Kpaytuo or with whom, though probably it would be in a hut or house without running water, a refrigerator, stove or indoor toilet. To prepare, I bought three tins of corned beef and three tins of sardines, a few packets of crackers—which in Monrovia humidity were stale the day they were unloaded at the port—salt, sugar, toilet paper, a flashlight (a must up-country), and a thermos that I filled with imported water.

Since I had spent the morning going from store to store searching out supplies, it was 12:30 P.M. by the time I arrived at the Nimba County Parking Station, from where I would secure transportation into the interior. By starting at that hour I was pushing my chances of arriving in Kpaytuo before nightfall. The prudent course would have been to delay my departure for a day, but as I wanted to sleep that night in Kpaytuo, I plunged ahead.

In my Peace Corps years the Nimba County Parking Station (Kpaytuo being in Nimba County, most populous of Liberia's then nine counties) was a dusty, vacant field. Whenever I approached it as a Volunteer, five taxi drivers had tried to wrestle my bag from my hand. The one who succeeded carried it, with me in pursuit, to his vehicle, where he tried to convince me that riding into the interior with him meant being transported, if not to Valhalla, then at the very least to my destination, promptly, courteously and safely. When I finally selected a driver, knowing full well he was neither responsible nor reliable, I waited until he had garnered enough other passengers, in a like manner, to fill his taxi. Then, and only then, did we depart. One usually waited hours in the torrid heat—ninety degrees and eighty to ninety percent or higher humidity—until the taxi of one's choice departed. There was also the matter, in those Peace Corps years, of dickering over the fare. Each passenger negotiated the best price he could, since the prices often fluctuated from driver to driver, especially for us whites, who were perceived, rightly enough, as immeasurably wealthier than the average Liberian. We were generally charged about ten percent more, for which we often received one of the more comfortable seats, usually in the front; the term "comfortable" was relative. (Following the Liberians' usage, I use "white" and "white man" or "white woman" interchangeably for a "Westerner," a "European" or an "American." Of course I'm aware that there are black Americans, many of whom prefer to be called African-American; and Asian and Hispanic Americans. But in the years of which I write, the aforementioned racial and ethnic groups were few and far between in Liberia, even scarcer in up-country Liberia. More on the subject, as it relates to black Americans, later in the story.)

Arriving at the Nimba Parking Station upon my return in 1982, I noticed, much to my surprise, that there was a system for securing passage into the interior. I entered a small shed, purchased a ticket (one never saw anything resembling a ticket in 1966–67), and received a receipt. My name was then entered in a log, proving to all the world I was a passenger, on a specified vehicle, bound for Ganta, beyond which I'd travel by bus the rest of the way.

And there was one fixed price, although I did suspect that I paid more for my load than a Liberian would have for a comparable load. Each vehicle was assigned a position in line, on a first-come, first-served basis. When the first vehicle in the line had the requisite number of passengers, then and only then could the next vehicle in line accept passengers. Of course there was no actual line: the taxis were parked all over the place. There were foul-ups and arguments (*palavers*, as arguments are known in Liberia and which are, I'd argue, the national pastime); and interminable delays, as both the drivers and passengers circumvented the regulations of the recently formed transportation union. But at least it was a beginning—a vast improvement over the old "system," if I may so abuse the word.

By the time we left the Nimba Parking Station it was 2:00 P.M.

Including the driver, there were eleven of us wedged into a Peugeot station wagon designed to seat eight; also our luggage, squashed together like the passengers.

◆   ◆   ◆

Monrovia to Kpaytuo is 205 miles, a journey that took between ten and fourteen hours when I lived there, depending on how often the vehicle broke down, whether the driver had bothered to bring along a spare tire and an operable jack (most vehicles had one or the other, but rarely both), how long the driver and/or passengers dallied at the villages and towns en route, how many and how long were the arguments that ensued between the passengers and the driver and among the passengers, and finally, and most crucially, the condition of the road.

One road, only a section of which was paved, penetrated the interior of Liberia from Monrovia to Kpaytuo, and that road had been completed in the 1940s. The paved section of it, when I lived there, extended 80 miles—from the capital to Totota, where, not coincidentally, President Tubman's farm (think of it as his Camp David) was located. During the rainy season, the extensive dirt section of the road, pounded by up to ten inches of rain a month and gutted by monstrous flatbed logging trucks, turned into a quagmire, making travel precarious and, at times, for hours or days, impossible. On many occasions the streams and creeks alongside the road overflowed. The news that an Italian company had in 1979 paved another eighty-eight miles of the road, the stretch from Totota to Ganta, was welcome, for it cut the tortuous journey from Monrovia to Kpaytuo, my Liberian home, by as much as half. (That gave Liberia, including the coastal area, about 500 miles of paved road, one of the lowest totals in Africa.)

Two-thirds of Liberia had originally been covered by dense, tropical forest—almost the entire country beyond the coastal plain, which runs about 30 miles inland. With time large strips of the jungle along the natural trade routes had been cleared. We sped through the rolling hills and the broad meadows of these secondary woodlands. But it was to the great forest, parts of which were still untouched and unmapped by humans, that I was heading.

We drove alongside the Firestone Rubber Plantation. As far as the eye could see were rubber trees—tidy rows of thin, fragile, striped trees, looking like thousands of zebra legs planted in the ground. Nineteen twenty-six was the year the Firestone Tire and Rubber Company, of Akron, Ohio, signed an agreement with the Liberian government, then as always desperate for cash. Firestone lent the Liberian government $5 million in exchange for which Firestone was granted a ninety-nine year lease on one million acres of land at six cents, then raised to fifty cents, an acre. On that land Firestone created the largest rubber plantation in the world. Rubber became Liberia's leading and just about only export crop, accounting in many of the pre-World War Two years for as much as ninety percent of Liberia's foreign earnings. What little social and economic development the government undertook in those years was made possible by the income generated by the Firestone operation. And after the Japanese conquered most of Southeast Asia's rubber plantations in World War Two, Firestone's rubber became one of the few sources of this crucial but scarce raw material available to the Allies: imagine tens of thousands of airplane and jeep tires, gas masks and life boats, all made from Liberian rubber. To gather it during the War, the United States government built an international airport outside of, and a deep water port in, Monrovia.

Given its long and ubiquitous presence in the country, it's easy to indict Firestone for exploiting the Liberian government and its citizens, paying the latter cheap wages and reaping large profits as a result of its agreement with the former. But until the 1950s, when iron ore became Liberia's most important industry, no institution, home-grown or foreign, was paying Liberians wages of any kind. It was Firestone that introduced the people to the cash economy. It was Firestone, far and away the largest employer in Liberia—with at one time 25,000 Liberians tapping rubber—that set the standard of wages throughout the country. And since the government was unwilling or unable to educate and train its healthy or take care of its sick citizens, it was left to Firestone from the 1930s to the 1960s to do so: and that it did, building housing and schools, even hospitals, for its workers and their families. To be sure, Firestone never has been a purely philanthropic organization: it came to Liberia to make money, and money it made. But in so

7

doing, Firestone became, inadvertently, a revolutionary force for change in modern Liberia.

◆　◆　◆

The hamlets, villages and small towns through which we passed were much as I remembered them, save that the people, with but few exceptions, no longer lived in circular huts with thatched roofs: they now preferred houses of mud-brick with A-frame roofs of corrugated zinc sheeting—the type of dwelling only a small percentage of the people in the interior had lived in fourteen years before, including me.

There being no structures other than homes in the village—no banks or hardware stores, no clothing or furniture shops, no drug or shoe stores, no government buildings, no signs, neon or otherwise—

A woman weaving a fishing net, sitting on a mat woven from palm fronds.

Julia Mah and her brother, circa 1966, returning to the village from the family farm at the end of the work day, rice and greens for that night's meal balanced on their heads.

the smaller villages of three hundred houses or fewer tend to appear rather similar, though by no means unattractive.

The scenes of daily life that flashed by were also as I remembered them: girls and women hauling loads of wood or buckets of water on their heads. Each wore a *lappa*, a long piece of colored cloth, formerly homemade, but now imported, wrapped around her body and tucked in under the armpit. Men in threadbare shorts, ragged T-shirts and plastic sandals were coming back from the small plots of land on which they raised rice, the staple of the Liberian diet. The men carried cutlasses, the machete-like tools with which they cut the bush. Old ladies sat in the shade of trees and under the eaves of houses, minding children and weaving mats or fishing nets from palm leaves. Scrawny chickens, goats and hogs and a few flaccid cows wandered about. And the glare of the sun, high in the sky, grilled everything and everyone beneath it. Onward we went, the luxuriant and thick green forest to our right and left. The day still hot, I felt, once again, the torpor of the tropics, the air, to quote the author Joseph Conrad, "warm, thick, heavy and sluggish."

About 20 miles from Ganta, the transfer point on the road to Kpaytuo, my luck ran out. The taxi lost speed and rolled to a stop. The car couldn't be out of gasoline—though the manner in which it gradually slowed to a halt suggested as much—because the driver had stopped for gas before we left Monrovia. (I could hardly have forgotten, given that it had taken about twenty-five minutes.) But I was giving the driver, an ill-tempered, devious member of the Mandingo tribe, too much credit. Rather than fill the tank, as we passengers had assumed, he had purchased only enough gas to go from Monrovia to Ganta—so he'd thought. He'd miscalculated, buying only enough gas to go from Monrovia to the point at which we now found ourselves, twenty miles short of Ganta. It was 4:00 P.M. I wanted to wring his neck. My chance of arriving in Kpaytuo before dark, slim though it had been when I set out, was now vanishing. Already hyper and anxious about my arrival, uncertain of what awaited me, I took my anxiety out on the poor driver, berating him for the delay.

Carrying an empty container for gas, the driver hopped a ride into Ganta with a fellow Mandingo. I stood by the roadside, hoping I too might hitch a ride into Ganta. But the few vehicles that passed were buses and taxis from Monrovia, all of them full of passengers. My fellow passengers, used to delays of this sort, sat quietly by the road. A few wandered off, probably in search of water. After marching up and down the road, every now and then kicking the gravel in frustration at my being there instead of that much closer to Kpaytuo, I eventually sat down and ate half the roasted chicken that I had bought the night before, as much to soothe my nerves as to assuage my hunger.

The driver returned in about an hour and a half, smiling no less, and said, "It is good to have friends," a reference to the ease with which he'd been able to hitch a ride to and from Ganta.

"It is better to have brains!" I said to him.

We arrived in Ganta at about 6:00 P.M., at least two hours from Kpaytuo. The paved road ends at Ganta, so the taxis from Monrovia go no farther into the interior—and knowing what the dirt road is like, who can blame them? A money bus was about to depart for Tappita, on

The ubiquitous transport in up-country Liberia, a money bus, at times about as comfortable as riding on an empty creek bed.

the way to which lies Kpaytuo. It was probably the last bus heading that day to Tappita.

Money buses (called mammy wagons in other parts of Africa) are like the small buses or jitneys seen on the streets of Atlantic City, New Jersey. They hold about twelve to sixteen passengers comfortably; but in up-country Liberia, with twenty to twenty-four souls and their bags and the occasional goat and the ever-present chickens routinely stuffed and wedged into them, the money bus experience was just a little bit more comfortable than riding on an ox-cart. I don't know why the Liberians called them "money buses" as opposed to buses; for the same reason, I suppose, they called a train "the real bus." In any case, it was by money bus that one traveled into and throughout the interior. Not everywhere, for there were still large areas of Liberia into which no road passed; if you wanted to reach remote villages in these areas, you trekked to them.

The money bus I found myself on that memorable day was typical of those I'd traveled on many times before in the interior: the shock absorbers were gone, the muffler shot, the front windshield cracked, the motor wheezing, the tires bald and wobbly. We passengers were jammed together on two unpadded boards that ran from behind the driver's seat to the back of the bus. The large glass windows on the sides of the vehicle had been removed, for they would have cracked the first time the bus traversed the unpaved, pitted and pock-marked dirt road. A tarpaulin was draped over both sides of the bus, though it would not adequately shield us from the clouds of dust raised by our own vehicle and all the money buses coming from the opposite direction. Liberia's rusty-red earth is laterite, a soil found in the tropics and rich in iron, from whence come the country's rich iron ore deposits. Iron oxides give the soil a reddish cast. Hours of traveling on a laterite road leaves every exposed pore and orifice of one's body filled with red dust.

Traveling on the road in a broken-down money bus without shock absorbers was, I remembered anew, like riding along an empty creek bed. And yet the scene up-country, as the sun began its descent, was beautiful: the red-tinted road weaved through the immense, emerald-green forest and the enchanting sky was powder blue, with streaks of purple beginning to appear. The country all around was peaceful, the labors of another day having come to an end as the people made their way on foot from their farms to their villages. There wasn't a factory or any other booming, polluting symbol of the modern, industrial world for hundreds of miles in any direction, though it seemed like thousands. The air was pristine, the atmosphere tranquil. All was radiant and quiet, save for the chirping birds. At that moment there was no other road in the world I wished to be on.

Though I expected to, I did not recognize any of the villages through which we passed. Even more to my surprise, when the bus sputtered into it, I did not recognize Saclepea, a town many times the size of Kpaytuo, that I used to visit often to buy supplies, and on the occasional weekends would visit to stay overnight with Peace Corps Volunteers stationed there.

It was dark as I began the last leg of my journey, the nine-mile stretch from Saclepea to Kpaytuo. Having no idea where I'd stay or with whom, I was playing Russian roulette, "Liberian style." I didn't know if I'd sleep that night in a bed or a hut; if my friend Tado Jackson were not in the village, I doubted it would be a bed. If I slept in a hut, it would be on a "country bed," which was a shelf of hardened mud constructed along the inside cylindrical walls and covered with hand-made mats. Nor, at that hour, was I likely to find food. It's not like there was a convenience store open; there would most likely be no store open, convenient or otherwise. Looking back on my state of mind, I'm surprised that I wasn't more anxious, even scared; but I was not. My adrenaline was surging at the thought of my "homecoming." And I looked on the brighter side of my situation: arriving in the dark, unannounced, after so many years away, added even more wonder and drama to my return.

We made two or three stops after Saclepea, and then stopped at a dark place like all those before it. The driver told me this was Kpaytuo.

"Where do you want to get down?" he asked.

I figured I'd get off at the "school" compound, near which my home had been located, but in the dark I couldn't see the compound—or much of anything else. It was obvious Kpaytuo still had no electricity.

So the bus stopped in front of a doorway from which emanated a dim glow. I walked around in front of the bus in order to see by the headlights how much money I was handing to the driver. I waited for the driver's assistant to remove the tarpaulin from the top and lower my bags. I then entered what turned out to be a small shop selling cane juice, lit by a hurricane lantern.

"Can Tado Jackson still live here?" I asked of the two small boys standing inside.

"Yes," one of them answered.

"Carry me to his house, yah?"

"I can do it-oh," answered the small boy, in that lilting Liberian accent I enjoy hearing. I left my bags in the shop.

As we began to cross the road I heard someone shout: "Cherry, is that you?" And before I answered, three figures, whom I could not make out in the dark, gathered round me. Amazingly, one was Tado Jackson, the very person I had asked for; and the other two were Arthur Wonyou, one of my ex-students, and Albert Kpeah, one of Tado's many relatives—all three old and dear friends. They had been standing and talking in front of Albert's house, which was only about twenty yards back from the road, when they had seen my figure illuminated by the bus's headlights. It was Albert, he proudly said, who'd guessed it was I. We hugged and shook hands. Standing there in the dark, in the middle of the one road that passes through Kpaytuo, I would have sworn it was a dream.

◆　◆　◆

We went to Tado's house—the very home the Peace Corps had rented for me when I lived in Kpaytuo (while Tado was away from the village upgrading his education). Since the home was built to Tado's size and budget, and he stood about five feet five inches, and I stood a smidgen under five feet eleven inches, instinctively I ducked as I passed through the doorway once more after an absence of fourteen years.

The first thing I did was walk about, even though with a small hurricane lantern I couldn't see much. I went into my old bedroom, tiny and insufferably hot. I walked about the center room, where my kitchen table once had stood; then to the back room, where Kamah had cooked and where we'd kept the kerosene refrigerator and kerosene stove, and the buckets of water for washing, cooking, cleaning and drinking. I saw no stove or refrigerator now. I made my way out back, once again bending my head at the doorway, and flashed the light upon the old outhouse and bathhouse, still standing—in what shape remained to be experienced.

Back inside I was greeted by a room alive with people: the news that I was back had already traveled. Some were former students of mine, others their brothers and cousins too young—or yet to be born—for me ever to have met. They had come to see the Peace Corps man.

A lantern was held up to a face, and collectively the group asked me if I knew the name that went with the face. I recognized most, for they were only older versions of the pre-pubescent and sixteen-year-old children I had taught. We smiled, laughed, and shook hands, snapping our middle fingers at the end of the handshake, as is the Liberian custom. To my knowledge Liberians are the only people who shake hands like this, and as they are friendly and exuberant, they shake hands with everyone, often with the same person three or four times in the course of an animated conversation. Some days it took me an hour to walk through Kpaytuo, which was only about two hundred yards long, so many people was I expected to greet and shake hands with. Day and night in Liberia one hears the clasping of hands followed by the snapping of middle fingers.

Andrew Karma, a former student who was about twenty-eight, asked if I remembered the time he, then about age thirteen, had climbed a sixty-foot palm tree for me.

"Of course," I said, adding that I also had the photograph of him doing it.

His cousin Johnson wondered if I remembered the night he came to my house—to the very room we were sitting in—to sing rice songs for me.

"Yes, I do," I said, "and I still have the tape."

Memba, another of the Karma clan, asked if I remembered the day a group of us had visited the farm where they pressed sugar cane for making "cane juice," a low-quality rum, and how afterward we'd sucked on the sugar cane in the fields. Indeed, I cherished the memory of that day and of those children, my houseboy Sammy's closest friends, whom

Andrew Karma, about 13 in 1966, who years later asked if I remembered the time he used a bamboo "ladder" to climb a palm tree for me; here is that photo, taken during one of many excursions into the bush I took with Andrew and Sammy Dahngbae and their buddies.

I have always thought of as African Tom Sawyers and Huckleberry Finns.

Ernest Yourmie recounted how his father had wanted to take him out of school, and how I'd persuaded the old man to let him remain. Peter Lankah, the goalie on the town's soccer team and the gentlest of people, who as a grown man stood before me with the build of an All-American halfback, wondered if I still liked to eat peanuts.

"Teacher Peanut," Andrew Karma sputtered in Gio, my nickname. Everyone laughed.

"Teacher, can you still throw the peanut in the air and catch it in your mouth?" Andrew asked.

"Yes, I can," I answered.

Someone said they'd heard I'd joined the army.

Not so, I said. "I can't like anyone telling me what to do," a declaration that made them laugh.

Knowing Liberians relish bravado, I was playing to the crowd. The bantering continued as all the while newcomers edged into the room, by now jammed with people. I was asked if I recognized the person who'd just entered, a man about my age. I didn't call out his name. Instead, by planting my feet firmly apart and raising my arms with one fist ready to jab and the other drawn close for protection, I recalled the many playful sessions of shadowboxing in which Edwin Siaway, the man in question, and I had engaged. The crowd howled. Edwin, Tado's nephew, looked thinner, but much the same.

Tado asked how my family was. My eyes filled with tears—not for the last time that night—and I could barely get the words out as I told him my mother, my "born Ma," as the Liberians say, was fine, but that my father had died six months before.

"Never mind, yah," they all said, employing the expression Liberians use to comfort.

Looking around the room, feeling as if I had never left, I said: "My friends in America wondered if the people of Kpaytuo can remember me."

We all laughed. After twenty minutes back in Kpaytuo, it was obvious that their memories of my stay were as vivid and pleasant as my own.

I asked if other Peace Corps Volunteers (mispronounced as "Peace Corpse" by many Liberians) had been stationed in Kpaytuo. Other than my replacements, a California couple who lived in Kpaytuo from 1968 to 1970, none had.

They kept apologizing that more of my old students were not in the village to greet me, for many of them lived and worked elsewhere. Almost everyone in a village the size of Kpaytuo is a blood relative. So the girls tend to cohabitate with or marry someone outside the village and usually live where their boyfriends or husbands live.

"When Sammy hears Bob Cherry is in Kpaytuo, he can come straight from Monrovia. For true-oh," said Andrew Karma.

Sammy, my houseboy and Man Friday, ever impetuous, had joined the army only days after the recent coup, when Master Sergeant (now Five-Star General *and* Doctor) Samuel K. Doe doubled the army's basic pay to $225 a month. The People's Redemption Council (PRC) may not have been composed of brilliant tacticians or theorists—one economist I met in the capital told me they couldn't distinguish economic policy from a Mercedes-Benz—but they were smart enough to keep the army, their power base, happy. I was sorry Sammy had joined the army. Knowing Liberia's army, I couldn't conceive of Sammy learning anything practical in it.

All the visitors who had crowded into the front room of Tado's home up to that point had been men and children. A woman then entered, Galonpoo, another of Tado's relatives, and one of my dearest friends. Galonpoo was my age, give or take a year, with a pretty, soft, round face and a smooth, creamy, caramel-colored complexion. *Poo* is Gio for the color white, thus this light-skinned woman was called Galonpoo. She and her husband and their children lived with her mother in a one-room round thatched-roofed hut. Theirs was the first hut I came to whenever I left my house to go to the village proper and in no other hut did I spend as much time. Galonpoo was still pretty but now hearty and hefty, by no means an unwelcome condition in Liberia. While I was conscious of weighing about ten pounds more than I had in 1968, and five more than I would have preferred, the Liberians were happy for my enlarged girth, signifying to them my good health and prosperity.

A few days before I had departed from Kpaytuo in January of 1968, Galonpoo's family had come to me with the news that she was "so-so sick." They had carried her to the *Zo*, whose country medicine had failed to improve her condition. They wanted to carry her to the Ganta Clinic, two hours away, but lacked money for transportation and the clinic, all of $5. No one in Kpaytuo had that kind of money on hand, except me. I gave them the money, and she was taken to the clinic, where it was discovered she had an ectopic pregnancy. Had she not received medical attention, she might well have hemorrhaged and died.

Next in walked Zoelay Retty Sonkarlay, who still looked, as best I could discern by the lantern light, remarkably attractive, if thinner. I was happy to see the years had been kind to my lover, whose age I estimate was thirty-six, give or take a year. There was much I wanted to ask of and say to Zoelay Retty, but with all those people in the room, I could only greet her and resign myself to waiting yet another day. Zoelay Retty and Galonpoo drifted outside, where, late though it was, Tado's wife, Mary, was preparing rice for me on the open fire.

As it was getting late, and my friends had to rise between five and six o'clock, they said goodnight, promising to visit when they returned from their farms the next evening.

Tado told me I'd be staying in my old bedroom, while he and his wife would sleep in the smaller room across the hall. No sooner had I shut the door, gotten into bed and turned off my flashlight than I thought I heard a rustling noise somewhere in the house and—even more upsetting—probably in my room. I heard the noise again, definitely in my room. Next I heard something like plastic tape cassette containers scraping along the floor. Then a gnawing sound, and something scurrying about. Tado's room is about twelve feet long by ten feet wide, so I lay no more than four feet from the spot from where it seemed the sounds came, though in dark I couldn't be certain. Was a bug or lizard trapped in the room? The problem with that scenario is that bugs and lizards do not make gnawing sounds. There was only one creature likely to make that sound in that place at that hour—a rat. Something fell to the floor, scaring the hell out of me. I jumped up in the bed, petrified, and unsure of what to do.

Tado and the rest of the household were asleep. I was reluctant to wake them. My flashlight lay on the floor next to the bed, but I was afraid to reach down for it, lest I brush against the prowling rat. I knew nothing of rat behavior, but it sounded as if this one was trying to eat its way into my Ghurka bag to get at the food contained therein. If I shined the light in its face I might scare it off; then again, maybe I'd arouse it to attack. I stabbed around in the dark, eventually locating my flashlight and one of my shoes—the latter a potential weapon. I shined the light around the room, even under the bed, but to no avail: I neither saw nor heard a thing. I turned the light off and tried to sleep, but within minutes I again heard the rustling and the disgusting sound of tiny feet scurrying around the room. I fished through my bag, the one the rat had been trying to eat into, and reluctantly took out a sleeping pill, fortunately a remedy to which I might turn about once every five years in the United States, and I swallowed it with the last of the cool water in my thermos. The devil with what was in the room if I could get to sleep.

Mercifully, at around 4:00 A.M., I drifted off.

But was I destined to wake up, like the character in Graham Greene's book on Liberia, with a rat sitting on my pillow, savoring the oil in my hair?

Chapter 2

The sound of people talking Gio woke me at seven o'clock. For some reason—certainly not adequate sleep—I wasn't tired. Lying in bed, the better to savor the thrill of actually being back in Kpaytuo, I listened to people outside talking and exchanging greetings loudly, which is the Liberian way: children shouting, crying and laughing; goats braying, cows mooing, and roosters crowing. From the front room came the whisk of a broom and from out back the swoosh of water being poured into a vessel. Peeking out of the tiny window I saw a child emptying a bucket of water into a 55-gallon drum.

By the time I got out of bed, at around eight o'clock, the village had long been awake. Standing at the side of Tado's house, I gazed down upon Kpaytuo, fresh and particularly lovely in the early morning. It would remain so only for another hour or so, by which time the oppressive heat would take command. Puffs of smoke rose about the houses. Women and children swept the area before their houses; others entered the bush, there to gather wood for the morning's fire. Their men, having taken a bath and, if there was food to spare, eaten, were off to the farms, the small plots of land one to three miles from the village proper on which they raised rice. Depending on the stage of the rice cycle, the women might follow in a couple of hours.

In the daylight I observed that Tado's house was still on the edge of the village, only about twenty yards from the bush. Flying over the interior once in a three-seater plane had enabled me to see how thick and immense was the rain forest—a billowy sea of green, dotted in a few spots by tiny brown clearings: these, the hamlets and villages of the hinterland, were few and far between.

As the path to the well for his quarter of the village ran alongside Tado's house, I again greeted the women and children going to and coming from the well as I had done so many times and so many years

21

Tado Jackson's house, February 1982—the house in which I lived alone as a Peace Corps Volunteer and in which I stayed with Tado and his family during much of my return visit. The latrine is visible behind the house to the right.

before. Walking to the well is a trek which takes, all told, twenty to thirty minutes—this for a bucket of water often unfit to drink.

"*Bobwah*," we said to one another as we met—which is "Good Morning" in Gio. And then those who greeted me, especially the children, broke into the warmest and most brilliant smiles.

The main activity at Tado's house took place immediately behind it, where the women and children had gathered round the fire over which was placed a large, black kettle filled with boiling rice. Sitting before it, on a chair no more than eighteen inches high, was Mary Jackson, Tado's wife, whom I had met the night before. Mary and some women I did not know talked and occasionally glanced into the pot, while about them wandered their children, goats, chickens and hogs.

The latrine constructed when I last lived in Kpaytuo was still standing, in what condition remained to be seen. Authors of many travel books rarely, if ever, refer to, let alone discuss, a subject that anyone who has travelled in underdeveloped countries knows is of utmost importance: where, and under what circumstances, the traveler goes to the toilet. The subject, I am not ashamed to acknowledge, was among my biggest concerns in returning to Kpaytuo, for the tribal people, especially in the villages with but few exceptions in that era, did not use latrines, preferring to do their business in the bush, women in one section, men in another. Being, for the most part, unaware of the relation between sanitation and health, the tribal people believed white people use toilets only because we don't want anyone to see our bodies. As for a wipe, soft leaves served as the only affordable toilet paper.

I wasn't about to enter the latrine in the dark the night before; I had urinated in the bush behind Tado's house. But it was now morning, and my bladder was full. With many women and children working behind Tado's house and others frequently walking by on their way to the well, I did not want to use the bush. The door to the latrine was open about five inches. Following the practice of the few villagers who'd built latrines, I kept mine locked, else it would have been soiled by unwelcome visitors in no time. But that lock—or any replacement—was gone. Gingerly, I entered. There was no odor, a good omen. In removing the circular, wooden top I disturbed the sleep or peace of about fifty cockroaches, each easily two inches long, who scampered about in all directions. Hurriedly they slithered back down the hole or dashed around the floor and scurried up and over the walls. When I'd lived in Kpaytuo, my home and latrine were almost cockroach-free, because Sammy, my houseboy, disinfected my house and latrine weekly. Other Liberian visitors apparently were not so fortunate, as Sir Harry Hamilton Johnston, the great Africanist, bore witness to when he wrote, "With horrible fearlessness they, Liberia's cockroaches, land on a human being as voluntarily as on any other substance, and course wildly over one's face and hand or get entangled in one's hair. . . . These insects, as elsewhere in the tropics, do not hesitate at night to attack human beings who are asleep. They creep to the corners of the mouth of the sleeping person to suck the saliva." Thanks for the good news, Harry.

I urinated, put the wooden cover back and left, determined to talk to Tado about the rat *and* roach problems. As for a bowel movement, I hoped I could hold out until evening, when under the cover of darkness, I would squat in the bush. That, after all, is what I had done my first month in the village until a carpenter hired by Tado, who disappeared for days at a time, finally completed my latrine, concrete brick by concrete brick, with its raised wooden platform on which I sat comfortably.

Next I entered the bathhouse, a mud-brick structure with thin-gauge corrugated zinc sheets for a roof, and a concrete floor with a hole for the water to drain into the ground. It was located about twenty feet behind the back of the house and adjacent to it was the latrine. I employed my old, but effective method of wetting my body by using a large enamelware cup to scoop a cupful of water from a bucket, then soaping up, and rinsing off with more cupfuls of water. Standing in that rickety bathhouse, feeling the water cascade over my body as I dumped the remaining contents of the bucket over my head—the final and most pleasant step of my bathing ritual—I could not believe it had been fourteen years since I'd been in Kpaytuo. It seemed more like a matter of weeks.

After my bath I was greeted by Tado Jackson, my host and friend.

"Bob, you can embarrass me the way you arrived last night," he said. "You didn't give me a chance to prepare my home. I was just standing there by the road in my dirty work clothes. I didn't even have my bath. Remember we are Africans and we never forget to give our guest a warm reception. And you did not give me the opportunity to inform the chief and the town you were coming." (Its citizens refer to Kpaytuo as a town, but given its size, I consider it a village, though in this account I and they use the terms interchangeably when referring to Kpaytuo.)

"Tado," I said, "there was no way to get word to you. I was happy with the reception I got. It was warm."

He explained apologetically why his house had deteriorated over the years: he was building a larger and nicer one on his farm, some miles from the village, and, once that house was completed, he intended to move there with Mary and his family.

As he was wearing tattered clothes and carrying a cutlass, I knew that Tado, probably awake since 5:00 A.M., had been in his vegetable garden, located less than a mile from his house. Tado grew rice, for that is what he and his family ate every day, but unlike most tribal Liberians—certainly almost everyone else in Kpaytuo—he was never content to grow only rice and then only enough for one's family to consume. He earned money by raising and selling cucumbers, squash, beans, egg-plant and peppers. And with obvious pride, he told me, in one of the many letters we had written to one another, a couple of years before he'd begun to raise and sell chickens. They were flown to Monrovia from the United States, and if they survived the trip up-country and lived to maturity, were larger, tastier and more tender than the scrawny, tough Liberian variety. He netted $600 a year from his chicken venture—a significant amount in a country where the annual income was about $300 per capita.

Tado was small and slight, about five feet five inches, with skin the color of a chocolate chip cookie, and still handsome at forty-six, though no longer in the teddy-bear kind of way that he'd been when first we met. He was gentle and soft-spoken but resolute and strong-willed. He had run away from Kpaytuo as a young boy when his father refused to let him attend school. He ended up at the Bahn Mission, there coming under the tutelage of the American Tom Jackson, a member of the Worldwide Evangelical Crusade, whose Liberian mission was called the Inland Church. In 1948, when he was thirteen-years-old, Tado became a Christian. He also, as is the Liberian custom, took the missionary Tom Jackson's last name as his own, an expression of his respect and gratitude toward his spiritual father. Next to God, Tado most admired what he saw as the ingenuity, the industriousness, the scientific and technological know-how, the disciplined, no-nonsense, let's-roll-up-our-sleeves-and-get-the job-done character of the American people, traits so woefully missing in his own culture.

By temperament, education, ambition and religious conviction, Tado was different from the average citizen of Kpaytuo. I never saw him drinking palm wine or cane juice, dancing or singing, and I could not conceive of him being with a woman other than his wife—all common and accepted behavior for adult Liberians. Yet Tado was not self-righteous or condemnatory. When something scandalous or ridiculous occurred, which is the norm in Liberia, Tado would shake his head and say to me: "Bob, you know our country people. What to do?" And then he'd laugh ruefully with the tolerance for humanity's foibles and weak-nesses that I find so appealing in Africans.

The author, 22, with Tado Jackson, 31, circa 1966. Tado would become my closest friend in the village—a man worth admiring.

More than anyone, Tado was responsible for the Peace Corps, in the person of me, coming to Kpaytuo in 1966. Working with the Peace Corps Volunteers stationed in a nearby town, Tado had convinced Peace Corps officials in Monrovia that his village—in truth no more or less deserving, interested in or committed to the idea than scores of other villages—was the ideal site for a Peace Corps Volunteer. Tado had the foresight to appreciate what it would mean to Kpaytuo if it had a Peace Corps Volunteer: it would then be the beneficiary of the seem-

The author, 39, and Tado Jackson, 46 in 1982. Tado was serious without being solemn or sanctimonious and often worked 10-hour days on his farm, after which he might teach adult literacy classes or participate in prayer service.

ingly endless educational bounty and goodwill of the United States, munificence taking the form of pens and pencils, chalk and paper, maps and globes, scissors and crayons, sporting equipment and medicine—all things the Liberian government was unable to supply. And best of all would be the Peace Corps Volunteer—idealistic, if at times naive and self-righteous, but in the main diligent, enthusiastic, honest and educated (four of the least likely words one might choose to describe most Liberian teachers in that era).

In 1965—a year before my arrival—Tado, who had reached the ninth grade, was Kpaytuo's only teacher, earning $40 a month. Helping him with the younger children in the school were two of his kin, both approximately nineteen years old, and themselves only in the fifth grade. Neither of them was employed by the Liberian Department of Education. Surely it was one of the happiest days of Tado's life when that year, at age thirty, he passed the entrance examination and was accepted into the Zorzor Rural Teacher Training Institute, a three-year program then under the auspices of the San Francisco State College's Department of Education, designed to upgrade the inadequate education of Liberia's teachers, urban and rural. While attending Zorzor or Kakata, the other teachers' training institute, a teacher received a monthly stipend of $40 (equivalent to his monthly salary). Once graduated and again teaching, however, the graduates were promised $75 a month, almost double the salary of a teacher with a high school education or less.

God works in mysterious ways, Tado must have thought, for only a month before he was to leave for the Zorzor Institute his wife of three years, Sarah, died giving birth to their second child, a boy named Nerwah. (It was his second wife, Mary, whom I had met the night before.) That period after Tado's first wife's death was naturally a dark and difficult time. His newborn son, Nerwah, and his other boy, two-year-old Lee, were going to be taken care of at the mission in a nearby town while Tado was away at the Zorzor Institute, so at least their immediate future had been arranged. But Tado still had to finish building and paying for the addition to his house needed for the Peace Corps Volunteer (me) who would arrive less than a month after his wife's death. And Tado had to prepare himself, emotionally and physically, to leave Kpaytuo, the village of his birth, for Zorzor, a town hundreds of miles away from his Gio people, among the strange tribes in Loffa County. (Think of a tribe as a social group comprising families and clans, with a name, a dialect, a government but subordinate to the central one, and its own territory, even if some members live outside that territory.) Finally, Tado had to make arrangements with a local man to tend the vegetable garden Tado had assiduously cultivated every day before and after teaching school.

Tado left for Zorzor a couple of weeks after I arrived in Kpaytuo in February of 1966, but he returned to the village at the end of the school year, where we got to know one another—and thus began one of the most satisfying friendships of my life.

By the time Tado graduated from the Zorzor Institute, I had been gone from Liberia a year. In letters from him, commencing as soon as I departed, I learned that I had been replaced by two Volunteers from California, Jim and Mardi Grisswold (the last Volunteers ever to be stationed in Kpaytuo), and that even though he had graduated from Zorzor he had not received his official appointment, entitling him to the increased salary, because of the colossal corruption and incompetence endemic—and epidemic—in Liberia.

His troubles had continued, as I learned when we spoke the morning of my first day back in Kpaytuo. He was then involved in a dispute over the ownership of land with a paramount chief; as a result of that land palaver (which he was to win after twelve years) he had lost his teaching job—thus farming was his only source of income.

Tado was the most reasonable, the most admirable and least argumentative Liberian I ever met. How typical of Liberia, and its worthless Powers-That-Be (tribal and Americo-Liberians, pre- and post-coup), that an honest, competent, energetic and dedicated Liberian teacher— in such short supply there (or anywhere)—one who actually preferred teaching and living in a village in the Liberian interior to the life in a larger town or the capital, was dismissed. I had helped Tado by sending him vegetable seeds, though Liberia being Liberia, where venal custom and postal employees have sticky fingers, most of the packages got through to him, though some did not.

❖   ❖   ❖

Having mentioned my concerns that first day back with clearing the rat (or rats) from the room in which I'd be sleeping and ridding the latrine of its cockroaches, Tado instructed the adorable boy next to him, his eight-year-old son Liberty, to bring him a "bony," the tiny fish found in the streams on the outskirts of the village at certain times of the year, which were dried before eating. When Liberty returned, Tado produced a package of powdered poison, which he mixed with water to make a paste, and then rubbed that on chunks of the fish. He placed the chunks under the bed and along the walls of my room and in various other rooms throughout the house, assuring me that when the rats ate the fish they would be gone in no time. As for the cockroaches, I knew that to be an easier matter: all we needed was disinfectant.

No sooner had I eaten a few bananas for breakfast that first morning than visitors began arriving at Tado's. (Until one has eaten a succulent freshly picked banana or pineapple, one doesn't really know the glories of these fruits.) The person I was happiest to see was Zoelay Retty Sonkarlay, my former lover. Zoelay Retty was accompanied by a woman I did not recognize, who turned out to be her closest friend, Garty. Wan and sickly in appearance, Garty looked ten years older than Zoelay Retty—the reason I failed to recognize her—though they were both in their mid-thirties. They stayed for about ten minutes and went

Kpaytuo in 1982, by which time corrugated zinc roofs were replacing thatched huts.

out back with Tado's wife, Mary, though not before Zoelay Retty and I set up a rendezvous.

I decided to take a stroll through the village. In the daylight I saw that Kpaytuo had grown to about two hundred and fifty homes. There seemed to be no pattern or thought given to where the new homes were built. Some stood less than ten feet apart, utterly without regard to drainage, a factor I'd have thought would have been much on their minds, given the considerable rainfall. Almost every home had a corrugated metal roof, as no one would be so old-fashioned as to build a new home with a thatched roof. Few of the homes, new or old, had shutters on the windows, and none had screens.

In my Peace Corps days, Tado's house was one of the few with a corrugated metal roof, which was uninsulated, and which the sun "baked" during the midday hours. Therefore, I tried to spend a portion of the midday hours visiting my students' families in the cool, dark interior of a thatched hut or, accompanied by a handful of my favorite students, in the pleasant surroundings of the cool rain forest. Still another comfortable place to escape the afternoon heat was under a palaver hut, a small thatched hut, about ten feet in diameter, with its sides open, in which the people settled palavers (arguments), discussed community matters, gossiped and drank palm wine. No surprise that tribal Liberians abandoned thatched-roofed huts. They wanted to be modern and being modern didn't involve living in a thatched-roofed hut, even though it afforded better protection from the brutal midday heat than an uninsulated zinc roof; lest I forget, it was also a perfect nesting place for rats, reason enough for the demise of thatched roofs.

Returning to Tado's after my walk, I ate chicken and rice cooked in palm oil, served with my favorite sauce, cassava leaf, which grows wild in the bush. (Soup is what the Liberians call the gravies and sauces they pour on rice.) As a Peace Corps Volunteer, I had eaten two mountainous platefuls of rice with chunks of antelope meat (which animal the tribal Liberians called a "deer") mixed with different gravies every night for dinner. The food was similar to that eaten by the country people, except that they could not often afford to buy, and so rarely ate, meat; they did so when a member of the family killed or trapped game. Then they devoured the animal, eating organs and parts we Westerners do not, including the nose and eyes. They would dry or smoke part of the animal over the fire in their huts, though that didn't always prevent the meat from spoiling, and days later they would consume what we Westerners, with much more delicate stomachs and palates, think of as rotten meat.

During my Peace Corps service, I devoted an inordinate amount of time to thinking about food, mainly because of the many hours required to secure and prepare it. It wasn't like stopping at a supermarket or convenience store on the way home from work and popping something into the oven or, easier still, eating in a restaurant. Kpaytuo wasn't even large enough to have a market, much less a restaurant. If anything were for sale—a bunch of plantains or a hindquarter of meat, for instance—it was hung from a hut and sold on a first-come, first-served basis. The longer the meat hung, the cheaper the price.

Every day after school Sammy, Kamah and I discussed the soup we'd have for that night's dinner, and in the afternoon Kamah looked for it—in the bush if it grew wild (like cassava leaf and collard greens), or by approaching one of the few people in town who grew vegetables (like eggplant, which was rarely available). At some point in the middle of the day one of them took a packet of meat out of the kerosene refrigerator to defrost. Since Liberians reckon time so differently than Westerners, Kamah could never understand my impatience if she showed up to begin preparing dinner an hour or two after she was supposed to. Likewise it was difficult in the beginning of our relationship for Sammy and Kamah to understand why I always insisted we have enough boiled water on hand and, when the boiled water was almost finished, to think about boiling more and actually boiling it.

To the Liberians Westerners dart about like ants and they find Westerners as difficult to understand as Westerners do them. They used to call Westerners' obsessive activity the "hurry-hurry palaver." While visiting a cemetery in Monrovia many years ago, a Liberian supposedly said, "Look at all those hurry-hurry people in the graveyard, and the work is not finished yet."

◆   ◆   ◆

Frank Siaway and Arthur Wonyou came to visit. Frank, who was Tado's half-brother, had been the handsomest, cleverest, most athletically-gifted, and most popular young man in Kpaytuo. He was about two years younger than I. More the pity to see what had become of him, for before me stood a shriveled old man of about thirty-six. I don't know what disease he had contracted, or what parasites decimated his body. Certainly he was anemic. As unfairly as fate had treated him, he was, as ever, pleasant and uncomplaining. Frank had married one of the girls from a nearby village and lived and farmed on the outskirts of Kpaytuo—not very happily, Tado intimated.

Arthur, like Frank, was around my age. Our girlfriends had been and still were close friends. Arthur had a kindly face, wore a full beard, as did I, and had a receding hairline, as did I. He asked me why the two of us, unlike everyone else in Kpaytuo, had lost so much of our hair. Would that I knew, I told him. I've posed the very question to God Himself. Now that he and another citizen had recently opened a clinic in town, the people of Kpaytuo called Arthur "Doctor."

We began to discuss the coup that had ended the decades-long dominance by the Americo-Liberians and during which President Tolbert and twenty-eight of his subordinates were murdered; and days later thirteen cabinet officers and other high officials were taken to the beach outside Monrovia, stripped to the waist, tied to a pole, and shot—the gruesome images of which beach scene were filmed and viewed around the world on television screens and in newspapers. Though I wouldn't call Frank or Arthur bloodthirsty or violent, the coup was an event in which they took pride, since it was tribal men their age, from the same culture and with similar backgrounds, who had perpetrated it. They hoped, of course, the coup would bring real and not just cosmetic change to the lot of the country people. They expressed the view that the junior officers decided to carry out the coup when they discovered President Tolbert planned to kill the opposition leaders then awaiting trial, turn the country over to someone—who, exactly, was never mentioned—and flee Liberia.

My two Kpaytuo friends believed that Tolbert and his family were involved in too many businesses—from growing rice to selling charcoal, from manufacturing soap to selling fish—and that the resulting financial web compromised President Tolbert's ability to rule justly and wisely. When the cost of rice and other foods began to climb, the Liberians concluded that it was Tolbert's fault, since, they reasoned, he and his family stood to profit most from the increased prices. There was some truth to their reasoning: the Tolbert family business had received $10 million in unsecured loans from the Bank of Liberia, one of the reasons the bank had collapsed following the 1980 coup.

Arthur, with Frank concurring, repeated the popular theory that on the night of the coup the junior officers had been smoking marijuana—otherwise, I was told by them and in time by others, they, the officers, would not have had the courage to pull off what everyone agrees was an astonishing act of daring. And in the midst of the brief but bloody battle for control of the Executive Mansion, President Tolbert supposedly shouted to one of the soldiers, "If you let me go, I'll give you half of my fortune." But the soldier refused. (I found this part of the story dubious, in light of the eagerness with which Liberian soldiers solicited and accepted bribes.) They also contended that the soldiers, knowing President Tolbert was immune to bullets, stabbed him to death. Frank insisted (with Arthur readily agreeing) that the coup would never have succeeded had Tolbert been able to reach the swagger stick he carried in public.

"Why not?" I asked.

"He would have disappeared," Frank answered matter of factly.

Tado, one of the more successful farmers in Kpaytuo—though the term is relative—joined our discussion, which turned to farming. Frank and Arthur were amazed when I said that in America the average rice farm is about four hundred acres, and that a farm could stretch from Kpaytuo to Saclepea, a distance of nine miles, or more. The average Liberian rice farm is a scant two acres, while Tado's vegetable garden would in time be twice that size. Tado said he had read there are even machines in America that thresh and clean rice, put it in a bag and, as incredible as it might sound, tie the bag shut.

"For true, Teacher Cherry?" Frank asked.

"For true," I said.

Arthur refused to believe there is also a machine that peels corn from its husk.

"It is so!" insisted Tado.

"It can be so," said I, adding that in America our farmers can produce so much food—rice, corn, wheat, barley and many other varieties—that the American government pays them not to grow certain crops, in this way keeping prices at an artificially high level.

Their eyes almost popped out at this news: they considered America the land of wonder, the mightiest, the most generous, the richest country on earth, but even in America surely there was not so much money and food that farmers were paid not to farm.

❖   ❖   ❖

On closer inspection I observed what Tado was referring to regarding his house, which had been in bad shape fourteen years before when the Peace Corps rented it for $450 per year. Now it was falling apart: the screens were torn in most of the windows, allowing mosquitoes to enter in great numbers. Lucky for me I had begun taking a malaria prophylactic before my trip and continued to do so. In addition to mosquitoes, I could expect flies, beetles and a large, wasp-like insect the Liberians called a "cow fly." At first, these were nuisances, but in time I'd get used to them, as I had once before. Since I was not staying long and since Tado intended to move to a "modern" home on the outskirts of town within a year, I could not expect him to repair the screens and upgrade the house on my behalf.

The front room of Tado's house, the room the Liberians call the piazza, was where I'd kept a bookcase, stocked with hundreds of excellent paperback novels and non-fiction books, courtesy of the Peace Corps office when a new post was opened; and a desk at which I sat and wrote in my journal during my Peace Corps sojourn; and where, on a manual typewriter, I improved my typing by composing five-page letters almost every week to either my sister or my parents, and corresponded with a few friends; and where I read and prepared my lesson plans at night by a kerosene lamp. The same faded, peeling linoleum was on the floor, the only floor in the house so covered; the others were cement. The desk and bookcase and my two chairs were gone, replaced by a set of four cheap chairs and a tiny, inexpensive coffee table. A cloth calendar from 1975 with a scene depicting New England in the fall, complete with a white-steeple church surrounded by a white picket fence and yellow- and red-leafed trees adorned the wall. There was also a framed picture of Jesus and one of Tado, taken upon his graduation from the Zorzor Rural Teacher Training Institute, hanging on the wall. In his starched white shirt and tie and jacket, he resembled an earnest young Negro graduate (as the graduate would have been called) from Howard University around 1910.

Tado's children and another child had slept on the floor of this room. In another tiny room, no more than eight feet by eight feet, Tado's mother-in-law slept. The room I was staying in (my old room) had a bed with a mattress about two inches thick, and a soggy old pillow. There weren't any real sheets, white or otherwise, but there was a large piece of cloth, of the kind Liberians fashion for their *lappas* and shirts, serving as a bottom sheet. Another one, rather musty, served as a blanket. There was also an old, wooden bureau, but it was moldy and full of Tado's papers and paraphernalia, so I kept my clothes and things in my suitcase and leather Ghurka bag on the floor. There were tape cassettes on the floor—the ones strewn about by the rat. The small room where Tado and Mary had slept, opposite mine, contained an old wooden bed frame without a mattress; that was all.

Toward the back of the house was the room in which I used to eat. A rickety card table was standing next to the wall, a chair in front of it. There was an ancient, wooden cupboard, in which were stored, amid the cobwebs, mangy-looking onions. One compartment of the cupboard held a box of wooden matches, a few cheap enamelware plates and a few tablespoons. In the room adjacent to this stood a half-empty hundred-pound bag of rice and a bunch of plantains.

I was fortunate I could stay with Tado. First, I enjoyed his company. We were kindred spirits. Secondly, educated by missionaries, Tado understood the *kwi* (modern) way. I could depend on him to instruct his wife Mary, a country woman who had never been to school, to be especially careful in preparing my food, washing my dishes and, most important of all, boiling my drinking water, even though I was fairly certain that *their* drinking water was not boiled. It wasn't that another household in Kpaytuo would be indifferent to my becoming ill. It's just that the average villager really didn't believe there are little things we can't see called bacteria that can make us sick; and few of the villagers accepted the correlation between sanitation and health. They may claim, though only to appear *kwi*, that water from a bad well could make you sick with diarrhea, but they didn't believe it: more likely they supposed you were witched, and that, not the bad water, was why your stomach hurt or—in the Liberian vernacular—your stomach ran.

Kpaytuo's school children lined up for food at recess circa 1967. The bulgur wheat and powdered milk were provided by CARE, the humanitarian organization. For many students it was their only meal during the daylight hours.

Chapter 3

I had no difficulty remembering the first time I saw Zoelay Retty Sonkarly. It was the opening week of school, March 1966. I had walked behind the schoolhouse to a thatched shed and observed a young woman bending over a black pot. When she stood erect, she was a lovely sight to behold. Wearing an old *lappa* and a canary-yellow blouse, she was sexy and pretty with a fabulous figure: a slim waist, large, pointed breasts pressing against her blouse, and (obvious when she had bent over the pot) a small, well-shaped posterior. Not without cause had the best-selling author John Gunther asserted in *Inside Africa* that Liberia's women had the most beautiful breasts in Africa. Zoelay Retty's skin was golden-brown, her face small, with high cheekbones, long eyelashes and slightly oriental eyes and full, sensual lips. In other words, a knock-out. And she was about my age. Attracted to her, I had no idea to whom she might be attached, if anyone, nor what my chances were—at some future time—of getting to know her, in the Biblical sense.

Zoelay Retty Sonkarly, about 20, circa 1966. I remember the first time I saw her—a lovely sight to behold.

Being a young and inexperienced Peace Corps Volunteer and representing the United States government, I was unsure of how the villagers would react were I to express an interest in tribal women. Besides, I had enough things to worry about, adjust to and deal with—primarily culture shock and a new job—without adding, right from the get-go, the potential complications of sex and romance to my life.

Little did I suspect that Kpaytuo's citizens would have thought my interest in the available unmarried women the most natural response in the world. Liberians, as I was soon enough to learn, approached sex as a need to be fulfilled. Which is not to say they took it lightly: just the opposite. Most crises in life—with the sole exception of death from old age—had, in their minds, sexual genesis. As George Schwab pointed out in his classic study, *Tribes of the Liberian Hinterland*, published by Harvard's Peabody Museum in 1947, failures in important undertakings were frequently attributed to broken sexual taboos—engaging in intercourse during the day, or having sex with a pregnant woman, for instance. Though I would have no inkling of this until many months into my tour, every father in Kpaytuo would have welcomed my loving his available daughters: better I, who could provide for the girl and her family, than some poor *schnook* of a bush farmer, the old man would have reasoned. Relationships and marriages were considered business affairs in Liberia—as they were in Europe and America in olden times—though that is not to say that individual fancy and love didn't enter into it on occasion.

❖   ❖   ❖

In my Peace Corps days, Zoelay Retty was our school's CARE cook, at a salary of $25 a month. CARE (Cooperative American Relief Everywhere) administered a school lunch program, which provided such staples as bulgur wheat, cornmeal and powdered milk free to the Liberian schools. Often this meal, which we served at recess, was the only one the children of Kpaytuo ate during the day, and not a few of the children, really too young to be in school, came only for this hot meal. Zoelay Retty's appointment as our CARE cook had more to do with her relationship with the then Supervisor of Schools for Nimba County, Charles Boayue, than her culinary skills: she was one of Boayue's girlfriends. In fact they had a four-year-old son, Tommy. But as Boayue lived in Sanniquellie, Nimba's county seat and eight hours from Kpaytuo, he and Zoelay Retty saw each other only every few months.

I was the keeper of the keys to the room in which we stored the CARE food. With the concurrence of a village elder, who functioned as a one-man school board, I declined to give the keys to the principal, knowing he would consume or sell much of the food, especially the vegetable oil. So I often came into contact with Zoelay Retty during the school day, when each morning she needed the key to open the storeroom. We began to banter and tease and then to flirt with each other, even though like most tribal girls her age (she was about twenty), Zoelay Retty had never been to school, and her English was limited.

One morning I entered the thatched shed behind the school where she prepared the food—we euphemistically called the place our CARE Kitchen—and, as she was making biscuits, found her arms immersed in a batter. I asked for my keys, since I needed to return to my house for something. Having no pockets in her *lappa*, as was her practice, she had placed the keys in her bra. She motioned with her head for me to retrieve my keys, since she obviously couldn't get them herself. Placing my hands next to her soft, warm, ample breasts, I found my keys, which for days afterward did not feel the same.

(It had been the custom of tribal women to go around topless, but by the late 1960s, one saw them topless only during the hottest hours of the day or in front of, or in, their huts or on their farms. And even then all but the very young and the very old tended to draw their *lappas* over their breasts in my presence, correctly sensing that most white males from my culture are obsessed with the female breast. Perplexed by our ways, Tado once asked me if it were true white men enjoyed looking at pictures of naked women. Yes, it was true, I told him; though, without being prudish or sanctimonious, I don't particularly; instead, I like the real thing.)

In time Zoelay Retty began to visit my house, first during the latter part of the afternoon, when she wasn't working on her people's farm, and eventually in the evenings. If the schoolboys were browsing through my picture books and magazines or just hanging out—and they usually were—her coming in the evening proved awkward. (At least I felt awkward.) There was no sense of privacy in the Liberian culture so the villagers found it odd whenever, day or night, I told them I wanted to be alone—whether to read, write, think or, in this case, be with Zoelay Retty. To avoid this, Zoelay Retty usually came around 10:00 P.M., by which time the children had gone home to sleep. She also occasionally cooked rice and chicken for me in her hut, and sent the food over with the dishes wrapped in her kerchief, an endearing gesture that Liberian women adopt towards their lovers. As we were not lovers the first time she did this, it was, on her part, a message—the significance of which I was at first oblivious to. (Remember, I was twenty-two, dumb and dumber in such matters.)

From that first glimpse in my first weeks in Kpaytuo, I was taken with Zoelay Retty, even though she spoke little English and was from a culture so different from my own. The chemistry between us was stronger than cultural differences. We appreciated each other's sense of humor, and I fancied her personality as well as her good looks and shapely figure. She could be aloof and cool (and I like my women warm), but you can't always find everything you want in a mate. Nor did I like her occasional visits to Boayue, but these I grudgingly accepted. Long after I would be gone from Liberia, she'd still need him as a benefactor. Likewise, she wouldn't have objected to occasional dalliances on my part. This was the Liberian way. In any case, about seven months after I arrived in Kpaytuo, Zoelay Retty and I became lovers.

❖   ❖   ❖

Upon my return in 1982, Tado told me that of the half dozen or so students in his adult literacy class, none were more diligent than Zoelay Retty. When I lived in Kpaytuo she could not read or write; because, like most of her generation of tribal women, she had never attended school. I wanted to see the book she was learning to read from, so later that day, after she had returned to Tado's house with a fat chicken as a gift, I asked her to go to her house for her reading book. When she returned I asked her to read. She was reluctant, but after much pleading, mock threats, and a promise to buy her a book in Monrovia, she agreed. Embarrassed and self-conscious, yet eager to demonstrate her new skill to me, she grappled with the words, whispering each of them, by way of practice, before actually repeating the word aloud. Gently I coaxed and prodded her along, conveying, I hope, how very much I wanted to hear her read. And methodically, laboriously, almost painfully, she gave birth to a few sentences: "Floumo . . . went to . . . church. The . . . church has a . . . zinc roof. Floumo . . . lives . . in . . . a . . . village. . . . . He . . . lives. . .with . . . his . . . mother, . father . . . and . . . five . . . . brothers . . . and . . . sisters."

A woman in her thirties, with four children, who had spent her life growing rice, chopping wood and carrying buckets of water, was doing what we in the West take for granted in a child of six. Zoe-lay Retty was ecstatic, having shown me—who more than anyone or anything in the world represented, to her, education and knowledge—how much progress she had made in the last few years; for to know "book" after all is the first and most crucial step in being *kwi* (or modern).

After dinner that second night of my return, Arthur Wonyou and I strolled through the town. The night was dark, the moon nowhere to be seen. No children were out playing, nor were any of their older brothers and sisters singing or dancing, as they would on moonlit nights. Arthur said he had something he wanted to talk about with me, but was afraid I'd be offended by the subject.

Zoelay Retty Sonkarly in 1982.

42

Nothing he could say would offend me, I assured him. It seemed that he and Edwin Siaway, another of my old students (the one whom I used to shadow box with) had been discussing the possibility of my having relations with some of the available women in Kpaytuo during my visit. Arthur looked at me, smiled, and sheepishly said, "But Edwin said it can somehow be embarrassing to talk the thing with you." I told Arthur I was not in the least embarrassed to discuss the subject.

"There can be plenty of fine women here who want to make friends with you, Cherry. Even the time you can be here. There can be too many women who want to love to you. For true-oh. But a woman cannot approach a man."

I thanked Arthur for his concern with my welfare, but told him I didn't think I'd need his or Edwin's help, being able to talk for myself in woman business. In fact, earlier that day I had asked Zoelay Retty if she had a boyfriend.

"Who told you so?" she'd said indignantly.

"No one," I'd answered. "I just want to know."

"I tell you later tonight," she said.

After my stroll with Arthur I intended to return to Tado's house, there to await a visit from Zoelay Retty. We'd be alone, for Tado and Mary and his family were spending the night at his farm.

I heard footsteps and then she appeared. She wore a white blouse with a freshly washed and ironed navy blue *lappa*. She and her son may have referred to her as an "Old Ma," her body may not have been as firm and ripe as when she and I had been in our early twenties, but she was still attractive and sexy. I brought out a chair for her. There was no awkwardness. With Zoelay Retty and all the people of Kpaytuo, it was as if I had seen them a month before.

She said, "When they come and tell me that you can be here-oh, I cannot believe it self. I come over, stand outside the house so. Look at you so. I can think it can be like a dream."

"It's no dream-oh," I said. "My one is back."

She had never married, though I've no doubt there were many suitors, for Zoelay Retty was fetching, a real catch. A single woman in Liberia had a much different and in some ways more enviable status then than her counterpart in the United States at that time. There was no stigma to an unmarried woman bearing children. (Nor, for the most part is there for most women in North America circa 2017.) On the contrary, a Liberian single woman who had borne a healthy child was ample evidence that she was fertile and thus commanded a higher "bride price." As for the children of an unmarried woman being illegitimate, the concept didn't exist among the Liberians. All children were welcome, the more the better. (This won't be the case when the majority of its citizens are involved in a cash economy, but back then it was.)

Zoelay Retty had borne two more children since last I saw her, both of whose fathers lived outside Kpaytuo. Charles Boayue, her one-time benefactor and the former head of education in Nimba County, had fallen out of grace after the coup. Even though he was a tribal man, he had risen to power under the Americo-Liberians and, like many tribal people, was more than willing to do their bidding. (Not, by any means, were all the people who fled Liberia after the coup Americo-Liberians; many tribal people left, too: among them a high school principal who, it turned out, owned two apartment buildings in Brooklyn, New York—not bad on an annual salary of less than $3,000.)

I surmised these were not the best of times for Zoelay Retty. Still, she didn't complain. I was ecstatic to see her, and very much desired to make love to her. I didn't know what her reaction would be, so, a little nervous and hesitant, I suggested we go to my bedroom. She followed, saying not a word. We sat down on my bed and shortly were engaged in an activity we had done in that very bedroom many years ago and many times before, to the delight of us both.

Chapter 4

The following day there came to visit me the brothers Karngbeae, Thomas and Augustus. They were in their late twenties to early thirties. I had taught them, and their younger brother, Jesse, as teenagers. Through considerable sacrifice on their and their families' parts, they had graduated from high school, a rare accomplishment in Liberia. They were proud of that, even more so that Jesse had attended the University of Liberia and was scheduled to graduate in a year, at about age twenty-eight—the first person from Kpaytuo ever to attend college. Neither Thomas nor Augustus lived or worked in Kpaytuo.

Thomas was well-built and handsome, with dark, smooth skin and a round head and receding hairline, more like a West African from Ghana in shape and feature than a Liberian. He taught elementary school in Zuatuo, a nearby village. Augustus, slighter than and not as handsome as Thomas, had a scholarly, sensitive bearing, accentuated by his spectacles and thin Lincolnesque beard. He would be spending the next two years upgrading his education at the Kakata Rural Teacher Training Institute, which like its counterpart in the Liberian city of Zorzor, trained primary and secondary teachers. It was the school vacation period, so they were in Kpaytuo helping their father on his farm, now that he was too old to chop down trees and cut the bush for eight hours a day: he had sacrificed for them; they were repaying the old man. In a non-cash economy, children, the more the better, were the best insurance policy for old age.

Since most of the students I had taught in Kpaytuo entered kindergarten between ages ten and fifteen, I assumed few of them would graduate from high school, especially the girls, who typically gave birth by sixteen. Even if they were determined and fortunate enough to graduate high school at age twenty-five or thirty, what kind of job could my students expect to secure given their ages and substandard educations? If these two strikes against them were not sufficient, there was the Liberian economy: I couldn't conceive of it creating jobs for even the relatively small number of tribal children graduating from high school and college.

My prognosis of what lay ahead for my students and their counterparts throughout the country was all too accurate for *most of them*, but from talking to Thomas and Augustus, I realized that for a small, ambitious and lucky group, of whom they numbered, I was wrong. I had failed to consider that in a country like Liberia, where almost every tribal youngster began school at age ten or twelve, with predictably numerous interruptions, it is the norm for a student to graduate high school in his or her late twenties; and college, for the fortunate few, in his or her mid- to late-thirties. I had also underestimated the ability of the Liberian government to absorb the small number of tribal children graduating from high school during the 1970s. Working for the government, in the capital of course, was the goal of many educated tribal Liberians—and, for that matter, the uneducated, too. One out of every six employed Liberians worked for the government.

Only about a dozen of the seventy-five students I taught still lived in Kpaytuo. Most, like Thomas and Augustus, had left for school or work. Sammy Gweh, who was my houseboy's close friend and also one of my favorites, operated heavy duty equipment in Monrovia—one of the more prestigious jobs for a tribal person. Another had

Thomas Karngbeae, one of my ex-students, who by 1982 had become a teacher. Teacher Thomas and I discussed the Liberian and American approaches to relationships, sexual and otherwise.

enlisted in the army after the coup, and he, like my houseboy Sammy, was stationed outside Monrovia. Paul Tuazama, everyone agreed, was a "big man," a major in the National Police Force. His brother, Joshua, was an "accountant." Liberians call a bookkeeper an accountant, a paramedic a nurse, and a nurse a doctor, so there was no way of knowing whether Joshua really was an accountant. But whatever he was, he and his father, whom I knew well, had much to feel proud about. Moses Grant was also a "so-so big man," who owned two taxis and was a security guard for the Liberian American-Swedish Mineral Company (LAMCO), the consortium that mined and exported the rich iron ore deposits from the Nimba Mountains in the north. No one knew where Betty Leeleh, my favorite of all the students I taught, lived or what she was doing. Kamah, my cook, was in Monrovia. So was Johnny (now Kyende) Bormentar, who worked for the Department of Public Health. His pretty, spirited sister, Rebecca, was studying to be a "nurse."

Having business to conduct in the village, Augustus left, leaving Thomas and me to discuss, among other topics, the universally interesting subject of the relationship between the sexes. To illustrate a common Liberian situation, Thomas cited Lucy Gbon. Lucy had been living with her boyfriend in the town of Yekepa when he lost his job. The boyfriend moved far away to the Bomi Hills mine area to look for work, while Lucy returned to her parents' home in Kpaytuo. During such visits home as Lucy's—which could last for months or even years— Lucy almost certainly would—and in fact did—become pregnant by a Kpaytuo man.

"What will happen," I asked Thomas, "when she goes to her boyfriend in Bomi Hills with the news that she is pregnant, or when he finds out?"

Thomas replied that the boyfriend has to accept it, knowing that a young girl like Lucy can't remain in a place like Kpaytuo without loving. He (the boyfriend) also has to be responsible for the child, even though it is not his and isn't written in tribal law.

"And if he doesn't accept it, I asked?"

Then, according to tribal custom, Thomas said, the father of the girl will try to harmonize the situation.

I then said to Thomas, "You stay in Zuatuo, and your wife stays in

Tappeta. [About two hours away.] And you have girlfriends in Zuatuo?"

"Yes," he said.

"And did you ever make your girlfriend pregnant?"

"Yes."

"In America," I pointed out, "if you were living in New York and your wife were living in Philadelphia, and you had a child with a girlfriend in New York, your wife is going to be angry."

"Of course," he agreed. "When it happened, she was angry. She was too vexed. But I begged her, because I am not the first African to do this."

"Where is the baby?" I asked Thomas.

"The baby is with the parents of the girlfriend."

We both broke out laughing at his answer. "The baby is with the parents of the girlfriend!" I exclaimed. "Where is the girlfriend?"

"The girl has gone on her way. I don't know where she is now," Thomas said.

"But who does the baby belong to?"

"The parents of the girl say the baby for them. And I say the baby for me. So it's just there. We have not come to any kind of conclusion. I help small, they help small."

"And how old is the baby?"

"Three years old."

"When will you judge the thing?"

"You know, here in Liberia, there are always people who can juggle the facts. When the baby misbehave, that's the time they will tell him that he has a father. But when he is progressing there, then they will say the baby for them."

He then asked me, "Is it true that the white women in the United States do not love to any other boyfriend except the one they are married?"

"Yes, I know a woman who married this man when they were twenty-one. She is thirty-eight, and has never loved to anyone else."

Thomas laughed.

"That can't happen in Africa?" I asked

"Not to my knowledge," he answered.

"In my country," I said, "it is a big-big palaver if a married man or woman loves to another person. Here it is not such a big palaver. Isn't that so?"

"It is so."

"When does it become a big-big palaver in Liberia?" I asked. "For example, Galonpoo is married to Albert. Suppose Galonpoo can love to somebody. When does it become a big-big palaver?"

Thomas said, "When Albert needs certain service from Galonpoo and Albert does not get certain service from Galonpoo."

"You mean sexual service?"

"Sexual service and around the house," he said.

"You mean if Albert needs water for his bath, and she says, 'No, I don't have time' then there can be a big palaver?"

"Yes," Thomas said, and added, "Then Albert says, 'You got to say so because I know you have another man to be served. That is the reason why you don't want to serve me.'"

"And suppose Albert is loving to someone else?" I asked. "When will the palaver come?"

"The palaver will come," Thomas said, "when the woman Albert is loving to does not give respect to Galonpoo."

"How does she show her disrespect?"

"Some time in the night a group of girls can go out to sing. While singing Galonpoo can be passing. Then they will sing some kind of song there relating to Galonpoo. Then the other girls will be laughing at Galonpoo. Then Galonpoo will come and ask Albert, 'Why such a person got to sing that kind of song to me?' Then palaver will come."

Thomas then observed: "Here in Liberia our belief is when you get married to a white woman, she doesn't play any fire with you, like, 'Let me go have another man there to love to.' So we all have the belief that when we have the money, we will all fly to the United States to get married there."

"Do Liberian women believe this about American men, too?" I asked.

"Yes. The girls also have the same belief. If a Liberian woman marries to you, Teacher Cherry, she has the belief that you will not play around."

"It depends on the person," I said. "Some Americans play around,

49

some do not. On the average there is more playing around in Liberia than in America."

Then Thomas asked me if he goes to the United States did I think he would be lucky enough to find someone to love?

I said I thought so.

At this he was pleased, for he said that he had never gone a month without a woman.

Chapter 5

My ex-student Arthur Wonyou wanted me to visit the clinic he and Sammy Wowah had opened recently. Arthur ran the clinic for Sammy Wowah, a Kpaytuo "success story" who worked in health care and lived in Monrovia. The clinic was located in the former home of Samuel (Sammy) B. Cooper, a wealthy and powerful—and Kpaytuo's only—Americo-Liberian resident. Cooper also owned a home in Monrovia, where his wife and family stayed, and a rubber farm in Totota. He was a successful and prominent member of the Americo-Liberian elite. In Kpaytuo he had built a fine cinder home, by far the nicest, and only remotely modern, structure in the village. Still, when I lived in Kpaytuo the home had no electricity or running water, though there were plans to build a cistern and bring in a generator. Cooper and two of his legitimate sons, Ben and John, who were my age, alternated one-month stays in the village during my Peace Corps years, overseeing the logging operations at the sawmill the Coopers owned on the outskirts of Kpaytuo.

Arthur Wonyou, my ex-student who in 1982 ran the Kpaytuo clinic. Arthur asked if I knew why he and I, unlike most males in Kpaytuo, had receding hairlines. To which I responded that I did not know but had posed the question to God Himself.

Though I was good terms with all the Coopers, I didn't see much of the family, preferring to spend my time with the country people.

Following the coup, Arthur said, Cooper "donated" his large, cinder-block home to the citizens of Kpaytuo, and his other less substantial home in Kpaytuo to Galonpoo, one of the prettier girls in Kpaytuo and with whom Cooper had fathered a child seventeen years before—one of two children Cooper had by two Kpaytuo women.

By this point in the story the reader should be aware that it is not unusual, or in any way condemned, for a married Liberian to father children with a woman other than his wife. The richer and more powerful the man, the more "outside children" he begot, especially in the case of the wealthy Americo-Liberians, whose wives—many hefty, but not all—contrasted unfavorably with the comely, younger and ever-willing and available tribal girls. Liberia's long-serving President, William Tubman, had one child by his wife, but mentioned six children in his will, and fathered who knows how many others. Indeed, tribal Liberians boasted of President Tubman's legendary potency: people who considered him the father of modern Liberia—which he was—may have been thinking literally as well as figuratively. The "outside children" of a wealthy Americo-Liberian—or, for that matter, any important tribal man—were accepted by, and often into, his "legal" family: they carried their father's name, and their education was paid for by their natural father.

◆　　◆　　◆

After "donating" his homes, Samuel Cooper and his sons, Ben and John, left Kpaytuo. Where they went no one in the village knew or cared. Resentful of Cooper, the villagers asserted to me that he had stolen their land for his logging operation. "You people shit on the trees. I'm going to make money from them," was allegedly the imperious phrase Cooper employed to justify his action. (Before making judgment, I'd like to hear Samuel Cooper's side of the story.)

When Arthur and I arrived at the clinic, a half dozen women with babies and children were already waiting patiently on a bench on the porch. Each day, he told me, as the news of the clinic spread, more people were coming from the hamlets and villages in the forest, off the main road, some three to ten miles from Kpaytuo.

I noticed the lock on the mahogany hand-carved door had been jimmied open, leading me to suspect Cooper's "donation" was not entirely voluntary. There was no furniture in the house, just four or five large, vacant rooms with high insulated ceilings, thick cinder block walls, finished with smooth plaster, and level windows, doors and floors.

Arthur had an office, of sorts, in one of the rooms. In the closet he kept his meager supply of pills and needles and vials of penicillin. The same Liberians who were reluctant to apply a disinfectant or keep a bandage on a cut, or regularly clean it to avoid infection, eagerly asked for, and submitted to, "an injection," preferably, though not always, of penicillin. They abused antibiotics even more than did Westerners and when they really needed the antibiotics, in a life-threatening situation, I wondered if their bodies would respond. In truth, it probably didn't matter, for in life-threatening situations most Liberians rarely were under the care of competent medical personnel, even in Monrovia. Forget about it happening in the villages and most towns in the interior.

The most common ailment he treated, Arthur related, was "runny stomach," the Liberian name for diarrhea. With obvious pride he pointed to a bottle of kaopectate, which he dispensed to the people until the "medicine," of which there was not a great deal, was finished.

Arthur was no dummy, far from it, but neither was he a nurse, let alone a doctor. But since the government, pre- and post-coup, had neglected Kpaytuo, two of its citizens, Arthur and Sammy Wowah, had opened a clinic—not a very professional or well-stocked one to be sure, but better than nothing. Arthur and Sammy's grand scheme, once the government gave its approval (I wasn't going to hold my breath waiting for that to happen) was a clinic with a staff of five, modern medical equipment, including an x-ray machine, shelves of antibiotics, and a delivery room. They had even gotten someone to draw up a blueprint of it. Liberian towns fifteen times larger than Kpaytuo could not afford such a clinic, but why spoil their dreams?

◆　◆　◆

I harbored, truth be told, no fear of returning to a country ruled by a military clique that had imposed and enforced a curfew in Monrovia, nor of traveling, alone, into the interior, nor even staying in a village I had not been in for fourteen years. What I feared in returning to Liberia was getting sick. And with good reason, for Liberia was one of the unhealthiest places on earth, though the reason that all Liberians don't die young is that many acquire immunity to many diseases. Nevertheless, bacteria and viruses thrived in its fetid air. Sewage disposal was inadequate in Monrovia, nonexistent in most of the interior. Most of the country's water was contaminated, from which the people contracted an assortment of waterborne and water-related diseases, including cholera, typhoid fever and amoebic dysentery. Tuberculosis debilitated, polio crippled, elephantiasis made grotesque, leprosy maimed and sleeping sickness killed the unlucky in Liberia. And then there was malaria, greatest of the pestilential fevers.

A disease like hookworm, with the parasite literally sucking blood from the intestine, is not by itself catastrophic, but can produce anemia, which lowers the person's resistance and leaves him susceptible to those illnesses—like pneumonia—that are life-threating. The nemeses of Liberia's children were—and still are—pneumonia and diarrheal infection, the latter caused by drinking contaminated water. A child with diarrhea becomes malnourished and dehydrated. The function of vital organs such as the heart and kidney can be disrupted, and then the child is in mortal danger. Pneumonia and diarrheal infection are still the largest killers of children in developing countries and are the main reasons fifty percent of the children born in Liberia do not live to age five.

The tragedy is that seventy-five to eighty percent of the illnesses Liberians contract are preventable. Exacerbating the health care situation, at least when I was there, were the myths the country people subscribed to. The ranking public health officer in Nimba County once told me, for example, that the tribal people believed a pregnant women was better off remaining thin than putting on weight; that if you fed a baby eggs, he would grow up to be a thief. (To be sure, there are many thieves in Liberia, but not from their eating eggs as children.) As for malaria, the tribal people believed you contracted it either by taking a cold bath, eating cold rice or sucking on oranges. They probably associated the cool feeling produced by these activities with the chills accompanying malaria.

Even before coming back to Liberia, I knew I wanted to do something for the people of Kpaytuo—exactly what remained to be determined. I wanted to see what was most needed, as opposed to most wanted. Upon my return, it quickly became evident that little had changed in Kpaytuo. And after my visit to the clinic, I pondered the idea of doing something in the area of health—specifically improving the quality of Kpaytuo's drinking water: after all, most of the diseases that afflicted the villagers were directly related to, or associated with, impure water.

I'd ask the chief to call a meeting of the town elders, at which I'd make my intentions known.

Chapter 6

My stay in Kpaytuo was turning out well. Tado and Mary were wonderful, doing everything they could to make me comfortable. Mary made certain I always had boiled water to drink, though I had to tell her when the water had boiled for twenty minutes as she did not tell time. Unfortunately, it took hours for the water to cool, and then was hardly cold. My being in the house meant extra work for Mary, this at a time when she was needed on the farm. I suggested to Tado we hire a village girl, whom I would pay, to help Mary for the duration of my stay. This we did. The poisoned chunks of fish Tado had placed about the house had killed or driven the rats away; likewise, the disinfectant rendered the latrine usable, though the two-inch cockroaches still inhabited the hole and hovered, menacing and ugly, on the walls. Nevertheless, I was enjoying myself, already immensely pleased with my decision to return.

Early morning from 7:00 A.M. to 9:30 A.M. was always one of my favorite times in the village, and again, from 5:00 P.M. to 7:00 P.M., but in between those periods the heat—combined with the humidity—was searing and unyielding. I was exhausted by the slightest effort, and did not remember, though I am certain it had been so, my first exposure to the tropics being so debilitating and trying. I drank five times as much liquid as normally. Still my body craved water day and night.

I usually got out of bed by 7:45 A.M., by which time the rest of the household had been up for an hour: Tado, Mary, Mary's mother, Martha Gweh (a family member) and whoever else happened to be staying there. Martha Gweh, an adorable girl about nine, swept the house with a broom made from palm fronds almost as tall as she. Even though Tado's house stood at least sixty yards from the road (many stood less than twenty-five), we were in the middle of the dry season, so a thin layer of red dust, kicked up by the money buses on the dirt road, settled all through the house. Mary Jackson, her mother, and Mellay, the fourteen-year-old hired to assist Mary during my stay, were usually out back. If they were lucky, they would have already eaten a breakfast of cold rice left over from dinner the night before. But, as often as not, there would have been no leftovers consisting of rice or eddoes (the root of a tuberous plant), so they would do without food until the evening while working hard during the ensuing twelve hours. Both younger girls had been to the well two or three times already, while Mary had been to the bush (which is what the Liberians called the tropical forest surrounding the village), bringing back firewood for the morning fire. During the day, more wood would be chopped for the evening fire.

By the time I was up, the women were usually washing the dishes from the previous night's dinner. They used a cheap bar of soap, one of the few items manufactured in Liberia. For my benefit, the dishes and pots were rinsed in hot, though not always boiling, water. (In my own Peace Corps household, Kamah, the cook, rinsed the dishes with boiling water.) So far my intestinal tract was in perfect condition, a testament to Mary's conscientious care.

I took a bucket bath in the morning, and I felt guilty when Mellay, half my age, or Martha, half my size, fetched water from the 55-gallon drum in which it was stored, poured it into a bucket and hauled the bucket, no easy task for them, into the bathhouse. I told them I wanted to do it for myself, but every morning these hardworking, sweet-dispositioned children insisted on doing it for me, an honored guest. While I bathed, I listened to hogs slurping from the puddle of water formed where my bath water flowed out of the bathhouse.

All the water for the household was stored in the drum. Water was scooped out of the drum with an enamelware cup to fill buckets for washing, cooking and drinking. During my time as a Peace Corps Volunteer, I had stored water in a similar drum—an empty 55-gallon drum was one of the first purchases a Volunteer made when opening a new post—but I'd also kept three buckets of water on hand in my house. That way, for example, if I wanted to wash my hands, I did not have to walk outside and back for water.

Considering how much manpower, or in this case, womanpower, was devoted to taking care of the needs of one person, I recognized again how difficult it was for the average tribal family, with an annual income of about $300, to maintain a way of life that would substantially reduce their chances of becoming sick.

Of course all Liberians should have boiled their drinking water, used latrines, eaten meat, fish, vegetables and dairy products, applied iodine to cuts and kept them clean and dry, regularly disinfected their homes and latrines, and eradicated the swamps around their villages and towns where disease-carrying insects bred, but it simply wasn't realistic: they couldn't afford the kerosene, never mind the stove on which to boil water for drinking. And the women and children couldn't spend all day boiling water over an open fire, for there was work to do around the house and on the farm—cooking rice and nursing children, planting and harvesting rice. They didn't have electricity for a refrigerator and couldn't afford to buy one if they had.

They couldn't keep their cuts clean, because they couldn't afford iodine and bandages. Their clinics, if such existed, were usually out of medicine. Even if townspeople were lucky enough to live in a larger town with a government clinic and the clinic's personnel had not stolen and sold the bandages and iodine, typical Liberians simply didn't have the time to devote to medical care, what with their daily routine of walking miles through the bush to and from their farms and performing long hours of physical labor. Liberians would not live healthier lives until their economic circumstances improved.

❖ ❖ ❖

After my morning bath, I ate breakfast, usually slices of pineapple or a couple bananas, both of which were cultivated for sale. I then typed up the notes I had been taking and wrote letters on the trusty portable typewriter I had bought a month before the trip. The man who'd sold it to me had boasted of many times selling the same model, an Olympia, to missionaries bound for India, where the heat, dust and humidity gum up lesser machines. He wouldn't let me consider any other typewriter in his shop. He was right, for it worked dependably. (And it is presently stored in my office closet in my Pennsylvania home, though I have never had occasion to use it since that trip. But like the madeleine phenomenon for Proust, it triggers memories whenever I open the closet.) I often typed in the shade of Tado's house, presenting, I imagined, a rather bizarre picture to the women and children walking to and from the well. My writing sessions were anything but continuous, for old friends and new ones were always stopping by to say hello. And the younger children hovered about, fascinated by the clacking sounds and words produced by the typewriter. I, in turn, was always moved by their marveling at my *kwi* contraptions. The one they seem to enjoy most was the aerosol can that dispensed shaving cream, for though in those years—and many thereafter—I wore a beard, I shaved under and around it.

By mid-morning Mary and Mellay had finished the work around the house, and they were off, Mary to assist Tado on the farm, Mellay to do whatever she did between 11:00 A.M. and 3:00 P.M.—probably help her own people. A couple times a week Mellay washed my clothes, taking each article and rubbing it so hard against a bar of soap I thought she was going to wear a hole in the fabric.

Lunch proved to be a problem, as I had expected it would. I didn't have bread or the facilities to bake it, so that eliminated sandwiches. I had bought peanut butter and jelly and a package of crackers in Monrovia, but even as I emptied the crackers into a glass jar I noticed ants tumbling out of the package. Tado's young children and their friends, understandably fascinated with my every move, investigated whatever I brought into the house. They had probably never seen a white person up close, or at any range; I was as strange and as exotic to them as a Martian (if such existed) would be to me. They had examined the two large glass jars with tops in which I stored crackers and salt, and had forgotten to put the tops back when they were through. Ants and humidity had entered. I ended up eating canned sardines with stale crackers for lunch, a meal I found neither appetizing nor filling.

It was also unpleasant to sit at the table in the center room (it was much too hot to eat outside at that hour) with tiny, harmless house ants crawling about the table and, occasionally, climbing on the plate and food, and flies and beetles buzzing about me. I was hungry all day until dinner, when finally I got all the food, fresh and delicious, I could desire. Consequently I lost weight, which was there to lose. When I returned to Philadelphia from Africa in 1968, people used to ask me if I missed my family and friends. Of course the answer was yes. But as much as I had missed them, I had never dreamed about them, while frequently I had dreamed about spaghetti with white clam sauce. Psychiatrists can make of that what they will.

◆　◆　◆

I had discovered a relatively cool place to while away the torrid midday hours—under the huge tree near Old Man Gbon's house. ("Old Man" and "Old Ma" were used by Liberians as terms of affection and respect.) Few trees stood in the village proper, though of course hundreds of thousands made up the rain forest that surrounded it. Upon my return I noticed that almost every home was now covered with a corrugated metal roof. Palaver huts—small palm-thatched, open-air kiosks that warded off the sun—were nowhere to be seen. So there were few spots in the village to escape the blazing sun. Fortunately, someone had had the foresight not to cut down the tree in front of Old Man Gbon's house. Under its shady branches, someone had built a bamboo bench (really a platform) about eight feet long, and there, almost every day after lunch, I went, carrying a book, my camera and a notebook.

When I walked to the shady spot under the tree on this day, sitting there were Marie Sonyah, a village girl, and Lucy Gbon, still another member of the Gbon clan and the younger sister of one of my ex-students, Jesse. Lucy, age sixteen, sat on a tiny chair nursing her five-month-old child, while Marie, eighteen, sat on a taller chair plaiting Lucy's hair, a favorite midday pastime of the younger tribal women. Marie's three-month-old child slept on a nearby mat. When Marie was finished, they would switch places, so Lucy might plait Marie's hair in the most intricate of designs.

I asked Marie where the baby's Pa was, and she said, "He can be somewhere behind Monrovia." Lucy's child began to cough. Lucy told me her child was sick, and I could hear that its chest was badly congested. She went into the house and brought out a bottle of laxative. The problem was with the baby's respiratory system, so I asked Lucy why she was giving the baby something that would cause the child to go to the bathroom. Her answer: "The baby's belly can be swollen."

It is a wonder all the babies in Liberia—not just half of them—don't die before age five.

Marie Sonyah, having her hair plaited, a favorite midday pastime of the younger women, when they aren't working on the farm or otherwise engaged in back-breaking work.

Chapter 7

As the sun was setting and I was about to enter the bathhouse, I heard my name being yelled from the direction of Andrew Karma's house about forty yards away. I turned to discover someone running toward me with outstretched arms. As soon as I made out the green army fatigues, I knew that it was Sammy, my one-time houseboy and Man Friday. We embraced. He had tears in his eyes. I was more reserved, none too pleased with the reports I had received from Tado about what had happened to the $400 I had sent to Sammy for trade school years before.

He was in his late-twenties. As an adult, he was still short, no more than five feet, six inches tall; but muscular, wiry and pitch black. He wore a mustache and one of his front teeth, those beautiful teeth that gave him that winsome smile, was missing, knocked out, he said, when he tried to stop a fight between two friends who had been drinking. He was self-conscious about the missing tooth, as he often placed his hand over his mouth when he spoke. Like that of so many Liberians, his body's normal development had been slightly retarded, either from a vitamin deficiency—the Liberian diet lacks sufficient protein, calcium, iron and vitamin A—or from a childhood illness.

When he'd learned I had returned to Kpaytuo, he'd begged his superior officer for a three-day emergency leave, claiming a relative was seriously ill. The first thing he wanted me to do was to visit his mother, so she and the other families in his quarter of the village might see us together again. Upon the death of his natural father in 1967 I had become what we in America would call Sammy's guardian uncle. And since after my departure from Liberia I had continued to help Sammy, to the Liberians (including Sammy) I had become his adoptive father—his Pa.

I tried to piece his life together from the time that I'd left Liberia—hardly an easy task with the country people, who don't place much

The author and Sammy Dahngbae, my ex-houseboy, then about 28, who had joined the Liberian army. February 1982.

importance on specific times, dates or even the sequence of events. Finally, I asked him to write it down for me, which he gladly did. In 1968–69, he was in Kpaytuo, helping my replacements during their first few difficult months as Peace Corps Volunteers. But they had decided to divide the work among the schoolboys and schoolgirls rather than to have a permanent household staff. Having reached the fifth grade with no money coming in, and no Liberian father to help him, Sammy had moved to Ganta in 1971, staying with his sister (same Ma, same Pa), who owned a tiny shop there. The following year he went to Saclepea, worked part-time for a Lebanese man who owned a store there, and attended school. He lived in Saclepea from 1972 to 1974, reaching the ninth grade. As the school he attended only went as far as the ninth grade, he was forced to move again, this time to Gbarngba, county

63

headquarters of Bong County. He remained in school for half a year, but because, in his words, of "so-so hard times," meaning not enough money for his school uniforms, shoes, housing, clothes and food, he had dropped out of school in 1975. By then he had reached the tenth grade. He ended up working in Monrovia with a French company that exported timber. That is where he had been working when we resumed contact in 1977. He liked the job, except for the low pay, twenty-five cents an hour, and the fact that his boss spoke only French and they often had to communicate in sign language. Then it was back to Ganta, where he worked as a nurse's aide after graduating from a four-month training course at the hospital there.

In May of 1980, less than a month after the coup, he joined the army for a five-year enlistment. Having completed a medical training course, he now worked at an army clinic. He had two children with his common-law wife. He also had a girlfriend, he told me matter-of-factly, as an American male might tell you he owned a car *and* a camper. He made me promise to come see the children, and told me he had no intention of marrying his common-law wife.

Tado and Zoelay Retty had told me Sammy was a lady's man: women literally threw themselves at him, most unusual because he was neither rich nor powerful—the two most common aphrodisiacs. What Sammy had was charm and confidence.

"Teacher, can I come to stay in America with you?" he asked.

It was a largely expected question, for I don't think there lived a man, woman or child in Liberia who did not wish to visit, and then find a way to remain in, America.

"How long do you want to stay in America?" I asked.

"Ten to fifteen years," he answered.

I smiled, imagining he was going to say a couple of years. "What about your children? They'll be so-so big people time you come back with gray head."

"I can bring them over."

"And what will you do in America?" I asked.

"I can work in a factory."

"And when time comes to return to Liberia?"

"I can buy coffee and cocoa and sell them here," he said.

As best I could determine, he knew nothing about buying and selling coffee and cocoa. I told him we'd discuss the matter when I visited him in Monrovia. Then Sammy told me what he knew about the coup. His version of what happened—and why it happened—was similar to Frank and Arthur's. But Sammy added a footnote concerning President Tolbert's wife, who was arrested after the coup and told that she was going to be murdered like her husband unless she revealed where Tolbert kept his money. Supposedly she told them that he had buried it in a box in the graveyard on his farm and wore the key to the box on a toe of his right foot. The soldiers, according to Sammy, dug Tolbert's body up from the common grave where it had been dumped, found the key, and uncovered the hidden treasure. (And Long John Silver, of *Treasure Island*, got his share.)

Another photo of the author and Sammy Dahngbae, my Liberian "son," in 1982.

❖ ❖ ❖

Why wasn't I happier to see Sammy? Part of the reason undoubtedly was his failure to use the $400 I had sent him to enroll in a trade school. He claimed the school discouraged tribal people from attending, which might have been true, but I doubted it. Tado Jackson's version of why Sammy never enrolled, corroborated by Zoelay Retty, was that Sammy had gotten in a "helluva woman palaver," and had had to use a good portion of the money to settle the palaver. He had squandered my gift and had never become an electrician, and I was disappointed. I was also none too thrilled that he had joined the army, where the only thing he would learn how to do, I feared, was to bully and to extort money from Liberia's already downtrodden populace. But what really shocked and bothered me, the truth be told, was that the adorable thirteen-year-old with whom I had passed so many pleasant hours was gone. He had been replaced by an adult—with adult needs and responsibilities and problems. The very qualities that had made Sammy a delightful companion and effective houseboy—his charm, ambition, aggressiveness and nimble mind—I held against him as an adult. I could hardly fault Sammy for the "crime" of growing up. But fault him I did—though only temporarily. In time I accepted his adult self—wasn't that grand of me?—and came to enjoy his company as I had so many years before. And over the years, I continued to help him.

Chapter 8

I could have chosen a better time of the year for my visit. I had arrived in February, at the beginning of the rice cycle, the first stage of which involved clearing a small tract of one's land of trees, vines, shrubs and undergrowth. Every morning from February through March, the men of the village would leave around six o'clock, and spend the ensuing ten or twelve hours clearing the bush. This they performed with cutlasses and axes, preferably to the beat of a drum and the singing of work songs. The work was exhausting. Imagine flailing away for hours at a tree three to five feet in diameter, and doing this day after day. While the men cut the bush, the women and children prepared the large midday meal, that is if any rice remained from the previous year's crop.

Before the bush was cleared in the old days, families approached a *Zo* (for want of a better term, a "medicine man") or a high official in the secret society, the latter an all-powerful social, religious and educational institution that regulated tribal society. Their influence waned, though they were still influential, after the Second World War.

Chickens were sacrificed and ancestors appeased to ensure the fertility of the soil and protect one and all from accident or illness during the planting season. As it was, if a man accidentally cut himself or some misfortune befell him, it was assumed his wife was the reason: she had cheated on him; thus the injury, which was duly investigated.

Until the bush was cleared, many families remained overnight on their farms, sleeping under temporary thatched lean-tos, so they didn't have to trudge the few miles back to Kpaytuo at the end of the long day. They usually returned to the village at dusk on Saturday. After my arrival in 1966, seeing the village nearly deserted during the day and most of the week, I remember asking where everyone was? The answer, though I didn't really understand it for weeks, was working and staying on their farms.

The fallen shrubs, vines and trees were allowed to dry partially and were then burned in late April or May, often more than once, as the ash from the fire provided the soil with minerals it needs, while the heat broke up the earth and served as a substitute, though not a very good one, for ploughing. Men, women and children hauled away the burned tree trunks and limbs. The fire didn't spread to the surrounding forest, for the uncut trees and shrubs were too green to burn.

Once the backbreaking task of cutting, burning and clearing the bush was complete, the men's work on the farm was finished. They had other tasks to complete: sharpening or repairing their tools and building traps for game; venturing into the bush in the middle of the night to hunt for meat. They passed much of the day sitting around with their friends playing a game they called "country checkers," and settling and often instigating palavers. Their habit of drinking palm wine, which comes from the sap of the palm tree left to ferment into a mildly alcoholic, slightly fizzy liquid that looks like soapy water, helped put them in the proper judicial frame of mind to resolve the palavers.

The women and children began planting by June, scratching in the rice seeds with short-handled hoes or sticks. The seeds had to be in the ground and taking root by mid-June else the heavy rains would wash them away and spell disaster for the family: there would be no food. Various "medicines" were concocted, sacrifices again offered to ancestors, and taboos (no sex during the day, among many others) enforced to protect the crop and increase its yield. The great fear was that someone or something would witch the crop, perhaps even an ancestor who felt neglected. While the seeds sprouted, the children stood watch during the day—like human scarecrows—frightening away the "rice birds," or weavers, intent on eating new sprouts and maturing grain. My male students, excellent marksmen with their homemade slingshots, fired at the birds when the birds were not frightened off by the scarecrows. While protecting the nascent rice crop, of course, the children couldn't very well attend school, a fact not all new Peace Corps Volunteers understood. Too many of us were offended when the students stayed away from school, little knowing or appreciating the extent to which the children were needed on the family farm at that phase of the rice cycle. I count myself among the guilty, at least during my first months in the country.

By September the rice began to mature, and then harvesting, another job for the women and children, commenced, reaching its peak in November, and sometimes continuing as late as December. The rice, during my day, was harvested by hand by cutting it off at the stalk with a tiny knife.

That's why November, better still December, would have been the ideal month for my visit: by then the rice would have been harvested—eventually to be cleaned by women and children, pounding the stalks with a five-foot long wooden pestle in a two-foot high wooden mortar. The people would have had plenty of food in their bellies (and in storage), and everyone would have had the time to remain in the village, relaxing during the day, and singing, dancing and dallying through much of the night. The school year also ended by mid-December, though it was not supposed to end officially until late December. (The Liberian school year began in late February; the first semester ran to July, the second from July to the end of the year.)

Many of the sons and daughters of villages like Kpaytuo, who had no choice but to attend high school elsewhere, there being no high school in Kpaytuo, returned to the village at the end of the school year. And those sons and daughters of the villages and towns who worked elsewhere, usually in Monrovia, also returned to their "hometown" in late December for the festivities and to reunite with family and old friends.

All these events were more than reason enough for feasts. And while they were at it, the Liberians celebrated the Christmas-New Year season, too, though not with "Jingle Bells" and Christmas trees, but with tribal singing and dancing; cooking and consuming enormous quantities of rice, goat and chicken; and for the richest man in a village, slaughtering a cow. (From picture books my students knew about Santa Claus, whom they referred to as "the White Man's Devil," meaning a powerful medicine man or witch doctor).

Even the weather in the interior was more tolerable to me, if not the country people, in late December. Though the year-round temperature averages in the mid-eighties, with a stifling relative humidity in the mid-eighties or even nineties, on many December nights the temperature dropped to the mid-seventies, with the humidity reaching a pleasant seventy degrees. In those circumstances I slept covered with a light blanket, and I closed the tiny shutters in my bedroom. I enjoyed waking up to a cool mist, though to the Liberians it was like being in the Antarctic. During my stint as a Peace Corps Volunteer, there were still more festivities on November 29, President Tubman's birthday, which was a national holiday. Days before and days after his birthday the country stopped: no work, no school, all government and private businesses closed. For all practical purposes, difficult as it may be to believe, Liberia pretty well shut down from about November 25 through the New Year. It didn't make for a productive society, but Liberians—and we guests—had a helluva lot of fun.

❖ ❖ ❖

Sunday is a day of rest and everyone is in the village, even for those people who the rest of the week remain at their farms overnight during the "clearing phase" of the rice cycle. So it was on this day, under the huge tree in front of Old Man Gbon's home, that I talked to the town chief, town elders and a dozen or so adult males about my interest in doing something for Kpaytuo.

Though there were wells in the various quarters of the village, they were shallow, dirty and, as they had no rim or cover or protective wall around them, easily contaminated. The women and particularly the children approached them so many times each day that it was not long before the ground around them turned into a mud puddle. Ironic, then, that no women were present at the town meeting; women were not included in such discussions in those times.

I told those assembled that I wanted to improve Kpaytuo's drinking water by building new and better wells. But before reaching any final decision, I wanted them to discuss my proposal, while I'd be looking into the best type of well to build. They were thrilled, and not a few of them spoke of me in terms that would have been inappropriate (and embarrassing) if applied to Mother Teresa, much less myself. Their praise notwithstanding, I wondered if many of those present—Tado Jackson and Old Man Tuazama excepted—believed me. Since it was a Liberian inclination to make promises and pronouncements that one had no intention of keeping, I understood the skepticism of my audience. Nor was philanthropy something the Liberians comprehended easily. Why should I or anyone want to help them? The more cynical among them probably thought I was proposing the well project in hopes of receiving better treatment during my visit. Or because my ancestral spirits had commanded me to do so. Or perhaps by building wells in Kpaytuo I would end up with potent magic or medicine.

The concern of those at the meeting willing to give me the benefit of the doubt regarding the well project was that I avoid channeling the money to them through any Liberian governmental agency. To do so, they were convinced from experience, would mean they'd never see either the money or what it was intended to buy or build. So in spite of the rhetoric and slogans since the coup two years before, the billboards in Monrovia exhorting Liberians to "Join Hands and Promote the Revolution," renaming a bridge the "People's Bridge," referring to the court as the "People's Court," and the optimistic talk about change, the same old—and monumental—corruption still flourished.

I reminded them that this was not my first day in Liberia, so I understood their concern. I knew the country, I told them—its good and bad points. I emphatically stated that I was not going to let anyone, in or out of government, "eat my money." On the other hand, I wanted—and needed—to receive assurances from the government that whatever I proposed to do in Kpaytuo met with its approval, lest my gift come back to haunt the people of Kpaytuo. I explained that I did not want the government telling the people of Kpaytuo some day, over an entirely different matter: "You want books for your school or medicine for a clinic, don't come to us. Go speak to your rich white man in America."

The chief, not a little taken aback by my frankness—tribal Liberians couched their feelings in imprecise language and took a circuitous path to ask a question or express an opinion—smiled and said, "Cherry, for true, you know our people."

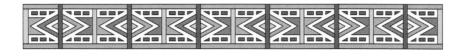

SACLEPEA

David, 71, and Maud Carson, 69, missionaries. David could fix just about any machine—from radios to generators, broken locks to typewriters. He was a founding member in 1938 of the Inland Church in Liberia, then part of the Worldwide Evangelical Council.

Chapter 9

Having decided to do something about the water situation in Kpaytuo, it was necessary for me to return to Monrovia, where I hoped to learn more about the project: Should I pay for the construction of a water system operated by electricity? Was that practical? Or should I pay for the construction of wells that did not depend on electricity? If so, what kind of wells? I didn't know a bloody thing about wells. Where would the parts come from, who would dig and install them? And how much was all this going to cost me?

Rather than make the trip down to Monrovia in one day, always a long and unpleasant experience, I decided to break it up by spending the night in Saclepea with David and Maud Carson, the couple who ran the Saclepea mission. Though surely I must have met the Carsons at some time between 1966 and the end of 1967, I did not remember them; but then when I, a wise man of twenty-two, lived in Liberia, I never had much to do with missionaries, believing them to be hopelessly misguided, puritanical old fuddy-duddies bent on converting the Liberians to their respective Western religions, and in the process destroying all that was worthy in tribal culture. I conveniently forgot that the finest Liberian I knew, Tado Jackson, was the product of a mission. Maybe it was I, at twenty-two, who was misguided?

The Carsons were friends, confidants and spiritual counselors to Tado—to them and their mission he delivered his two young children in 1966 for safe keeping after the death of his first wife. Tado suggested I talk to Mr. Carson about the water project, since Mr. Carson had built his own water system at the mission.

◆　◆　◆

Christianity has played a large role in Liberia's history, more so than in most African countries. The early supporters and members of the

American Colonization Society were devout Christians and many were ministers. There was something evangelical in forming a society whose purpose was to resettle freed persons of color on the shores of West Africa. In 1820 there were about two hundred thousand freed persons of color in the United States, of whom about twenty thousand eventually settled in the area that would become Liberia.

Among the leading figures in the early days of the colony (later the Republic of Liberia) were the Rev. Samuel Bacon, one of three white men to accompany eighty-eight blacks on the voyage of the *Elizabeth* in 1820—the first venture of the Colonization Society; and the Rev. Jehudi Ashmun, who arrived in Liberia in 1822 and was probably responsible more than anyone else for keeping the small, embattled and disgruntled colony from disintegrating. The influence of religion in Liberia continued well into the twentieth century: prior to the coup, Liberia's President, William Tolbert, was a Baptist minister and once headed the World Baptist Alliance.

When the settlers declared Liberia an independent country in 1847, the country was looked upon as the Promised Land, to which it was hoped, in the words of the Liberian Constitution, "the dispersed and oppressed children of Africa" would return, a goal not unlike the dream of the Jewish people to return to Zion. Nor was the evangelical fervor to be confined to Liberia. Her Founding Fathers saw their mission as an even more challenging task: "to regenerate and enlighten this benighted Continent." Not for nothing was Liberia called the "Missionary Nation."

Alas, like so much of what was written in the Liberian Constitution, this never came to pass. The task of converting the tribal people was left to white missionaries, with most of them coming from the United States (further cementing the special relationship between the two countries) and Canada. Supposedly circa the 1960s there were more missionaries per capita in Liberia than in any other country. As it was, it was only in the twentieth century that the Americo-Liberians granted the missionaries permission to preach in the interior, and then on one condition: that the missionaries establish and maintain schools. This they did and well into the 1960s mission schools bore the brunt of the task of educating tribal children. During my Peace Corps service and during my visit back, mission schools were the best—in truth the only decent—primary and secondary schools in the country. (The only exception was the American Cooperative School, an expensive private school in Monrovia with grades one through twelve. That is where the Americo-Liberian elite, families of the diplomatic corps, and many foreign philanthropic organizations' personnel, like CARE, sent their children.)

While most of the tribal people were animist, about ten percent had converted to Christianity, though many converts continued to believe in and practice native rituals and medicine. The powerful Chief Towe can serve as an example. He publicly announced his conversion to Christianity, but before attending church one day he wanted to sue thirteen of his wives who, he believed, had witched him. But others, of whom my friend Tado Jackson was the paradigm, believed to the letter, and tried to lead their lives by, the Bible. Upon my return I sensed that the more dependable, hardest-working, civic-minded tribal Liberians tended to identify themselves as Christians. (With one exception, that would be the entrepreneurial Mandingoes, who were Muslim and comprised about five percent of the tribal population. While they were hard-working, they preferred to keep among themselves, so I wouldn't call them civic-minded, at least not in Liberia in those days.)

❖   ❖   ❖

That afternoon I waited alongside the road in Kpaytuo for a money bus bound for Ganta, on the road to which is Saclepea and its mission, my destination. As there was no money bus schedule—pigs will fly before that day comes—one never knew if the wait for a bus up-country would be thirty minutes or three hours. That being the case, a few villagers almost always kept one company during the roadside vigil, more so when I, a special visitor, was waiting. After about an hour's wait, a truck rumbled into view. I flagged it down and observed that it was a government vehicle with about ten passengers piled on top, along with their bags of rice and bunches of plantains. The driver agreed to take me to Saclepea for 75¢, the same fare I would have paid on a money bus. One saw government trucks hauling wood and sand and bricks and chickens and corrugated metal and bananas and passengers, but rare was it to see a government truck actually transporting only what it was supposed to—in this case the bags of cement on which the ten passengers sat.

The driver invited me to sit in the cabin with his fat girlfriend and him, and their child, and his girlfriend's even fatter girlfriend. Even though it was infinitely more comfortable to ride in the cab of a bus or truck on the roads of Liberia, I was reluctant to join them for lack of space. But the driver would hear none of my reservations and would have been offended had I turned down his invitation. So by straddling my legs around the gear shift and moving them according to the gear he was in, we five all fit in, snugly to be sure. A challenge all Westerners faced in a country like Liberia was to guard against believing—and then acting as if—one deserved the best seat on the money bus or taxi, solely because of our white skin.

With its lush foliage and vivid colors, the Liberian interior was beautiful, but it was a natural beauty. Liberians would never think of planting a tree or flower to improve the landscape. Growing up amid nature's bounty, they didn't find flowers and trees especially enchanting; rather, these were ever-present elements in the environment, like the sun and the sky. George Schwab, an acclaimed Africanist, captured the Liberian attitude in his book, *Tribes of the Liberian Hinterland*, when he quoted one of them as saying, "Whoever heard of anyone being so foolish as to plant trees! That's God's palaver."

The sites in the interior where minimal gardening or landscaping had been undertaken were so much the lovelier. Such was the case with the Saclepea mission, located about three-quarters of a mile from the town proper. The mission complex was three hundred yards off the dirt road, far enough away so the clouds of red dust continually raised by the money buses and logging trucks thundering up and down the laterite-rich road did not reach it. As I approached the mission complex I saw well-groomed shrubs, flowers and palm trees. And nestled among them, at the end of a circular dirt driveway, stood the main house.

Walking up the dirt driveway towards the house, I observed a skinny man in Bermuda shorts and a T-shirt, with skin the color of alabaster, standing on a ledge twenty-five feet off the ground. He was peering into one of five barrels. A Liberian, who was watching him, turned as I approached and said, "Look at that old man up there." That "old man" was David Carson, paterfamilias of the Saclepea mission. He was inspecting the mission's water system.

I yelled up and introduced myself. "Yes," he said, "Tado had mentioned you were in the country." He added that I would find Mrs. Carson inside and something to drink, his Irish accent sounding especially pronounced in that setting. Then he turned back to his task.

I found Mrs. Carson, who after a few minutes insisted I call her Maud. With her was Susan Smith, a Canadian-born missionary in her mid-twenties who lived with the Carsons. Maud, also Canadian-born, immediately offered me freshly baked oatmeal cookies, which I devoured while gulping down four glasses of water.

After I rested for a short while, Maud Carson took me on a brief tour of the mission, beginning behind the house, where three girls, about age fourteen, were cooking that evening's meal on an open fire for the thirty-three girls and eleven boys who boarded at the mission. Another sixty-six children attended school at the mission, but did not live there.

The older resident girls took turns cooking and cleaning, while the boys fetched water and wood. The boys also had a vegetable garden in which they worked most afternoons until 5:00, at which time one of the Carsons would blow a horn, signaling the end of the work period and the beginning of the play period, which in Liberia for a young male meant one thing—soccer (though like the rest of the world, they called it football).

Maud showed me their chicken house, which provided them with large, fresh eggs. I never saw a chicken coop in Kpaytuo and rarely an egg, fresh or otherwise. And since the local hunters knew the Carsons were always in the market for it, the household always had freshly killed antelope meat on hand. Though Maud, who was nearing seventy, felt weak from what she suspected was malaria, she never slackened the frantic pace at which she bounded about the place. She was in and out of her kitchen supervising the girls cooking that evening's meal for the household, then outside to make certain the girls cooking for the students were not fooling around, then back inside the house, where the mother of a student had come, unexpectedly, to discuss a problem.

There was medicine to apply to a student's infected sore, and a man at the back door selling freshly caught fish, an argument to settle between two schoolgirls, and still she had to prepare for her next class. She had stopped teaching years ago, but because one of the missionaries was in the United States on medical leave, Maud was teaching her classes until the woman returned at the end of the month. And there was the ever-present challenge of advising the Liberian girls to avoid pregnancy out of wedlock—as easily accomplished in those years as plugging up Niagara Falls.

She flapped around the place like a hen clucking after her wayward chicks. I wondered what the Liberians made of her peripatetic manner and shrill voice. Probably they were mystified, though by now used to her ways, also grateful that she and her husband gave so much of themselves in their (and surely they would add, God's) work.

The house, which Maud told me her husband had built, was of mud brick, although I'd have sworn it was made of cement; the walls were nicely plastered, about a foot thick, and painted an apricot hue. The ceilings were high and well-insulated, the windows four feet high (about twice the height and width of those in Tado's home), all of which made sitting in the home bearable in the hottest hours of the afternoon. In the living room were a sturdy wooden sofa and two wooden chairs and a fireplace, all designed and built by Mr. Carson. There were some paintings on the wall and a plaque that read, "He that dwelleth in the secret place of the Most High shall abide under the shadow of the Almighty."

The rooms were large and clean, including the one in which I would sleep, which normally was the habitation of the female missionary then home on medical leave. Besides the three bedrooms, there was a tiny room off the dining room area that served as an office of sorts, containing Mr. Carson's tools, a short-wave radio, and hundreds of old books and pamphlets, all of them religious in nature. The dining room had a large, solid wood table, around which six could sit comfortably, and high wooden cabinets. The kitchen had a kerosene refrigerator, four kerosene burners on which Maud cooked and baked, the usual assortment of pots and pans one finds in the kitchen of a resourceful cook, and a large counter running along one entire side of the room, with bowls filled with grapefruits from their own trees, limes, pineapples, bananas and rice.

The Carsons and Susan were members of the Worldwide Evangelization Crusade (today called the Worldwide Evangelization for Christ), an interdenominational organization with missions in thirty-two countries. (And, though I was unaware of it at the time, the Mission's headquarters were in Fort Washington, Pennsylvania, about a forty-five minute drive from my home.) In Liberia the Worldwide Evangelization Crusade was called the Liberian Inland Mission and was founded by eight white Westerners in 1938. The only surviving founder in 1982 was David Carson, who at seventy-one had the energy of a man forty years younger. He could fix just about any machine ever designed—from radios to generators, a broken lock to typewriters, as the Carsons instructed the mission girls in rudimentary typing. (The time of which I write predated the availability of inexpensive computers, much less ubiquitous smart phones and tablets.) The only doors I ever saw shut properly in the interior of Liberia were the Carsons'. He'd cultivated this knack for mending things in his native Ireland, where as a young man he'd earned his living repairing watches. Aside from building the house, he had wired it and the rest of the mission for electricity. The generator was down, though, during my visit, while a part was in Monrovia for repair.

Using a small motor, he had also hooked up a rudimentary, but effective, water system. Hitting water thirty feet down, he sank a one-inch pipe attached to a piston water pump driven by a gasoline engine. That pumped the water to the foot of the water tower, and then up about thirty-five feet into the five 55-gallon drums. Other pipes carried the water into the Carsons' bathroom. The water drunk at the mission, by both the missionaries and the students, passed via another pipe through a chemical filter, removing harmful parasites.

Mr. Carson—I never could bring myself to call him Dave—told me that a generator-driven system for Kpaytuo would have to be more powerful than his. That being so, he did not believe Kpaytuo's citizens could keep such a system in operation for very long. He suggested I think in terms of simple, but dependable, draw-bucket wells: there were fewer parts to worry about breaking. The main consideration would be to dig wells deep enough, with a sturdy cover and a concrete lip to prevent mud and debris from winding up inside.

For dinner Maud served canned meat, homemade cole slaw, homemade potato salad, baked beans and, for dessert, fresh pineapple and bananas. They drank hot tea; I drank water, of which I could not drink enough. Maud apologized for the meal, explaining that they ate their hot and big meal, usually rice and meat, in the afternoon. I had no complaints, I told her. Coming from Kpaytuo, it was like dining in the Ritz. Each of us even had his or her own linen napkin.

During dinner Maud told me the story of Sarah, Tado's first wife. After the difficulty of carrying her first child, Lee, Sarah was terrified of becoming pregnant again. But pregnant she became, and, sure enough, there were complications. She was taken from Kpaytuo to the Ganta Hospital. Maud never did make it clear to me what was wrong with Sarah. The Ganta missionaries, who ran the hospital, contacted the Carsons via shortwave, telling them they should summon Tado from Kpaytuo, as his wife was fading quickly. Maud said she remembered the day as if it were yesterday, and not sixteen years before. When they reached Kpaytuo, Tado was working in his garden, so someone was sent to fetch him. They—the Carsons and Tado—drove the two hours to Ganta, but arrived too late: Tado's wife had died. Tado was devastated, according to Maud, crying like a baby. Mr. Carson pointed out that crying for a Liberian male is unusual, since it is considered something that only children and women do. Maud also told me, much to my surprise, that in 1969, Tado's last year at the Zorzor Rural Teacher Training Institute, he had a nervous breakdown. "He was cuckoo," she said, "but in time he recovered."

It was obvious the Carsons were extremely fond of Tado. So much the worse for the news I had to tell them. I had discovered, for he made absolutely no effort to hide the fact, that Tado regularly took the tranquilizer Valium, three 5-milligram tablets during the day, two before bedtime. I told Tado that Valium, no matter what the quack in Monrovia who'd suggested or sold them said, was not the answer to his problems. (One didn't—and still doesn't—need a prescription to buy antibiotics or drugs like Valium in Liberia; all one needs is money.) I told Tado that he could become—and indeed probably was—psychologically and physically dependent on them. He was shocked, having no idea of the potential harm related to continued use of them.

Maud said Tado was very naive. "He trusts people too much," she said. She recounted that Tado had been elected to the board of the coffee and cocoa co-operative, which was headquartered in Saclepea. Government auditors had approached Tado recently and told him that unless he agreed to give them $5,000 they would swear that their audit revealed he had stolen money from the co-operative. Tado refused to give the scoundrels a penny. True to their word, they accused Tado of embezzling money from the co-operative. The palaver was then in the courts. Tado could ill afford to take time from his work to travel to San-niquellie, the county seat, for the trial. Nor did he have money to hire a lawyer, assuming there was even one to be hired in Sanniquellie. The case (one has to know Tado and see how modestly he lives to appreciate what a calumny the charge was) was driving the overburdened man to Valium. (Fortunately, in time, Tado was eventually to break his dependency on Valium.)

◆　◆　◆

In 1938, when Mr. Carson had arrived in Liberia, there was no road into the interior, let alone kerosene refrigerators and generators to produce electricity. This skinny, unprepossessing man had walked thousands of miles through swamps, over hills, through the rain forest, to the remotest hamlets and villages of Liberia to preach the word of his Lord. It was an impressive feat of dedication and endurance—especially since he survived to recount it.

He reminisced about the days before the motor road was completed in the 1940s, when the tribal converts of the Inland Mission thought nothing of walking great distances, sometimes as much as fifty miles, to attend special mission convocations. Then the motor road was built and tribal members would come to the meetings only in a vehicle. At one point the Inland Mission owned a small airplane, though they later sold it. "It is just like the Liberians to go from the extreme of walking fifty miles to attend a meeting to saying that unless they were flown in, they would not attend the meeting," Mr. Carson observed ruefully.

Mr. Carson was direct, taciturn and devout. He had no time for small talk or pleasantries—for there was always work to be done on the mission—and could not care less about politics, economics or sociology—the bogus "religions" of our enlightened day. He was a hard, though fair, taskmaster. I probably wouldn't have taken to him when I was twenty-two, but at thirty-nine, with little in common, I very much liked and admired him.

After dinner, while the Carsons were busy with something or other, Susan, the other missionary in the household, diplomatically asked me what my relationship was with God. I responded by saying I had none. I told her I was Jewish, though more culturally than theologically. And that was the end of our brief conversation.

❖　❖　❖

I knew there was a female Peace Corps Volunteer in Saclepea named Barbara Gastian, but that was all I knew. Excusing myself from the Carsons but promising to return before their evening prayer, I headed to Barbara's house in the dark. After asking a passer-by for directions to the Peace Corps woman's house, I knocked on the door of a large home and a hearty-looking woman in her mid-to-late twenties with blond hair, wearing a caftan, answered the door. It was Barbara. She asked me how I got her name, and I told her it had been given to me by a Peace Corps staff member in Monrovia.

"I'm no longer a Volunteer," she said, somewhat miffed that the Peace Corps continued to think of her as a Volunteer.

Barbara had served her two years as a Peace Corps Volunteer. Then, tired of living on the meager Peace Corps salary of two hundred and fifty-two dollars a month, but still interested in her work, if somewhat less encouraged about doing it in Liberia, she had accepted a job with the Nimba County Agricultural Development Project (NCADP), a program funded by the West German government. (In 1982 Germany was still divided into two countries, East and West Germany.) Barbara's job, the same one she had performed as a Peace Corps Volunteer, was to develop fisheries in the area—that is, to teach the people how to farm fish, some of which they could eat, and some of which they could sell, subsequently improving their diets and financial conditions.

The daughter of a United States Agency for International Development (USAID) economist, Barbara had lived most of her childhood in South America. Her contract with the Nimba County Agricultural Development Project almost over, she hoped to return to Panama, preferably as an USAID employee, doing there what she had been unable to do in Liberia. Within fifteen minutes a young white man drove up on a motorcycle. It was Richard Kodl, a Peace Corps Volunteer working with the Nimba County Agricultural Development Project. He was developing irrigated rice projects. Sitting on Barbara's porch, we talked, smoked cigarettes and drank Club beer, Liberia's national brew, just as I had on so many occasions with my Volunteer friends years ago.

They asked me about Saclepea in the old days. I told them I used to visit the Volunteers stationed there and buy my supplies at the store owned by a Lebanese man named Riad. Barbara mentioned that the Lebanese merchants in Saclepea, who owned all the retail stores, had recently been driven out by the Mandingoes. (The Mandingo tribe was spread throughout West Africa. In Liberia, they made up about five percent of the population and were petty traders.) One Lebanese merchant, she said, had died in Saclepea under mysterious circumstances, another back in Lebanon under equally mystifying circumstances— both supposedly poisoned at the hands of the Mandingoes. This prompted the surviving Lebanese merchants of Saclepea to flee while they still could.

Neither Barbara's nor Richard's work took them to Kpaytuo, so what little they knew about the place came from a Liberian field technician with the Nimba County Agricultural Development Project assigned to a cocoa project in Kpaytuo. Apparently the field technician found Kpaytuo's citizens difficult to work with. In fact, he claimed to have found human skulls lying on the ground in a cemetery there and refused to work in Kpaytuo. Like so many events in Liberia, it was difficult to uncover the truth of the story. No doubt the Liberian field technician refused to return to Kpaytuo, thereby depriving its citizens of the benefits of the cocoa program. But what was the reason? Had he been involved in "woman palaver," as most Liberian men at some time in their lives were? Had he tried to extort food or money from the town in return for performing his job? Such behavior by Liberia's civil servants was hardly unusual. Or maybe, as he claimed, he had stumbled upon a secret society ritual that he felt—rightly or wrongly—threatened his life. I asked Richard and Barbara how my ex-students who had remained in Kpaytuo felt towards those of my students who had left and were presumably better off working for various government agencies and European and American concessions.

"They would probably like to poison them," Richard said. There was a man, he told me, who had a fish farm. The people in this man's village routinely defecated in his fish pond. One day there was a palaver in the man's village between two girls. When the man tried to break up the palaver, the villagers, according to Richard, seized on this as an excuse to beat the hell out of him. According to Richard, that's how envious they were of the man using a *kwi* method, such as a fish farm, to better himself, and how fearful they were that he might succeed.

As Schwab observed in his classic book on Liberia, jealousy and hatred, mostly based on fear and the instinct for self-preservation, are common traits of the Liberian tribesmen. He wrote: "Since success depends upon the favor of unseen powers, and the favor of these powers can be obtained only be means of powerful medicines or magic, a neighbor more powerful than oneself obviously possesses a more powerful medicine. He is, therefore, a potential enemy."

That isn't to say every native wants to poison every other Liberian: for, to quote Schwab again, "As with us, there are men and women of good and bad disposition; those who are amiable, peaceable, long suffering; those who are quarrelsome and quick tempered. Some are ambitious, neat, and cleanly; some shiftless, slovenly, and dirty. Some are easily satisfied, contented, and generous; others dissatisfied, constantly finding fault, nagging, miserly. One finds the trusting, confiding, and well wishing; the suspicious and jealous. There are persons who are diplomatic and courteous; and those who are blundering or bully trouble-makers." The master Schwab was right on the money.

Barbara and Richard felt that Liberia was in much worse shape in the two years since the coup. Whatever the faults of the Tolbert government and the Americo-Liberians, Barbara and Richard contended, at least the government had had direction, some commercial activity and a stable, if despicable, ruling bourgeois. Now there was a new, though equally repellent, class in power, little commercial activity and little stability. Barbara predicted the economy would come tumbling down in the not so distant future.

❖   ❖   ❖

Returning to the Carsons' mission, I found them with Susan in the living room about to read from the Bible, as was their custom before retiring. I took a place among them. I am certain that Susan told the Carsons that I was Jewish and of my relationship with God, such as it was, for before reading Mr. Carson said, "Robert, you should realize that all of us will be called to meet our Maker some day." He also said they believed, as it has been prophesized in the Bible, that Israel would be on the verge of destruction by the Arabs—this would be Armageddon—whereupon the Messiah would appear to save Israel from doom. Recognizing the Messiah as their true and only God, the Israelites, he said, would repent and convert to Christianity. He did not say when Armageddon would occur.

Mr. Carson read from *John: 3*, a conversation between Nicodemus, a ruler of the Jews, and Jesus. Jesus tells Nicodemus that unless a man is born anew he cannot see the kingdom of God, and reminds him that "God so loved the world that he gave his only son, that whoever believes in him should not perish but have eternal life." While Mr. Carson read, I gazed about, hoping to fix in my mind's eye the special moment: the room was bathed in a soft, golden light and there, so far from civilization, I felt a peacefulness and spirituality the likes of which I had never experienced. If I've ever felt God's presence, it was in that room, with his servants, David and Maud Carson.

MONROVIA

Major Paul Tuazama, in worldly terms probably the most successful, certainly the most influential, of my ex-students, Monrovia 1982.

Chapter 10

Monrovia, Liberia's capital, was named in honor of James Monroe, during whose presidency the movement to resettle American slaves in West Africa commenced. It is one of only two world capitals named for a U.S. President, the other of course being Washington, D.C. With a population of about 350,000 in 1982, Monrovia was far and away Liberia's largest city, home to about a third of its population—the cultural and political heart of the country. Monrovia also ranks as the world's wettest capital, with an average annual rainfall of 180 inches a year; and during the rainy season it might receive more rain in one month (30 inches) than London receives in a year!

Before leaving Saclepea for the trip to Monrovia, I had introduced myself to a supervisor of the Nimba County Agricultural Development Project. He told me that if I wanted to learn about the water situation in the interior, I ought to speak to a certain Dutch hydrologist at the Liberian Hydrological Office in Monrovia. That was where I was heading, when the other passenger in the taxi, whom I did not know, got out at his destination, a two-story building. (It was common in Monrovia to share taxis with two or three people going in the same direction.) Men in smart-looking uniforms milled about the surrounding ground. They were members of the National Police Force. Also standing idly about were scores of young men and children. The larger and the more important the governmental building in Monrovia, the greater the number of people who milled about outside. What, I often asked myself, were they waiting for? Perhaps the money being ill-used inside to find its way outside.

One of the vehicles parked on the grounds was a beat-up yellow Peugeot 504 station wagon, the make and color in that era of most of the larger taxis in Liberia. The words "Paul Tuazama and Sons" were painted on its side. In one of those serendipitous moments I enjoy— and seem to experience more than most people—I had, apparently, stumbled upon the car I assumed belonged to Paul Tuazama, another of my former students. He had washed and ironed my clothes during my first year in Kpaytuo. Paul and I got along both in my classroom and outside. He was bright, strong-willed and, at times stubborn, just like his father, an influential and well-meaning town elder. As everyone in Kpaytuo upon my return was quick to tell me, Paul had become a major in the National Police Force, probably the most well-known, certainly the most powerful, of all Kpaytuo's sons.

I asked the taxi driver to wait while I searched for Paul, explaining that I had been Major Tuazama's Peace Corps teacher many years before when he was about fourteen. The National Policemen gathered there, of course, knew Major Tuazama, but none of them had an inkling where in the compound he was. One suggested he might be in his office at the Congo Town Police District. But since Paul's car was here, it was reasonable to assume Paul was, too. Another policeman offered to take me around the compound to help me look for Paul, and I accepted.

For fifteen minutes we went from office to office, knocking on each door and asking if Major Tuazama was there. Finally we opened a door and I saw my old student. No sooner had I peeked into the room than Paul yelled, "Teacher Cherry!"

We embraced and slapped hands together exuberantly, snapping our fingers at the end of the handshake, Liberian style. He told the somewhat bewildered people in the room that I had been his teacher many years before in Kpaytuo—a situation they might have been able to identify with, probably coming from small villages not unlike Kpaytuo where they might have been taught by Peace Corps Volunteers or missionaries. We hugged again.

Paul was a handsome, even dashing, man in his late twenties. He wore an Errol Flynn-like mustache and had some of the famous film actor's elegance and bearing. After a few minutes it was obvious that even though Paul was probably one of the seventy-five most powerful men in Liberia, he was not haughty or imperious nor did he put on airs, as was so often the case with Liberians of any authority or power, tribal or Americo-Liberian.

I told him I was on my way (with a taxi waiting for me below) to

see someone at the Liberian Hydrological Office to discuss constructing new wells in Kpaytuo.

"Thank you, teacher, for not forgetting Kpaytuo," he said.

Excusing himself from his meeting, Paul insisted on carrying me—
to use the Liberian vernacular—to the office. During the half hour that
had elapsed looking for, and talking with Paul, my taxi driver had quietly waited for my return. Since taxis are not equipped with meters, my
search for Paul had cost him time and money. I apologized for the delay,
told him I would not be going, and gave him extra dollars above the
agreed-upon fare.

Paul and I and his aide drove in his station wagon, which sometimes
served as a taxi—thus the sign painted on the side—to the office, only
to discover that Eric, the hydrologist, was out. I left a note explaining
why I had come and said I'd return some time that afternoon. Then,
we headed for the home of Mary Pratt, another old friend from Kpaytuo. But Mary was at work. I left a note promising to return that
evening.

After lunch I returned to the Liberian Hydrological Office, this
time with better luck. Eric, the Dutch hydrologist, was in. He was in-
trigued at my returning to Liberia and, even more, by my desire to help
Kpaytuo's citizens.

"It's no big deal," I said. "I have the desire, the time and the money."
I explained that it takes a Peace Corps Volunteer two to six months for
his or her head to stop spinning from culture shock and adjust to life in
Liberia and the tropics. For those Volunteers like myself, who had
opened new stations and who lived alone, it took even longer. (Most
Volunteers had roommates, and in the larger towns or cities two to four
Volunteers were stationed.) And then I had been so involved with teaching and the effort to build a new school, and was sick part of my last
year in Liberia, that I hadn't had the time or energy to do all that remained to be done. I told Eric of my belief that a curious metamorpho-
sis occurs the longer one lives in an underdeveloped country: one is no
longer shocked by the conditions and deprivations under which the
people live. One accepts the abnormal—babies with swollen stomachs
and people walking twenty minutes for a bucket of contaminated
water—as normal. One forgets, or becomes less outraged, that people

live like tribal Liberians; but the reality is that hundreds of millions of people in Africa, Asia and South America live in such conditions. Upon my return to Kpaytuo, before the shock and revulsion at the quality and unfairness of the people's lives dissipated, I had vowed to myself, and then the town folk, to do something about it.

Eric said there were two types of wells found in Liberia: a draw-bucket well and the more expensive pump well. A pump well cost about $1,500, compared to $200 or $300 for a draw-bucket well. (That would be about $3,750 for the pump well and roughly $500 to $750 for the draw-bucket well in 2017 dollars.) Not surprisingly, a pump well was more efficient and its water purer—when it was operating. That was the rub. In Liberia, he said, fifty percent of the pump wells did not work. I wouldn't be surprised if the figure were closer to eighty percent, either because the wrong parts were installed or, more likely, because the wells were not properly maintained. A ten-dollar part on the pump well went bad, he said, and because no one cared to replace it or could afford to, the well was out of operation. Or in the unlikely event that someone actually ordered the correct part, it could take a year to arrive, by which time the pump had rusted beyond repair. When a pump well was inoperable, the water from it was completely inaccessible, and the people were forced to use their old wells again. Those, lying stagnant for some time, were inevitably full of rank water. Echoing the sentiments of the missionary David Carson, Eric said: "If you want to help the people in your village, pay for draw-bucket wells."

Eric, who was married to a Liberian and employed by UNESCO, had lived in the country for five years and swore that he had never seen as much corruption in any country as in Liberia. He speculated that the idea of "eating money" was probably introduced by foreigners, possibly the Americo-Liberians. His contention was that tribal society, say in the seventeenth or eighteenth century, had to have been trustworthy, else it would have collapsed. I don't know enough about Liberia in centuries past to agree or disagree with Eric's hypothesis.

We, of course, have corruption in the West, though not to the degree of most Third World countries. In the time of which I write, Liberians and Third World people in general hadn't transferred their allegiance from family or clan to the state to the extent we had in the

West. And, to a degree, that is still true today. Indeed, years ago one wag described the countries in the Middle East as "tribes with flags."

To illustrate the point, consider a road project: the money and material destined to repair or maintain roads in American cities would be used for that purpose, though some of it may be skimmed off or squandered. Not so in Liberia: most, if not all of it, would be "eaten." The Liberian responsible for maintaining the roads would see his first—and perhaps only—obligation as that to his family. Another difference between corruption in the United States and Liberia is well illustrated by a remark of my friend and fellow Peace Corps Volunteer, Bill Fickling, who said: "In the West we bribe someone to do something illegal. In Liberia, you bribe someone to do his job."

◆ ◆ ◆

That evening, after a short visit with Mary Pratt, an old friend from Kpaytuo living in Monrovia, I hailed a cab to take me back to my hotel. I shared the cab with two other people. There were no meters, and the fare, theoretically, depended on how many boundaries you passed.

Most of the taxi and bus drivers, circa 1982, were Mandingoes, usually from Sierra Leone and Guinea, Liberia's neighboring countries on the west and north, respectively; for, as a rule, Liberians were not considered dependable, even by fellow Liberians. (This was also a reason the Liberians despised, and were envious of, the Mandingoes.)

Though the taxis' drivers were African, the owners were usually Lebanese. But since Liberian law prohibited an alien from owning a taxi or bus, and since only blacks of African descent were—*and still are*—eligible for citizenship under the Liberian Constitution, the vehicles were registered in the names of the Liberian wives or girlfriends of the Lebanese owners.

By coincidence—I wonder if the reader will think I "created" these coincidences, but I assure the reader that I have not—the taxi I was in on that night was driven by the same man who earlier in the day had waited so patiently for me at the National Police Headquarters while I searched for Paul Tuazama. Driving from 6:00 A.M. to 10:00 P.M., he took in $30 a day, of which he received from his "boss man" at the end of the week $25. He asked if I was interested in buying a car, because, he explained, he wanted to "drive for a white man." I think he meant he wanted to drive for an American.

The other passengers were a man in the front seat and a woman in the back with me. When we dropped the woman off at her destination she handed me a note she had apparently scribbled during the ride, a ride in which we had exchanged nothing more than "hello."

Her note said in full: "Miss Judith Harris. Please call me. Tel. 222068. I really like you. Thanks."

Appreciative of Miss Judith Harris' invitation, I never took her up on it.

Chapter 11

A couple of weeks before, fresh off the jet from New York and during the one-hour ride from the airport to Monrovia, I was asked by my taxi driver to which hotel I wanted to be taken. I mentioned the Ducor, then a part of the InterContinental hotel chain, and the only modern hotel I knew of in Liberia from my time there as a Peace Corps Volunteer. Probably from the tenacity with which I haggled over the price of the trip from the airport to the capital city, the driver had suggested the Holiday Inn, saying it was not "so-so dear as the Ducor can be."

I was surprised, though pleased, that Liberia now had a Holiday Inn. As soon as we drove up on that first occasion I realized it was not *that* Holiday Inn: someone had appropriated the name of the famous hotel chain for a rather ordinary-looking hotel of about forty rooms in the center of Monrovia. Upon entering I had been welcomed by a bellhop who wore a faded, red jacket much too small for him and who resembled the American author James Baldwin—a resemblance I took as a good omen for any literary endeavor that might develop from my return to Liberia. That first occasion I ended up staying there for a few nights before heading up-country for my memorable return to Kpaytuo.

On that first stay—and on subsequent trips to Monrovia during my 1982 visit—I was assigned room 304—a spacious, comfortable, though not especially modern or luxurious room with a Queen bed, a sink that worked, a toilet that flushed, an air conditioner that cooled, and a shower that refreshed. There was also a worn rug, battered furniture, a musty-smelling closet, and the plastic shell of a thermostat, sans mercury gauge, nailed to the door. I was charged $38 a night (equivalent in today's dollars to almost $100), which I thought was a lot of money for a hotel room in a poor country like Liberia, where the average annual income was then about $300 to $500—though still about half the Hotel Ducor's rates.

Since there wasn't a uniformed guard or any restriction on who might enter the Holiday Inn (unlike the lobby of the more exclusive and prestigious Hotel Ducor), every imaginable type wandered into the lobby: newspaper vendors who sold Liberian papers alongside African magazines (most, if I remember correctly, published in London) and the International Editions of *Time* and *Newsweek*. There also were young boys hawking African gimcracks and American junk, such as combs or cheap key-rings; German, Indian and Lebanese businessmen, who day and night quickly passed through the lobby to the adjacent nightclub, there to gawk at and lust after the Middle-Eastern belly dancers (a fresh crop of these nubile beauties was flown in monthly); gold and diamond merchants; high-ranking government officials and higher-ranking soldiers (remember, since the coup two years before, the country was ruled by soldiers); and finally, adorned in their flowing sky-blue or white gowns, which gave them a regal appearance (and looked so appropriate and comfortable for the African weather that I wanted to wear one), were male members of the Mandingo tribe, a handful of whom seemed to pass most of their time between the nearby mosque and the lobby of the Holiday Inn.

About fifteen people fit comfortably in the Holiday Inn lobby, which was approximately forty feet long and eighteen feet wide. There was a sofa on each side of it and six white metal chairs with cherry-red plastic seat covers. The lobby turned out to be an ideal spot for meeting people. Usually there were only four or five people there at any one time. Aside from people-watching and meeting new acquaintances in the lobby, I enjoyed gazing at a fish tank, which also fascinated the Africans. One night after a tribal woman peered intensely and silently for about five minutes at a rather gruesome-looking catfish swimming about the illuminated tank, she turned to me and said, "If a pregnant woman eats that fish, her baby will come out ugly like the fish."

That it was air-conditioned was part of the lobby's appeal. Only the more expensive Lebanese retail shops and jewelry stores on the main street—where in the latter one could find relatively inexpensive but high-quality gold jewelry—the better foreign restaurants, the offices of the highest Liberian government officials, the U.S. and other embassies, the Peace Corps office and the offices of the international agencies, and the one movie theater in town, were air-conditioned; and these were places the average Liberian rarely had occasion to enter, save for the movie theater which showed dreadful Kung Fu movies Liberian males hooted and hollered over. The Holiday Inn's air-conditioned lobby made the scorching days and the humid nights in the capital easier to bear.

◆　　◆　　◆

The young man from Guinea whom I saw almost every time I entered or left my Monrovia hotel. Sitting on a chair next to the hotel's entrance 12 hours a day, he sold Juicy Fruit gum, five cents a stick. He earned $4 a day.

As a Peace Corps Volunteer I ventured to Monrovia about once every four months, usually to buy supplies that were unavailable in the interior. I stayed for free in the Peace Corps hostel, exchanging news and gossip with Volunteer friends I might not have seen in six months or more.

In my early twenties, I didn't like Monrovia. I found the capital city expensive, hotter and more humid than the interior; also noisy, dirty and full of beggars, cripples and garbage. Additionally, I wanted to explore and learn about tribal culture full throttle, so I remained up-country as much as possible. If those weren't reasons enough to avoid it, Monrovia was also the bastion of the Americo-Liberians, who tended to live in Liberia's coastal cities where their ancestors had settled almost a century and a half before—the most in Monrovia but also in Harper, Greenville and Buchanan, the latter named after the last white governor of the American Colonization Society and brother of a future president of the United States, James Buchanan. But upon my return, at age 39, I enjoyed Monrovia, not least for the modern amenities available there, like running water and flushing toilets, drug stores and restaurants, retail shops and neon-lit appliance stores. And last, but of course not least, the excitement and adventure found only in a city.

The city snapped, crackled and popped. I had only to stand on the sidewalk in front of the Holiday Inn to feel Monrovia's vibes and savor its buzz. African music loud enough to hear a half block away blared from the bar a few doors down. Music was everywhere: pulsing from speakers on passing buses, issuing from tape recorders and radios (then called "boom boxes"), blasting from speakers outside stores. It was mostly African music—called "high life" in that era but also Jamaican reggae and black American funk.

Always sitting on a chair next to the hotel's entrance was a young man from Guinea who sold Juicy Fruit gum, five cents a stick, and Marlboro cigarettes, two for 15¢. He spoke little English, so we only exchanged greetings as I entered and left the hotel. He sat there from noon to midnight, six days a week, earning $4 a day. Across the street, Mandingo tailors hunched over their sewing machines, making colorful *lappas*, dresses, shirts and suits. It will be a drab day when Africans, in the name of being "cultured" and "sophisticated," wear only Western-style clothes, but the change was already on the way. Few women under forty in Monrovia wore *lappas* and almost none the colorful kerchiefs or head ties, both standard dress of Liberia's tribal women and girls decades before. Next to the Mandingo tailor shop was a bar with customers overflowing onto the sidewalk and street. And on the other side of the tailor shop was a general store with a huge icebox stocked with Coca-Cola and Fanta, as well as shelves filled with tins of sardines, bars of soap, bottles of bleach, boxes of toothbrushes and wooden matches.

Above the bar was the City Commercial Institute, one of many private schools in Monrovia offering classes in typing, shorthand and accounting. (Today they no doubt offer courses in computers.) Country girls who dreamed of working as a secretary in a government office—the finest job they could imagine—or for the really lucky and talented few, working with a foreign-owned business or international aid agency—earnestly marched up the stairs to the City Commercial Institute. So it was with the immigrants of my grandparents' generation, trudging to night school after a day's work in a sweatshop to learn the skills that would give them entry into the booming American economy of the early twentieth century. At least there were jobs for the would-be secretaries and bookkeepers and accountants and lawyers in America; not so, I feared, for the Liberians.

Day and night the sidewalks and streets were packed with brightly-dressed Africans who laughed, shouted, sang, danced, argued, flirted and made assignations. Many lingered on the street and sidewalks near the hotel until around midnight sipping beers, the men—and they were mostly men—sharing a laugh with buddies. Then it was time to think about setting off for home. No one wanted to be caught outside past the 1:00 A.M. curfew. At best, that meant a fine; at worst—so people said—it meant being detained for the night and perhaps getting cuffed about. Nearly two years before, the curfew had been imposed after the coup that had brought Samuel K. Doe and his People's Redemption Council to power.

Realizing it was too late to find a taxi or money bus home to beat the curfew, many a lovely woman stopped me on the street at 12:30 A.M., as I was returning to the hotel, and asked if she might spend the night with me: one even followed me into the hotel lobby, at first refusing to take no for an answer.

Before the coup and curfew many of Monrovia's citizens, especially on the weekend, rarely went to sleep before 4:00 A.M. On one such night circa 1967, my friend and fellow PCV, Bill Fickling, was sitting at a picnic table outside with other Volunteers, enjoying the tropical night and drinking beer. There being no toilets available, when the moment came they relieved themselves in a nearby alley. One of them had the misfortune of being seen by a policeman. Sensing some quick money, the policeman told the Volunteer he was going to arrest him. Of course no one should urinate outside, least of all we Peace Corps Volunteers, who were supposed to set an example, but there were so few places with working indoor toilets in the city. It was not uncommon to see scores of people urinating, not at all discretely, day and night. The policeman informed the Peace Corps Volunteer that for $50 he'd forget about the violation of a public ordinance. The Volunteer, always strapped for money on a monthly salary of $163, laughed. The policeman—even more strapped for money than a PCV—continued for a while to dicker over the price of the "fine," finally settling on the sum of 50¢.

◆　◆　◆

Over a lifetime of traveling to fifty countries, I've never been in a city where it is easier to meet people than in Monrovia. I could not walk down the street without people saying hello, often approaching and shaking my hand, and, of course, snapping our middle fingers at the end of the handshake. The uniquely Liberian handshake reflects the country's origins, so the story, which may be apocryphal, goes: supposedly in centuries' past the slave traders broke the middle fingers of their newly enslaved captives—both as a symbol of subjugation and as ready identification, lest the slaves escape. When the freed slaves returned to Liberia from America and founded the Republic in the nineteenth century, they defiantly snapped their middle finger at the end of a handshake to show their independence and celebrate their freedom, thus "creating" the Liberian handshake. And ever since all Liberians—indigenous or Americo-Liberian—have been exuberantly snapping their fingers away, in a state of blissful independence.

I'd often end up at Waterside, the site of the largest market in

Liberia, checking out the huge variety of foods and products for sale: fruits and vegetables grown in the interior, dry goods and electronics offered by Lebanese and Indian merchants, the wide miscellany of items hawked by African vendors. Everywhere the sidewalks were cracked and some of the streets strewn with paper and garbage. On the sidewalks in every direction at Waterside were people making "small market"—women peeled oranges with their penknives, selling them to Liberians who sucked rather than ate them; men and women, boys and girls, sold single sticks of chewing gum from Denmark; tea bags (two for 10¢) from China; aspirin (also two for 10¢) from England; evaporated milk from Holland; cooking oil from Singapore; and cigarettes, candy, crackers, biscuits, and bread, usually by the item, since few people could afford to buy a whole pack of crackers or biscuits or a bag of bread. While their mothers made market, some of the children, about seven or eight years old, stood alongside the road with their arms out-

A boy, "making market" by selling biscuits in Monrovia, 1982.

stretched, signaling to taxi drivers that they had change for sale—90¢ for each dollar. Using their mothers' market money, these children brought in a few extra dollars a day.

I passed by a barber shop with a sign in the window that said "Dr. of Hair," and walked by stores in which I could buy decent, even custom-designed, gold and silver jewelry—a specialty of the Lebanese. There also were animal hides for sale and wood carvings, all of them mass produced and undistinguished.

Other Africans, one jammed next to another, occupied rickety wooden stands on the sidewalks, selling pots and pans and socks and handbags, belts, batteries, cassettes, tape recorders, umbrellas, blankets, radios, combs, hats, wallets, shoes and pants, most imported from then-Communist Poland and most inexpensive and shoddy. Lastly, there was the creative entrepreneur who sold brassieres. He wore one over his dark T-shirt, the better to display his wares.

◆ ◆ ◆

Even though the People's Redemption Council had then been in power for almost two years, it was insecure about its hold on the country and thus exhibited the paranoia of revolutionary regimes. (For more examples see the sorry records of paranoia in the French, Russian, Chinese and Iranian Revolutions.) Illustrating this was a recent incident much publicized in the Liberian newspapers: six students at the University of Liberia had sent a petition to Samuel K. Doe, Commander-in-Chief and head of state, asking him to reconsider his ban on political activity. Doe pointed out to the students that their petition itself was a violation of his ban. The students were arrested and sentenced to die before a firing squad. Tensions were high in the city, with many people fearing another coup or at the very least riots if the sentences were carried out. Hours before the scheduled execution, Doe pardoned the students. They apologized, promising never to bring up the subject of political freedom again. The episode reminded me of an anecdote recounted by my fellow Volunteer, Bill Fickling. One day one of his students said to him, "Liberian democracy is the same as America's. The only difference is we Liberians can't criticize our government."

Chapter 12

Exhausted by the slightest effort, I wondered whether I was coming down with a "little fever," the playful paw-strokes of the wilderness the author Joseph Conrad spoke of before the more serious onslaught arrives in due course. I took a cab to the Peace Corps office, but neither the doctor nor the nurse was in. Manning the office was a Liberian named Isaac, whose principal job was peering into a microscope all day, examining the stools of Peace Corps Volunteers who were or felt ill, either condition always lurking in the tropics. That's what Isaac was doing—looking into a microscope—as I entered the inner office. I told him I felt weak. Removing his plastic gloves and washing his hands, he took my temperature, which he said was normal, and gave me some aspirin. He suggested that my body had yet to adjust to the tropics, and advised me to drink plenty of liquids and get lots of rest. Eventually, he assured me, I'd feel normal. I returned to the hotel around 11:00 A.M. to lie down, as I was good for nothing else.

That afternoon, still feeling debilitated, I attended an affair in honor of the Peace Corps' twentieth anniversary in Liberia. It was held in one of the modern, spiffy, air-conditioned offices of the United States International Information Service (formerly called the United States Information Agency). There were representatives from the Liberian Ministries of Health, Rural Development, and Education, each of whom predictably thanked the Peace Corps for its support those past twenty years and, even more predictably, asked for more support and money. Chuck Martin, Liberia's soon-to-retire Peace Corps director, pointed out that there were three thousand former Liberian Volunteers and eighty thousand former Peace Corps Volunteers—a rather substantial number. There are circa 2017 about 200,000 former PCVs. With all our mistakes and sometimes naive ideas, I am proud to be one of those 200,000 ex-Peace Corps Volunteers.

◆ ◆ ◆

When as a Peace Corps Volunteer on the occasions I ventured down to Monrovia, I looked forward to a meal at Diana's, in my opinion the finest restaurant in Liberia and one of the finest restaurants I have ever eaten in. Diana's, like most of the retail shops, restaurants and businesses circa 1967, was owned by foreigners: in Diana's case, Lebanese. Historically, the Americo-Liberians, the only Liberians with the capital to enter business, were contemptuous of it, gravitating instead to law, government and, most of all, politics. The explanation lies in the early days of the Republic, when the approximately twenty thousand freed slaves and other blacks repatriated to Liberia in the early-to-mid nineteenth century—most of them unlettered and unsophisticated—chose as their role models, having no others, their former masters, the leisured Southern aristocracy of the antebellum South. Not for the Southern gentry, nor the Americo-Liberians who aped them, something as plebian as trade. As for agriculture and working with one's hands, that reminded them of slave days. This attitude was evident to the members of the Harvard Expedition of 1926, one of whose members wrote: "Everything that grows well and requires no cultivation and almost no attention may be found, but the Americo-Liberians are not good agriculturists or gardeners. Physically they are lazy, and the amount of agricultural produce raised by them is exceedingly small. Those who can afford to, live chiefly on imported and tinned foods." (An admirable exception, in the twentieth century—and here I speak from first-hand knowledge—was Samuel Cooper, who owned the sawmill outside of Kpaytuo and a rubber farm elsewhere; more about him and his family later in the story. And, to be fair to the Americo-Liberians, I'm sure there were others through the years who partook in trade and were not lazy.)

So for much of Liberia's modern history the wealthier and more ambitious Americo-Liberians, taking advantage of political connections they had formed as the new aristocracy, amassed huge land holdings (some illegally and at the expense of the tribal people) on which rubber was grown. But the rubber farms were actually run by Ghanaians and West Indians, rarely the Americo-Liberian owner—still less often a tribal Liberian: his lot was to toil on the farm, often against his will and without remuneration.

Few tribal people entered business either, certainly not on anything but the smallest scale. They had neither the education nor the capital. (Nor the brains and inclination, the more arrogant and ignorant Americo-Liberian would have added, the words, ironically, white racists employed to justify discrimination for so many years toward American blacks.) My Peace Corps colleague, Bill Fickling, observed that the Americo-Liberians, during our time in the country, treated the indigenous tribal people the way many southern white Americans treated blacks before the Civil Rights revolution. He knew whereof he spoke, having grown up in the American South during the 1950s.

Thus in Liberia, even more than in the colonial possessions of the French, the British, the Germans and the Portuguese, the indigenous tribal people rarely developed an entrepreneurial class. The Mandingoes were an exception of sorts. But they were an island within the body politic of Liberia, comprising no more than five percent of the population, and they operated as merchants on a small scale. It was the Lebanese who controlled commerce on the retail level in Liberia circa 1967.

◆　◆　◆

Diana's fare in my Peace Corps days was continental, with a Middle Eastern bent. The specialty and my favorite dish was roast chicken basted in a garlic and lime sauce. In subsequent years I have eaten this dish in Middle Eastern restaurants in Cairo, Tel Aviv, London and New York, but in none of them was it as delicious or memorable as at Diana's. (Diana's hamburger, with just the right mix of Middle Eastern spices for my palate, was also among the best I've ever tasted.) I am willing to grant that my coming to Diana's from four or more months in the West African bush, where I ate rice every night, and, after a hot shower at the Peace Corps hostel, and sitting down to a square meal in a restaurant with air conditioning, no less, might have had something to do with the fervor with which I anticipated, and for many years afterwards savored, the pleasure of eating there.

Finding myself on Broad Street, a few blocks from Diana's, I decided to eat there for the first time in fourteen years. When I entered, two Liberian waiters each beckoned me to accompany him to a table. The patron decided which waiter to follow.

What looked like a rust-colored Styrofoam cave caught my eye, a garish addition to the restaurant since my last visit many years before. I chose the front room, with its more modest decor. A few rice dishes, prepared in the tribal style, were on the menu, a change for the better. I can't remember a single African dish on the menu during the 1960s. For that matter, one did not see Liberians eating in Diana's, save for Americo-Liberians. The clientele, by and large, was composed of foreigners—either members of the large American contingent in Liberia (working for the embassy, the United States Agency for International Development or the Peace Corps); or staff of the international organizations, like the United Nations; or white males, mostly twenty-five to forty-five, who owned or worked for businesses. But upon my return most of the patrons in Diana's were Liberian—tribal Liberians.

I ordered the chicken, then walked to the counter and introduced myself to the owner, who thanked me for coming back (so, too, did my waiter) and I bought the international edition of *Newsweek* and *West Africa*, a monthly African publication. Street vendors periodically came in selling American newsmagazines, combs or key rings—walking five-and-dime stores. That part of Liberia hadn't changed. The meal was good, but not as good as my remembered ones. (Is anything ever as good as we remember it to be?) The chicken was tough and small. Charging only $6 a dinner ($15 in today's money), the owner, it would seem, wasn't using the best quality birds. But his prices were at a reasonable level, for his African clientele couldn't afford more expensive meals.

My hotel, the Holiday Inn, was located on Carey Street, named after Lott Carey, a freed slave who'd become a distinguished early settler, and was one block from the bar and nightclub district on Gurley Street, named after the Reverend Ralph Gurley, another influential figure in the country's early days. Hoping a beer might pick me up, though I am not much of a drinker, I went to a nearby bar, where I met Lydia.

Lydia was her *kwi* name. Her tribal name sounded as if it were pronounced "Oh-ooh." Born in the town of Cape Palmas of Liberia's Grebe tribe, Lydia yearned for the excitement of a big city, so at age fifteen she left home and moved in with her older sister in Monrovia, where she still lived. She was eighteen, already the mother of a two-year old, and was in the eighth grade. Beautiful, if a trifle skinny, with an ebony complexion, she had fine, delicate features.

Lydia was a bar girl, meaning she was hired by the bar's owner to hustle drinks. Aside from the pittance they were paid, bar girls frequented bars for a good time, not least because, being exclusively tribal girls, from eighteen to twenty-five years old from hamlets and villages, they thought that it was the most exciting and glamorous experience in the world to sit in a neon-lit room until late at night—the music thumping, the lights flashing, and the drinks and laughs flowing. And from the money they earned, they could dress seductively each night in a mini-skirt with a low-cut blouse to show off their nice figures.

I'm certain that missionaries and preachers, among others, had warned girls like Lydia that bars were sinful places: so much more reason for girls to be attracted to and hang out in one. If she fancied you, the bar girl invited you back to her home—always her home—once the bar closed to have sex with her.

On my occasional trips to Monrovia as a Volunteer I didn't take part in the bar or bar girl scene, so I rely on my Peace Corps buddy Bill Fickling's memory, which from experience I know was peerless. Bill was twenty-four when we served in Liberia. He recalled that he stayed over at his favorite bar girl's home (more like a hovel) many times. Bill emphasized that bar girls were not prostitutes, if you define a prostitute as someone who performs sex for money. Bar girls never asked him for money, he said. That was confirmed by many Liberian Peace Corps Volunteers from that period, who enjoyed the favors of bar girls. A Volunteer who saw the same girl all the time was sometimes looked on by the girl (and her compatriots) as her boyfriend. Still, a Peace Corps Volunteer, on a meager salary of $163 a month, couldn't spend much in a bar drinking inexpensive Club beer, Bill recalled. It was the better-paid foreign businessmen who were the more profitable clients of the bar girls. Nevertheless, the bar girls liked—and were attracted to—the friendly young Peace Corps Volunteers, on whom they showered their favors. (All this, I hasten to add, occurred before the time of AIDs, when Liberia was for young, single males a sexual paradise. As for the Peace Corps women, some of them dated Lebanese men or fellow Peace Corps Volunteers; you'll have to ask one of them if that experience qualified as a sexual paradise.)

❖   ❖   ❖

Here I was on that night in 1982 with Lydia. I ordered a beer and bought one for her. Apropos of nothing, Lydia asked if I wanted to smoke marijuana. I declined her offer. I was stunned by the question. Drugs were not prevalent in Liberia in 1966 and 1967, at least to the best of my knowledge. Obviously the situation had changed by 1982, for she said that all she had to do was walk outside to buy one marijuana cigarette for $1. She also swore that Samuel K. Doe, before his ascendancy to Commander-in-Chief and head of the People's Redemption Council, when he was a poorly paid, lowly army officer, frequented many of the bars and clubs in Monrovia. And in them he smoked and sold marijuana. By the look on my face she saw that I found this hard to believe.

"I can talk true-oh," she said. "The man could sell it self. They can all smoke too much. Today self."

Still feeling lethargic, I thanked Lydia for her company, which I enjoyed, gave her a $10 tip, but told her, as I was tired and wanted to sleep, I was going back to my hotel—alone.

She walked me outside, where a young man approached us, saying hello to her. He wanted to engage in conversation but I cut him off, politely. When he walked away, Lydia told me that two years before the boy had named himself Tolbert, after then-President William Tolbert. The day after the coup, Lydia said, the boy announced, "My name is Doe."

Chapter 13

Paul Tuazama, my ex-student who was a major in the National Police Force, offered to take me to Camp Schieffelin, where my ex-houseboy, Sammy Dahngbae, was stationed. So that morning I hopped a cab over to the Congo Town police station, of which Paul was in charge. That section of Monrovia had been settled in the early nineteenth century by Congolese who had been taken from slave ships by the United States Navy after the ban on the importation of slaves into the United States went into effect in 1808. The Congolese and some 5,000 similarly transported other Africans had been deposited in Liberia—thus the name of the neighborhood, Congo Town. Many of the Congolese intermarried with the Americo-Liberians, forming the lower stratum of that dominant social class.

When I arrived, Paul came to meet me. Everyone saluted him as we walked through the small station to his office. Sitting there were Paul's assistant and the assistant's six-year-old son, and two women and their children. During the fifteen minutes we were in Paul's office, the women did not say a word. Nor did Paul introduce me to them.

On our way out of the station we were stopped by a white man, the employer of a Liberian then in police custody as the suspect in an air conditioner theft. When arrested, the boy had told the policemen that the stereo in his possession was his own, paid for from wages earned by working for a white man. The white man stood before us, having come to the police station to confirm that part of the boy's story. Since the stereo was neither stolen nor evidence in the air conditioner case, the man wanted to take it to his apartment for safekeeping until the boy got out of jail. All of us knew why the man did not want to leave the stereo in police custody: it would have disappeared from the station by that next morning, never to be found. Paul assented to the man's request, which I like to think he would have done even if I weren't present.

❖ ❖ ❖

Arriving at Camp Schieffelin, a forty-five minute ride from Monrovia, we were stopped by armed soldiers at the gate. Paul told them we had come to see Private Samuel Dahngbae. Had I been alone I probably would not have had any trouble getting permission, it just would have taken an hour or so. But traveling with Major Tuazama, probably among the seventy-five most powerful men in Liberia, we received permission to enter within ten minutes.

About six hundred soldiers were stationed at Camp Schieffelin, along with their families, bringing the total to some two thousand residents in all. Privates lived with their families in rooms 10 feet by 10 feet, about ten rooms per barracks. Sammy's room had a working ice box, of which he was enormously proud; his bed, a radio/tape recorder; and, on the wall, framed certificates from the Ganta Clinic and Army Basic Training. Water was provided from a spigot out back, which the residents shared when it was turned on in the morning and then again in the evening. The soldiers' wives—like their husbands, poor tribal folk—cooked chop (which is what the Liberians call a hot meal) on small grills on the porch out front. Latrines were out back for the adults, whose responsibility it was to clean up after their small children, who defecated on the grass around the barracks. The soldiers' wives and girlfriends, most of them between sixteen and twenty, were everywhere, either pregnant or nursing a child. Hundreds of children ran about, giving this part of the post the appearance of a day-care center.

After showing me his home and introducing me to his "wife," a sullen young woman, and his two children, Sammy, ever conscious of my harping to him about the importance of personal hygiene and the need for a career, proudly showed me the clinic in which he worked. The clinic was open not only to the military personnel at the camp and their families, but to non-military residents in the vicinity as well.

Referring to me as his sponsor, Sammy introduced me to his immediate superior. He, in turn, assembled the clinic's staff in a line, introducing them to me by rank and enumerating each one's responsibilities in the operation of the clinic. Sammy's superior showed Paul and me the waiting room, the laboratory, the drug dispensary, which was poorly stocked, and the injection room—imagine a Liberian clinic without a place to inject its patients. (To remind the reader, in those days tribal Liberians thought a penicillin injection was the road to health, to the point that they didn't appreciate the efficacy, for example, of keeping a wound clean or covered, ignoring the dictum, an ounce of prevention is worth a pound of cure.)

From there we walked about the post, stopping while Sammy introduced us to the camp's commander, whom we found sitting with some cronies on a porch. Like most of the people in power in the "New Liberia," the commanding officer was in his late twenties or early thirties. He appeared to be in a stupor, either from drugs or alcohol, and to demonstrate his authority, this contemptible, tin-pot Napoleon ordered Sammy to drop for ten pushups.

On the way to Paul's car, Sammy and Paul lamented that although it was March neither of them—along with all the other civil servants in the country—had yet to receive their February paychecks.

"When we don't get paid," Paul told me, "we can say, 'The Eagle is still flying.' When the money comes, we say, 'The Eagle has landed.'"

The eagle to which he was referring is the bald eagle, symbol of the United States government, whose foreign aid undoubtedly kept the Liberian economy, such as it was, afloat. (In fact, when I was a PCV, I was told that Liberia was the largest per capita recipient of foreign aid in Africa.)

Since there was no phone at the camp to which Sammy had access, it was difficult for us to make plans, more so as I did not know when I was heading back up-country or coming down to Monrovia again. I suggested to Sammy he stop by the Holiday Inn in a couple of weeks. Then, as he wished, I could meet his brother, Hastings, and we could discuss Sammy's future.

On the ride back, Paul told me he wanted to resume his studies in agriculture, preferably in the United States. I told him he would be better off, as it would be less costly, studying in Nigeria, where I had been told there were many fine universities. But Paul, like most Liberians, wanted to see the United States. He said he did not wish to rise too high in the National Police Force, for when the next coup occurred—he didn't say if, but when—he did not want to be, in his words, "taken to the beach," a reference to what had happened to thirteen cabinet ministers and other high officials of the Tolbert government—among them the Foreign Minister, the Speaker of the House and the Chief Justice of the Supreme Court, who ten days after the coup were stripped to the waist, tied to posts, and, before a stunned public, executed on the beach.

Chapter 14

One day in the lobby of the hotel I struck up a conversation with a distinguished-looking African. His name was Fafa E. M'Bai. Educated in London, he was a barrister from The Gambia, an English-speaking country in West Africa. He was in Liberia on behalf of his wife, who had ordered a shipment of palm oil. She had given $20,000 to a relative who resided in Liberia to pay for the oil and $5,000 more for 600 drums in which to transport it.

Palm oil is popular in West Africa as a cooking oil—cassava leaf cooked in palm oil is my favorite African dish. The oil is exported to the West as an ingredient in vegetable oil, candles and soap—thus the name fashioned at the beginning of the twentieth century for what was once the world's most popular soap—Palmolive, made of palm oil and olive oil. The product became so popular that the company that manufactured it, the B.J. Johnson Company of Milwaukee, eventually changed its name to Palmolive and today makes up part of one of the world's great consumer product companies, Colgate-Palmolive.

Shocking as it may be to some, Mr. M'Bai's wife's palm oil was never delivered from Liberia to The Gambia as contracted: it was nowhere to be found, nor was the $25,000. Mr. M'Bai had spent the past five weeks in Liberia, he recounted, waiting for his suit against his wife's relative to be adjudicated. (As soon wait for the sun to rise in the west.)

He related to me, more in amazement than anger, his experiences with the Liberian Ministry of Justice: every time a secretary there was asked by the appropriate person to type a document relating to Mr. M'Bai's case, she asked Mr. M'Bai, before proceeding to do her job, for a bribe, or as it is ubiquitously known throughout Liberia, a *dash*. "But once she got around to typing it," he said, "she did an excellent job, provided I gave her something. Far better than our secretaries at home," he added with no rancor in his voice.

Every time Mr. M'Bai entered the Minister of Justice's office, there were at least ten people sitting or standing silently, observing whatever went on (or more likely, what did not go on). And every time he entered or left the room, Mr. M'Bai recalled in a tone of stupefaction, he was expected to shake hands and snap fingers with everyone in the room.

"Someone will come in with a complaint and, after shaking every hand in the room, will be told to come back tomorrow," he told me. "And the person comes back the next day, and the day after that, and always, it is the same message: 'Please come back tomorrow.' And no one is angry at this kind of thing in this country," barrister M'Bai said. "I, myself, have my moody days. But never the Liberians. They are always happy—like children."

He added: "When I finally get to see the Minister, he picks up the phone, pretending he is telephoning someone regarding the disposition of my suit. But from experience, I know that in all probability, there is no one on the other end of the phone. Or, if there is, it is the operator or one of his girlfriends. Then the Minister turns to me and says that as a result of the just concluded phone conversation, he is sending his personal vehicle over to the appropriate person for the documentation needed to prosecute my case. I am told to return that afternoon at 2:00 P.M. The information will be in the office. I return at 2:00 P.M., but neither the information nor the Minister are there. We go through this every time I see him. There is no country in Africa like Liberia. It is like the South Sea Islands I have read about, with everyone happy-go-lucky."

Chapter 15

The people of Kpaytuo had told me that Kamah Fendahn, my ex-cook, was living in Monrovia, though no one knew her address. When she came to work for me at about the age of fourteen, Kamah was like a young, untamed, good-natured colt—seemingly all legs, with a soft, round, milk-chocolate face. She was on the verge of becoming a woman. Even though she was around my houseboy Sammy's age, she spoke far less English than he, especially in front of me, of whom, at first, she was afraid and in awe. She didn't read and write, having only entered school the year before I arrived. Her family realized that working for me was an opportunity for her to earn more money ($5 a month) than a girl her age could possibly earn under normal circumstances, so they gladly consented to her becoming my cook. Knowing how Liberian parents were likely to interpret such a request, they probably assumed that I also intended to bed her. Because of her age and my being her teacher, I never would have considered it and never did.

After her initial fright, Kamah took to the job. The chemistry among Sammy, Kamah and me was ideal. She was quiet, almost timid, and Sammy, devil that he was, enjoyed teasing her—especially making fun of any lapse in her rudimentary English. But she knew that he was just playing. On more important matters—like explaining the strange world of the white man—Sammy acted as her guide. Kamah was fascinated by my manual typewriter. Whenever I sat down to type, she always came into the room, peering at the wonderful machine that made words. The more comfortable she felt in my house, the closer she dared come. It was not long before she was confident enough to kneel on the floor beside me, her chin resting on my desk, the better to observe this marvelous contraption that "knew book." Kamah also liked to suck on ice. She was never much of a student, but one of my most vivid impressions is of her, having finished her chores around the house, languorously lying on her side in the front room, where I used to work, sucking on an ice cube, flipping through the pages of a magazine and occasionally looking up at me with those large, brown eyes.

◆　◆　◆

Liberians identified houses in Monrovia by landmarks. Few streets in the poorer sections of the city, where Kamah was likely to live, had street signs, forget numbers on homes. The best Kamah's mother, who still lived in Kpaytuo, could come up with is that Kamah lived on Twelfth Street in the neighborhood of

Kamah Fendahn, my cook, wearing "makeup," circa 1967.

Sinkor, near the high school. Her mother suggested I go to that spot and ask where the Mano people lived. Since almost everyone in a village the size of Kpaytuo (anywhere from 700 to 1,500 souls) was a blood relative, its citizens married someone from outside the village. Kamah, like almost everyone in Kpaytuo, was Gio, but she lived in Monrovia with a man from the Mano tribe, a larger tribe closest, both geographically and linguistically, to the Gio.

I took a cab to the cluster of homes on Twelfth Street opposite the high school. There was no dearth of people to approach. Most of the houses did not have electricity, and the houses were usually stifling, forcing people outside to seek the somewhat cooler and fresher air. Since it was unusual for a white man to be in what I could tell was a none-too-fashionable section, every eye followed me as I approached and asked if Mano people lived there. One of the women led me through a yard full of trash to another home, where a young girl standing before a mortar (with which to beat rice) said she was Kamah Fendahn's "sister," which could have meant she was actually her sister or possibly her cousin or niece. I did not know her, so I introduced myself as the Peace Corps man for whom Kamah had cooked many years ago in Kpaytuo. She said Kamah was at work, but would return around 5:00 that evening. I left a message telling Kamah I'd be back between 6:00 and 7:00 P. M.

That evening I returned and walked down a narrow path through a weed-infested yard to Kamah's house. About ten people stood before it, among them Kamah's "sister." She shouted into the house in Gio, and out came Kamah.

"Teacher Cherry!" she yelled. "You can come back to see us. We thank God." Kamah introduced me to the people who had gathered around us, including her "husband," a young man named Moses, and her two children, Paupee, a boy about seven and Gbo, a girl about five. Kamah suggested we go inside, where it would be easier to talk. We walked to the end of the house, to the room that Kamah and Moses rented for $35 a month.

We settled into the small room, Kamah sitting on the bed, Moses on a chair, I on another chair facing them. Kamah and Moses slept on the bed, their two children on the floor. Other than a three-foot-high ice box, which did not work but served as a cupboard, and a rack on which they hung their few articles of clothing, there wasn't space for anything in the room, even if they owned more things, which was unlikely.

The house did have electricity, though none of the many families who rented its rooms were paying for the service. Had the Monrovia Electric Company known, the electricity would have been turned off. Kamah turned on a tiny electric fan, which did little good, for the room was sweltering. Under normal circumstances we would have sat outside, where on many nights it was delightful, but as this was my first visit, the polite gesture on my part, as on theirs, was for us to remain inside.

Liberians tend to be slim, often as not because they are riddled with intestinal parasites, but Kamah, I was happy to see, radiated health. She was broad-shouldered, indeed looked like a swimmer. Her face was fuller. She was, there is no better term than the wonderful Yiddish word,

Kamah Fendahn, my ex-cook, then about 28, with two of her three children, in 1982.

zaftig (plump, buxom and well-rounded). She'd lost a couple teeth on the side of her mouth. (I'd often wondered how the Liberians, with little or no dental care, managed to have such beautiful teeth. The answer is that the children do, but by the time they are adults, Liberians do not.) Kamah was still pretty, though bearing three children, and being pregnant with a fourth, had taken its toll. Kind and sweet as a fourteen-year-old, she remained so as a mother and grown woman of about twenty-eight.

Kamah told me her first "husband" had died of kidney failure. She said, with pride, that had he lived he would have graduated from high school by now. "He was too fine and too smart," she said. Because Moses, her second "husband" was present, I felt uncomfortable by the rhapsodic terms with which she described her deceased husband; but neither of them seemed in the least uncomfortable.

120

Under tribal law, children belonged to the father and, if he died, to his family, so the offspring of Kamah and her first "husband" lived with the child's grandmother in Kakata, about 35 miles north of Monrovia. Had Kamah been married by the church, in all likelihood she would have been granted custody of the child. As it was, she was not in the least embittered that her firstborn was being raised by the child's grandmother, explaining to me that her dead "husband" had been the woman's only child. Kamah had been with her present "husband," Moses, for six years. She'd reached the ninth grade and wanted to return to school. She cooked, cleaned the house and minded the children of a well-off Liberian couple, the man a banker and the woman a nurse. Laboring from 7:30 in the morning to 6:00 in the evening, six days a week, Kamah earned $31 a week (about $80 in today's money).

If Kamah was hearty, Moses looked like his body had been chiseled from marble. He was twenty-two, approximately six years her junior. It's unusual in Liberia, as in most countries, for a woman to be older than her mate. Moses attended a school funded by UNESCO, where he was studying auto mechanics. While a student, he received a small stipend and supplemented this by selling tie-dyed cloth with his cousin and some friends in front of the Sinkor supermarket. Their customers were members of the international community—wives of diplomats, their children, Peace Corps Volunteers, U. N. personnel, and the like.

I was pleased that Moses was learning a marketable and useful skill. Ever since my Peace Corps experience, I have felt that what countries like Liberia need most is citizens with skills in modern farming techniques, small business operations, plumbing, electricity, carpentry, masonry, lathe operation, welding, auto mechanics, television repair, health care and, of course, computer operation and related technologies: not more people pushing papers in offices, some with fancy titles.

I was happy that Kamah was with someone who seemed responsible and hard working. He was also handsome and polite; and was learning a trade that would likely guarantee him employment.

When Moses left to buy soft drinks, Kamah told me that her Auntie had predicted that Moses would leave her once he was earning good money as an auto mechanic for a woman who "knew book," and had a good job that would bring more money into the family coffers. In

Moses' defense, however, Kamah said: "He can be a good husband. He treats my family with respect."

Moses returned with the soft drinks and ice. While we talked and drank the sodas, I noticed that Kamah lay across her bed in that inadvertently seductive manner of hers, sucking on an ice cube.

Chapter 16

The Holiday Inn was the most unforgettable hotel I've ever stayed in. I was told that it was owned by a Lebanese man, but after the 1980 coup he had grown fearful for his life and supposedly sold it to a Mandingo. Once the Lebanese had decided that Liberia was relatively stable again after the coup, he'd tried—and some say succeeded—to regain control of his hotel. I never figured out who owned it, for there was both an African and a Lebanese manager. The rooms and the lobby were under the domain of the Mandingo manager, while the bar/dining room/nightclub next to the lobby was run by the Lebanese manager. Though there must have been forty or so rooms in the hotel, I had the impression it was never more than a quarter full, if that. The nightclub, featuring Middle Eastern belly dancers and the requisite booze, attracted large crowds of males each evening—mostly European or Lebanese businessmen but some Liberian politicians and army officers—and that, rather than the hotel trade, I suspect, filled the coffers.

Whenever I left or entered the hotel, I invariably encountered Alhagy Mansano Dabo, a Mandingo diamond and gold merchant from The Gambia. He always looked regal in the white or powder-blue gowns favored by the Mandingoes. I'd guess his age at about fifty-five. He had thick, black glasses (which were rare to see on Africans in those days), white hair that glistened against the backdrop of his coal-black face, and teeth that were rotting and reddish-brown from chewing on kola nuts. He had recently arrived in Liberia from Zaire where he had searched, unsuccessfully, for diamonds to buy. He told me that most of the diamond merchants in Liberia used the Holiday Inn lobby as their office, though final transfer of goods and cash occurred elsewhere. That explained the letter taped to the wall of the lobby, which follows, with spelling, syntax and punctuation intact:

The management is hearby warning that effective immediately No visitor, diamond businessman neither any ordinary person is allowed to sit here. Only hotel guests are allowed to sit here. Visitors if you come to see any diamond buyer and do not know the office of that person, please contact the receptionist on duty to have said person contacted for you rather than sitting where our guests should be sitting. The situation many times crippled our business here.

Of course everyone ignored the letter and the lobby teemed with both guests and non-guests of the hotel, including The Gambian diamond merchants in their colorful, flowing robes.

I found it hard to believe that Dabo was a gold and diamond merchant, for he never seemed to have any money. Whenever we met, he

Alhagy Mansano Dabo, a Mandingo diamond and gold merchant from The Gambia. He was always broke, so I'm not sure how successful a diamond and gold merchant he was.

inquired in broken English about the status of the water project in Kpaytuo, asked me if I wanted a kola nut (the Africans like the caffeine contained therein) or a cigarette, and always exhorted me to marry an African. And then, at some point in the conversation, he'd ask for a dollar.

Against my better judgment, I lent Dabo $100, though only after he promised to pay the money back that very night and gave me as collateral three swatches of lovely white cloth. He said the cloth, of the kind the Mandingoes used to make their gowns, was worth more than the $100. He needed the money for an emergency, though of what nature I never got straight.

That night he did not repay me the $100, nor the next day or night, nor the day and night after that. On each occasion he offered an excuse, though I did not understand him because of his faulty English.

I was angry at him for breaking his word. I was angry enough to bring the matter to the attention of his cousin, the Mandingo manager of the hotel, adding that if I did not receive the money within forty-eight hours I was going to contact the police. Dabo and his cousin were in my room when this transpired. The cousin, obviously miffed with Dabo, asked him if what I said (regarding the loan) was true. Dabo sheepishly acknowledged that it was. The cousin said to me that I had to give the old man a chance to redeem himself, else Dabo would be shamed before his young relative (the manager). I must, the cousin said, give the cloth back to Dabo so he could sell it, in that way demonstrating that he had spoken the truth when he said the cloth was worth more than $100.

"Forget about the $100; it is nothing," the cousin said. "I can pay you in a moment," and, proving his point, he withdrew a wad of dollars from his pocket.

I was in no mood to save Dabo's face, much as I cared for the old rascal. I intended to go up-country in a few days: I wanted the money before I left. So I refused the cousin's proposition.

Realizing I was not going to change my mind, the cousin gave me my $100, and I gave Dabo back his cloth.

The next time I saw Dabo in the lobby, he asked me if I wanted a cigarette or a kola nut and said I ought to marry an African.

Chapter 17

When we first met, Neil Huff, CARE's country director in Liberia, was forty-eight years old with a neatly-kept British officer's mustache and a trim, muscular build. But for his bald head, he looked like a man in his thirties. He had managed or been the assistant director of CARE missions in Turkey, Iran, Algeria, India and Sri Lanka. So he knew his way around the then less-developed world.

Asked how Liberia compared to those countries, he said to me, "This place is like Mars."

Apropos of my plan to pay for the construction of draw-bucket wells in Kpaytuo, Neil said that, at one time or another, UNICEF, USAID, CARE and the EEC (the European Economic Community) had been involved in building wells in Liberia.

"The program was a disaster," he said. "The Liberian government never put money into the budget to maintain the wells. And the people would steal bits and pieces off the pumps. There was one type of pump that had a bolt on the handle. This bolt happened to be a standard size and fit the presses the Liberians use to process sugar cane into cane juice. The bolts were always being stolen from the pumps and used to make booze."

Neil said that someone from UNICEF had calculated that it had cost $16,000 to install each pump well in Liberia.

"How much should it have cost?" I asked.

"About $2,000," he said.

Matters weren't any better for the less complex, and less expensive, draw-bucket wells—the kind I intended to fund in Kpaytuo. Though they should have cost about $300 to $400, they had cost about $5,000 each, Neil said.

"We have poured money into Liberia with little effect," Neil said. "The donors change—one time it's CARE, the next the [West]

Germans, then the State Department—but nothing of substance has been achieved these past twenty years. The people won't work for themselves. They expect handouts."

◆　　◆　　◆

At the time of my return to Liberia, approximately one-third of the country's income came from foreign aid and grants, with the United States being its largest benefactor. The United States government gave Liberia approximately $91 million in economic and military assistance by fiscal year 1985, making Liberia, by far, the highest per capita aid recipient in Africa (and one of the highest, per capita, in the world). That figure was appreciably higher than the $19 million in aid we gave to Liberia in 1979, when William Tolbert was in power.

These figures didn't indicate that the United States preferred the Doe regime and its military rule to Tolbert's and civilian rule: I'd say the opposite was the truth. The increase in aid only showed that, however much we regretted the coup and a military government and Liberia's inefficient, corrupt and exasperating ways, the United States government, because it wanted a subservient, dependable ally in West Africa, and our unique relationship with Liberia, had done everything in its considerable power to keep the country stable and afloat.

Like so many of us, Neil Huff found Liberia and its inhabitants fascinating. "In spite of the privation here—and I'm not talking about people starving to death; there's none of that—I mean the difficulties and harassments of life after the coup—the people are unfailingly cheerful and basically optimistic. Even though they have a military government, the people still know they have rights that have not been taken from them. And they exercise them. They have a kind of sturdy independence."

I knew, first-hand, how beneficial CARE's many programs had been in Liberia, even with the abuses by the Liberians and the Liberian government. During my assignment in Kpaytuo, CARE's school lunch program often provided the only meal the children ate during the day. I kept the keys to the CARE storeroom, as otherwise the principal and the other teachers would have helped themselves to the food. But ultimately it had to be Liberians who held the keys, figuratively and literally. However, by 1982 they still were not up to the task. As Neil and others pointed out to me, the CARE food was not reaching the school children for whom it was intended. Instead, it was ending up for sale, often on the very day it was delivered, in local markets; or it was "mysteriously" disappearing, usually out the back window of the schools. CARE had reluctantly ceased the school lunch program, Neil said. I took no pleasure in hearing, as Neil derived none in telling me, that CARE, no longer willing to tolerate the Liberian government's sticky fingers, intended to close its Liberian mission.

◆　◆　◆

At the behest of my ex-student, Major Paul Tuazama, we drove to Painsville to see the Minister of Rural Development. Paul wanted me to discuss my plans for the wells in Kpaytuo with this gentleman, who turned out to be, like Paul, in his late twenties. He was handsome and intelligent, and seemed competent and decisive. He told me that if I paid for them, they (meaning the government) would be glad to order pump wells from the Ivory Coast.

Much as I was tempted to, I knew that the more complicated pump wells were not right at this point in Kpaytuo's development. I told the Minister I would let him know if I decided to go that way or remain with my first plan, to install draw-bucket wells.

Whatever route I chose, he said, I could count on the government supplying workers for the project. (Wonderful—the very people I wanted nowhere near the project. Better for Kpaytuo's citizens to provide the labor for the wells.) Nevertheless, I was pleased that I had conferred with him. No one, in government or out, could claim later, at least not truthfully, that the government had not been consulted or failed to approve the project to build wells in Kpaytuo.

It was time for me to return to Kpaytuo, there to report to the chief and elders my findings concerning the water project.

KPAYTUO

Mary Jackson, Tado's wife, dressing Kuahn, one of their children, 1982.

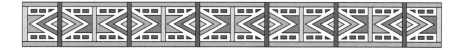

Chapter 18

The ride up-country to Kpaytuo was not too difficult, considering what some of them were like, but it was still grueling. The difficulties began even before the last leg of the trip started. We sat in one-hundred-degree heat for an hour in Ganta, where the paved road ended, until the money bus was full. I dared not walk about, for I might have lost my "choice" seat on the uncushioned plank on which I and my fellow passengers would ride, if not my spot on the bus altogether. Then, once we set off, the driver stopped for gas—heaven forbid that a money bus driver filled up *before* rather than *after* securing passengers. While he stopped for gas, a few male passengers hopped out to go to the bathroom in the nearby bush. That resulted in an additional fifteen-minute delay, while those of us who remained inside the bus sweltered and grumbled. Then there was a palaver between the driver and one of the passengers. The passenger claimed he should not have to pay the full fare for his daughter, who, for lack of room, sat atop packages and bundles on the floor. Eventually, we would complete the two-hour trip from Ganta to Kpaytuo, during which I had plenty of time to recall my other experiences with the Liberian national pastime, the palaver.

Liberians were the most argumentative and litigious people I'd ever encountered—as well, paradoxically, as the sweetest-natured. They argued passionately, and frequently, though not violently, on the farm, in the village, in stores, on the football field in the village, in the football stadium in Monrovia, in money buses—especially when boarding—and in the hut or home. Most palavers were settled on the spot, usually by a third party, after much sound and fury were expended by all concerned—and all concerned usually included most of the bystanders. The more serious palavers reached the town elders or the chief; and the most serious, the tribal or *kwi* courts. The run-of-the-mill palaver, the twenty-minute argument over whether someone had insulted you, provided a non-violent release for the innumerable frustrations of life in Liberia; and served as well, in my opinion, as a diversion and form of amusement.

Liberians thrived on palavers, which is not to say they were taken lightly. I made *that* mistake my first months in Liberia. One day during recess, two of my students, around age eighteen, got into a palaver. After recess I began to conduct class, but the two boys wanted to "talk the palaver." I insisted they resolve it after, not during, school hours. As I later learned, I was wrong: in their culture palavers were "talked" immediately. Also, I had shamed the boys in front of their peers and especially the younger members of the class, for I had acted as if their palaver, and thus they, were of no account. Remember, it was common in second-grade classes to have students aged all the way from ten to twenty.

Liberians employed riddles, proverbs and parables to score points in a palaver—the training would make them formidable lawyers. (The word "palaver" dates from Portuguese in the mid-eighteenth century, signifying talks between African tribal people and Portuguese traders, in which parables were used.) For example, David and Memba had a palaver over wages. David asserted that Memba had failed to pay him for working on Memba's farms and Memba asserted that David had stopped working and that was the reason he was not paid. David might say to the person judging the palaver, "An empty rice bag can't stand up." That is to say, "If you don't pay a man, don't expect him to work."

A palaver must be settled to the satisfaction of the parties directly involved, as difficult as that sounds. And once a palaver is settled, the antagonists and their supporters, who minutes before were shouting and cursing and threatening to sue one another, are laughing, shaking hands and snapping fingers, as if nothing had happened.

One day I bawled out one of the older students, Peter Menlae, for being negligent in serving the CARE food during recess. After school he brought a chicken to me by way of an apology. Even more ignorant than I was self-righteous (and amidst the mitigating circumstances of culture shock) when first I arrived in Kpaytuo I was offended at what I perceived, quite incorrectly, as the boy trying to bribe his way back into my good graces. When I rejected Peter's gift, the acceptance of which, to him, would have signified that the palaver was "fini"—he had been as mystified by my behavior as I was by his. In time, after struggling through many misunderstandings, I came to see and like their way. Not in everything, but in this.

Mary Jackson, Tado's wife, cleaning rice, 1982.

Chapter 19

As was my custom in the middle of each day in Kpaytuo, I parked myself on the bamboo bench that stood under a shady tree near Old Man Gbon's house. I was reading when two young Liberian men came over and introduced themselves as field technicians for the Nimba County Agricultural Development Project (NCADP). They acted—theoretically, if not often actually—as liaisons between the community and the NCADP office in Saclepea. One of the field technicians, Winston, who was assigned to Kpaytuo, worked on coffee and cocoa projects, while his friend worked out of Saclepea on fisheries. (Winston was his *kwi* name; he had a tribal name but, like most Liberians dealing with non-family members and wishing to appear "modern," he used a Western name.)

Having access to motorcycles, Winston and his fellow technicians raced up and down the dirt roads of Nimba County, trying to and usually succeeding in impressing people, particularly girls, with the power and importance of their positions.

Both complained that the country people wanted the Nimba County Agricultural Development Project to do everything; but for a project to succeed, they averred, the community had to participate. That sentiment would have gladdened the heart of Peace Corps, CARE or UNESCO personnel. I wondered if the two technicians, neither of them foolish, really believed what they were saying or whether, as I suspected, they were just parroting what they knew we Americans and Europeans, who funded the aid projects, wanted to hear.

Joining the conversation was a Kpaytuo man named David, who earlier had shot an antelope and given me one of its hindquarters as a present. The four of us discussed "tribal medicine," a subject that cropped up inevitably in almost every conversation with a Liberian. To quote Schwab, "It is impossible to conceive of any circumstance in the life of a primitive African which cannot be influenced by medicine, or

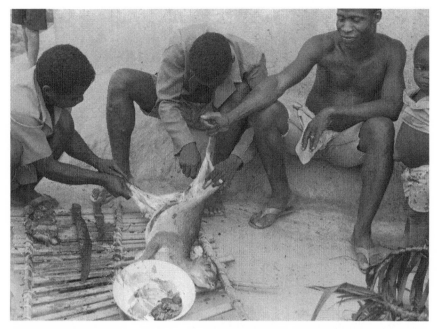

By 1982 meat was becoming scarcer in Liberia's interior, the animals driven from the forest by increased logging and farming. Here, village men skin an antelope that one of them had killed, a hindquarter of which was given to me as a gift.

for which no medicine exists, or in which there is no need for medicine." Anything with a hidden power is considered medicine, and anyone who knows how to combine or control hidden powers is a medicine man—or *Zo*.

David related a story of a medicine man with the power to repel bullets. Seeing my skeptical expression, Winston, one of the technicians, said that his father, like me, had doubted the man's prowess. So the medicine man told Winston's father to bring his own gun loaded with his own shotgun shells. Winston's father loaded the gun and, as ordered, fired at the man. Not a hair on the medicine man's body was disturbed, according to Winston, making a true believer out of his once-skeptical father.

"Why do you think the PRC [the People's Redemption Council]

killed Tolbert [the President, during the coup] with a knife?" David asked.

When I said I did not know, he answered: "Tolbert can have someone make medicine for him so no one can kill him with bullets."

I smiled, for this was what my ex-student Frank Siaway had told me a few weeks before about the events surrounding the coup and a variation of a story my students, circa 1967, used to swear by. But in the 1967 version the target of the bullets wasn't a high official assisted by a medicine man, but a common criminal. And instead of repelling the bullets, he caught them in his teeth. I had heard the story countless times. And also the one about the medicine you rubbed on the bottom of a tree that magically caused a snake in the top of the tree to fall to the ground immobilized; or the story about the woman in a nearby village who had given birth to a child fathered by a goat. (I'm willing to acknowledge there are many people in this world—I've even worked with a few—fathered by jackasses; but goats, never.)

A pioneer in explaining the psychology of the Liberian tribal people was Diedrich Westermann, a German Lutheran missionary and well-known Africanist who lived in West Africa around the time of the First World War. In his book on the Kpelle tribe of Liberia, written in 1921, Westermann observed: "If we realize the fact that for the tribesman there exists no boundary between the reasonable and the unreasonable, between the natural and the supernatural, even between the possible and the impossible, his religious activities will be intelligible according to our understanding. If he seeks to gain the favor of a person by means of friendly persuasion or exhortation, we can comprehend it; but when he attempts to do the same with a tree or stone, then it is nonsense to us. If he catches a leopard in a trap, we call that sensible, but when he seeks to appease the dead leopard by means of sacrifice, that appears irrational to us."

❖　❖　❖

Winston, the field technician, explained, and the others gathered round us readily agreed, that the white man wants his name carried far. So, were I, for example, to discover a cure for malaria, I'd tell the world of my discovery. Not so the African. Winston contended—and the others agreed—that an African would, and indeed has, carried his discoveries to the grave. I had heard this sentiment expressed by countless Liberians—one of their explanations for Africa's backwardness vis-à-vis the West.

Dr. George Way Harley, a medical missionary and anthropologist who for thirty-five years worked among, and wrote about, the Liberian tribal people, concurred. "I am willing to advance the hypothesis," Dr. Harley wrote, "that the lack of progress of these West African tribes and similar people has been due in no small measure to their socialistic totality, pulling down and destroying the progressive individual, or sacrificing him deliberately to their conservative ideals. Inventive genius was not only suppressed, it was taboo in such a system."

A young girl, with a baby tied to her back, working on her family's farm, 1982.

Chapter 20

Konvali Kamara was one of the few members of the Mandingo tribe living in Kpaytuo. Slight (about five feet, two inches), pitch black (like most Mandingoes), dignified and scrupulously honest, Konvali had a soft voice and a horrible hacking cough, courtesy of his chain-smoking. He was always serious, and I never bantered with him, as I did with most Liberians, who had fine senses of humor. Compared to most Liberians, the Mandingoes were a serious, no-nonsense, disciplined lot. Maybe because we didn't speak a common language, I found them aloof. Pressed to say why, I think the distance I felt between myself and Mandingoes was cultural—mine Judeo-Christian, theirs Muslim, African variety.

When I lived in Kpaytuo, Konvali was, relatively speaking, a prosperous citizen, the proprietor of a tiny general store and also a tailor shop. I bought salt, onions, cans of tomato paste and toilet paper from his store, but given the size of Kpaytuo—no more than a thousand people—I don't imagine Konvali earned much. Apparently hard times had hit him, for by 1982 he no longer had his store or tailor shop. He farmed, just like the Gio citizens of Kpaytuo.

Upon my return to Kpaytuo, Konvali came to Tado's house and asked me for a favor, an unusual act. I never remembered Konvali asking me for anything, which is more than I can say for most of Kpaytuo's residents, who were not shy about asking for favors. That's not a knock on Kpaytuo's residents. Relative to them, I had so much; they so little. Konvali wondered if, when I returned to America, I might send him an English-Arabic dictionary and an English-Arabic Koran. Not for himself, as he was illiterate. The books were for his son, who presumably was learning English in Liberia's schools. Mindful of his heritage, Konvali wanted the boy also to learn Arabic. I told him that I would be happy to do it.

Mamadu Kamara was Konvali's younger brother. I remembered

Mamadu as a quiet, introverted, inoffensive, extremely polite boy of eighteen in my first-grade class. Mamadu spoke so little English, as did most of the Mandingoes at that time up-country, that I did not say much to him, but as he'd been unfailingly courteous toward me, I'd always liked him. How sad, then, upon my return, to see what had happened to Mamadu. He had been robust: now, around thirty-two years old, he was emaciated, especially his head. He reminded me of a concentration camp survivor.

Recognizing me, he feebly held out his bony hand, which was covered with a white, chalky country medicine. A few years before, he had been stricken with a fever from which he'd never recovered. He was coherent one moment, delirious the next. Whatever had struck him down—malaria, which can affect the brain or, my guess, sleeping sickness—he was a wreck. He sat by the side of Konvali's house for hours on end in a torpid state, mumbling senseless words or staring silently into space. In the evenings, he prowled the village, speaking nonsense.

Shocked by Mamadu's condition, I spoke to my old friend and former student, Edwin Siaway, about him. Not surprisingly, the villagers believed Mamadu's illness was caused by a demon. Edwin said that some people can say (it is always "some people can say," when a Liberian really means he and his neighbors) that Konvali's mother wanted Konvali, her eldest son, to be rich, so she went to a medicine man and struck a Faustian bargain. The plan backfired (Edwin and the villagers believed), resulting in Mamadu becoming an invalid and Konvali, once one of the wealthier people in Kpaytuo, losing his store and tailor shop.

I asked Tado if Konvali had taken Mamadu to a clinic after he'd become ill, and Tado said no. The reason, according to Tado: Konvali and Mamadu had the same Ma, but not the same Pa. I found this to be nonsense. When I asked Konvali, he said that, of course, he had taken Mamadu to clinics and doctors, all to no avail.

◆　　◆　　◆

Since Tado's house was too hot to sit in, even at eight o'clock at night, by which hour the sun had set, he and I ate on the patio—an open-air addition built in front of his home, composed of a concrete floor surrounded by a three-foot-high concrete rail, with an opening to enter and leave the home. (The patio was added to the house in the years between my living there and my return visit.) Tado and I ate in the dark, lest the insects molest us. As Sir Harry Hamilton Johnston so accurately put it: "It is the mission of all insects in tropical climates to make themselves as odious to man in any way that occurs to them."

Women and children did not, as a rule, eat with the men in Kpaytuo, so, after serving us, Tado's wife, Mary, her mother and Tado's children ate out back next to the fire, where tribal women and children spend so many of their days and nights.

Tado liked to listen to the news on the battery-powered radio—Liberian and foreign news broadcasts on ELBC, the government-operated station; and Liberian news in the Gio dialect on ELWA, a mission-operated station. There were no newspapers up-country, and even if there had been most Liberians in those years—certainly those over fifty—did not read well or at all. Therefore, radio and—especially—word of mouth were the means by which the people learned what was going on in their country or within their extended families and circle of friends or enemies. Most tribal men had no interest in international news, but Tado did, so he listened to the broadcasts of the BBC, the Voice of America, and English-language stations of the then-Soviet Union and The People's Republic of China. I recall the sense of betrayal felt by the Lebanese and Syrian Liberian community in 1967 at the suddenness of the Israeli victory in the Six Day War: they, the Lebanese and Syrians, had all been listening to reports on the state-operated Egyptian radio station. According to that source, the Arab armies had been on the verge of entering Tel Aviv and obliterating the Israelis.

Radios were new and rare up-country in 1966–67, whereas by 1982 radios and tape recorders were common. I well remember the people in Kpaytuo gathered round a radio listening to news broadcasts in Gio in 1966. Signaling the beginning of the program, the radio announcer would say, "*Bobwah*," the Gio word for "Good Morning." And, in unison, the villagers would answer back: "*Ah-oh*," the traditional response.

Joining us after dinner on this night was Edwin Siaway, whose house was near Tado's, and Sammy Marwiah, the young man—I don't think he was more than twenty-four—who was the principal of the school and whom I had met upon my return. He was intelligent, ambitious, and seemed to care about the school. He was not a braggart or impudent, both common traits, in my experience, of Liberian principals. That Sammy Marwiah had been born and bred in Kpaytuo also had something to do with it: most of the principals and teachers did not teach in their own villages or towns, so they did not have family and friends (or a secret society) to act as a moderating force on their behavior.

Liberians possessed an insatiable curiosity about anything American. Being a live, willing source of information, I was questioned day and night about my culture.

"Teacher," Edwin asked, "is it true there are people in America who don't know book?" He asked apologetically, as if I would find the question absurd.

Even before I could answer, as if given the courage to ask what he considered an even more preposterous question, Sammy Marwiah said, "Mr. Cherry, they tell me there are poor people in America. I can't believe it. Is it so?"

They were equally perplexed and aghast when I said the answer to both questions was yes—there were poor people in America, some of whom were illiterate. Though I doubt it clarified matters, I explained that the Americans they came in contact with—Peace Corps Volunteers, missionaries, USAID technicians, engineers, doctors, nurses and mechanics—did not represent the entire population of the United States. In fact, I said, there were more poor people in America than there were people in Liberia, Sierra Leone, Guinea and the Ivory Coast. And (circa 1982) there were about twenty-five million Americans who couldn't read or write. But poor people in America, I pointed out, didn't work in or visit other countries. I acknowledged that the foreigners with whom Tado, Edwin and Sammy came in contact "knew book," and had money, although they were by no means wealthy.

This they refused to believe. I understood why, for even I, when a twenty-two-year-old Peace Corps Volunteer, owned more *kwi* things— a camera, a tape recorder, a typewriter, clothes, books, and (back in America) a car and so on—than they could have accumulated in three lifetimes. The Americans with whom they came in contact were, compared to them, very rich, and very educated.

Edwin then related seeing in Monrovia a movie named *Cornbread*. He said that people told him that the story was not true, and he wanted to know if that was so. Yes, I told him, the movies they see in Monrovia (most of them of the Kung Fu garbage genre) are not true. They are stories that someone made up.

"It is so," Tado chimed in. "I read a book three times named *Robinson Crusoe*. It can be so real. But people tell me it is only a story. For true."

"That's because *Robinson Crusoe* is so well written," I said. "Nevertheless, *Robinson Crusoe* is not a true story."

Then Sammy Marwiah asked if the houses and cars destroyed in the movies were real. To answer this was embarrassing. In a culture like theirs, which has so little, it was inconceivable to destroy—as people did in James Bond movies—cars, boats, planes, furniture, jewelry and even houses. I tried to explain that it cost millions of dollars to make these movies, but if they were successful, the people who made them earned many millions more dollars. Therefore, I explained to Tado and Edwin and Sammy, the people who made the movies decided it paid in the long run to destroy some cars and some houses and some boats, if they could make more money by doing so. I also said that many of the objects destroyed in the movies were made of plastic or wood, but not all.

Try as I might, I don't think I ever convinced them that there are poor people in America.

Chapter 21

A few nights later, having just come from my bath, I was sitting on the patio in the dark with a towel wrapped around my body, waiting to cool off before going inside my room to dress. It was dark, save for the weak light from a hurricane lantern. While waiting for our supper, Tado and I discussed our favorite subject, the differences between America and Liberia. I heard footsteps coming towards us on the narrow path leading from the road to Tado's home. The person walked over to where I was sitting, bent over and hugged me. Though I could barely see in the dimness, I knew it was Betty Leeleh.

From the moment I'd arrived back in Kpaytuo, I'd inquired about Betty, the favorite of all my students. In 1966 she had been about twelve when I'd taught her in the second grade, the shiest student I have ever seen: by staring at her for more than a second, I would make her turn away blushing. When I called the roll alphabetically each morning, on purpose I'd occasionally omit Betty's name, even though she was present. Afterward looking to the right and left of where on the bench she sat, but never directly at her, I'd say, "Is there anyone whose name I missed?" She'd fidget and worry that I had marked her absent, but was too shy and respectful to point out my error. The girl sitting next to her, usually her close friend, Anna Nuah, urged her to speak up, lest Betty be counted among the absent. Betty caught on to my game after a while, and knew that I had, in fact, marked her as present. As I got to know the students better, I often called them by their "country names," telling them that their tribal names were lovely and they had no reason to be ashamed of using them. I sometimes called Betty by her tribal name, "Fanta."

Being Tado's niece, Betty lived with one of her aunts in our quarter of the village. She and Anna Nuah passed by my house many times daily on the way to and from the well, and—like almost every student and certainly every young girl—always treated me with the greatest respect.

Anna Nuah, about 13, on the left with her closest friend, and my favorite student, Betty Leeleh, then about 12, circa 1966.

And when Betty had an ugly, oozing tropical ulcer a half-inch deep and larger than a half dollar on the inside of her ankle, she came to my house every day after school for weeks where I applied sulfa powder, sterile gauze and tape until months later it was gone, though a scar remained.

I never knew—or really inquired—why Betty was not living in her mother's village: probably because there was no school there. And no student was more enthusiastic about learning than Betty. So much the worse when Tado wrote me in 1969—a year after I left Africa—that

Betty Leeleh, whose father, desperate for money, had married her off at 15 to a much older Mandingo. But Betty had refused to accept her fate. Here she is, about 28, in 1982.

Betty's father, needing money, had married her at about age fifteen to an old Mandingo. What I didn't know, and learned only after I returned to Kpaytuo, was that Betty had refused to accept this as her fate and had run away from the man—not once but twice. Rather than return the bride price, Betty's father had exchanged one of her more docile sisters for Betty.

When I asked about her, as I had done the first night and day back in Kpaytuo, Tado had had no idea what she was doing or where she was living, though he had heard she might be living in Dunpa, the tiny village a day's walk from Kpaytuo where her parents lived. I wished to go there, but my body was not yet ready for an all-day trek into the bush. Tado had last seen her a year before, while the two of them were waiting for a money bus in Sanniquellie, the county headquarters many hours north of Kpaytuo. I found his losing touch with her peculiar, since she was his kin and he had once held such high hopes for her. I knew how hurt and disappointed Tado had been at Betty having to withdraw from school, especially given the circumstances. Nevertheless, I sensed something faintly condemnatory in Tado's voice, as if what had happened were somehow Betty's fault. Or maybe he disapproved of her recent lifestyle, especially if it did not include a married relationship and regular church attendance. Then again, perhaps I was reading something into the situation, and Tado and Betty, for whatever reason, had just lost touch.

Once back, I had sent a note to Betty, to no avail, via a man who claimed he was going to Dunpa. Then, during my journey to Saclepea (when I stayed with the Carsons), I had run into a relative of Betty's, who had told me Betty was living in Ganta. I promptly wrote Betty a note, which the relative had promised to deliver, though, this being Liberia, there was no guarantee the relative or the letter would reach Betty within two months—the length of my projected stay. But obviously the letter had reached its objective, for otherwise Betty—shy, sweet, special Betty—would not have been standing before me.

Self-conscious that my ex-student should come upon her former teacher covered only by a towel, I excused myself to put on walking shorts and a T-shirt. Soon after dinner Tado and Mary left for the school, where Tado taught night school, on the most elementary level, to a half dozen adults, most of them women in their twenties and thirties wanting to learn how to read and write English. Except for an occasional visitor, Betty and I were alone for the next two hours.

At my urging, she told me about her life since I'd left Liberia. It seems her father, a devout Muslim, believed that if Betty continued in school she would not be interested in Islam, and that, more than anything, was why he had withdrawn her from school in 1969. She did not mention that he'd also married her off then. I think she was ashamed. I'd never realized Betty was the child of a Mandingo man and a Gio woman. I should have suspected as much years before, since her country name, Fanta, is a Mandingo name. But, circa 1967, Betty was being raised in a decidedly Gio ambiance; as for religion, the influence there was her uncle Tado Jackson's Christianity.

While living in Dunpa, she took up with a Mandingo boy, giving birth in the early 1970s to a child. She believed that once she was living with this Mandingo boy he, unlike her father, would encourage her to return to school. But that was not to be. So after a while—it was difficult to pin her down, but I surmised it was around 1975—at around age twenty, she left him. She informed her parents that she intended to return to school (after a six-year absence). Furthermore, whether she remained in school or not, she had no interest in becoming a Muslim. This incensed and frightened her father, who believed that if Betty were an infidel, it reflected badly on him, considerably diminishing his own chances of entering Paradise. (I would have advised him to forget about Paradise and prepare some day for a long stay in Hell.)

By 1977 Betty was living in Sanniquellie, there taking up with a school teacher by whom she had a child in 1980. But that relationship ended, for the man was, though she didn't put it so bluntly, a bastard, who failed to support her or his child. Betty had recently left Sanniquellie for Ganta, which brought the story up to date. There she rented a room in a house. Her two-year-old lived with Betty's mother in Dunpa, while the older child, who was, I think, about nine, lived with the father in Saclepea. Betty, who long ago would have graduated but for the interruptions, was in the tenth grade. She hoped to bake and sell donuts after school during the week to make ends meet.

By the light of the new day, when she again visited, I saw that Betty had grown up to be a remarkably attractive woman. Her face, which had changed little, was as shiny and black as an ebony mask, with full lips, sparkling, large and inquisitive black eyes, long, sensual eyelashes, and a warm smile. She exuded a quiet strength and intelligence. Though the mother of two, hers was the lithe figure of a maiden. The most striking thing about her was an aristocratic bearing, even in her worn shoes and a tattered dress. (A real African Cinderella, the quintessential Jewish grandmother might add.)

Without my asking, she straightened my room, made the bed, and cut up a pineapple for me. Then she went out back to help Mary Jackson with the morning chores. We didn't speak much during the day, for she and Mary spent it scrubbing and cleaning the house, literally removing every item from inside and disinfecting the floors with Clorox.

I spent the morning writing up my experiences and impressions—as I tried to do each day—and listening to Mandingo and other West African music on my tape recorder, which incidentally was about one-twentieth the weight and one-tenth the size of the clunky tape recorder I'd used circa 1967. I devoted most of the afternoon to speaking with Thomas Karngbeae, who had arrived for the weekend from Zuatuo, where he taught school. Thomas, who was in his late twenties, was one of my former students. I hadn't seen Thomas since our memorable conversation early in my trip on the sexual mores of our respective cultures.

Thomas was mildly upset. He had heard on the radio that two Ethiopian scientists, having discovered eight planets missing, had predicted the Earth was going to explode the previous week. I tried to console Thomas by pointing out that we were not speaking in Heaven or Hell, but in Kpaytuo, so obviously the Earth had not been destroyed.

Switching to the subject of America, Thomas asked: "Is it true that Americans cannot stay with their brothers and sisters for a long time?"

I had been asked that question frequently by my Liberian friends.

"It is so, Thomas," I answered. "If you and your family were catching hard time, you would go live with one of your brothers. And while you were there, you and your family could help him and his family. But in America, if I went to stay at my sister's house, how could I help? If I had children, they couldn't bring water for her. My sister turns a faucet in her kitchen for water. She doesn't need wood for cooking. I couldn't help her husband on the rice farm, because he doesn't make a rice farm. He teaches in college. If I am in financial difficulties I can stay with my sister and her husband for a couple of weeks, but not for months or even years. Then her husband will say, 'I don't want your brother staying here for a year.'"

To which Thomas replied: "If I go to live with my sister and the husband tried to tell me that he didn't want me to stay there, I will accept that and pack my load and go on my way. But when I see the husband, too, maybe something will happen somewhere, and he'll have to come to me for help. I will tell my sister, 'No, I don't want to see your husband here. Let you and your husband go.'"

"But if the man lets you stay with him when you are having hard time," I said, "then when he is having hard time, he can come stay with you."

"Yes," Thomas answered, "that is what we do here."

"But we Americans don't do that."

"I don't know which system is better," Thomas said. "For me, my system is good. If I am catching hard time, I have to go to my sister for aid."

Before leaving, Thomas asked if he could write a letter to my mother. That letter, with his punctuation intact, follows:

Dear Mrs. Cherry:

I am very grateful to all mighty God who makes everything possible for us to have lived now. I am also thanking to him to have let Bob Cherry as your son.

This is my special thanks to you for granting him permission to fly to Liberia, most especially to Kpaytuo. This is the first of its kind in the history of Kpaytuo.

From the visit that your son took to Kpaytuo, the people have warmly welcomed every member of the Cherry family to Kpaytuo to become part of us.

I am taking this chance to give this African name to him. He is now called Gaylah and you are also called Galahlay which means Gaylah's mother.

I hope this letter finds you in good health and you read it with understanding. Thanks.

Happily yours,
Thomas Karngbeae

Chapter 22

H aving to return to Ganta, Betty left the next morning, a Sunday. She looked fetching and moved gracefully in her *lappa*, which exposed her beautiful shoulders. Africans look more attractive in African clothes than in Western garb, to me at any rate—as I think Westerners look better in Western, rather than African, clothes. I did sometimes wear flowing Liberian-style shirts when I lived there; not so when I returned.

After lunch, I headed for the shade under the tree in front of Old Man Gbon's house. On the way I stopped in at Marie Sonyah's father's house, hoping to borrow a chair on which to sit under the tree. Six or seven adults and countless children and babies were present in the sparsely furnished house. All the homes in Kpaytuo had a large room—for want of a better term the living room, though I never saw in any homes I visited during my 1982 return any tables, lamps, shelves, sofas, or any of the accessories one associated with the term. Additionally the houses had three or four smaller, unfurnished bedrooms.

Marie's mother was washing her grandchild in a metal tub, while Marie was braiding the hair of a girl holding her own baby. The baby defecated in the girl's lap. Rather than change her *lappa*, the girl—whose hair Marie had been braiding—casually rose and washed the spot twice with water and a dirty rag and then again sat down so Marie could resume braiding her hair.

While talking with Marie, Tado appeared to tell me the town elders and the chief had gathered so we might discuss the status of the well project. We proceeded to the tree in front of Old Man Gbon's, where we were greeted by the town chief, Michael Bleeton, the town elders—who select the chief—and about twenty adult males interested in sitting in on the discussion. The chief said they were pleased that I wanted to help them, and they thought the idea of building new wells was a good one. The chief then asked to hear what I had learned in Monrovia.

I told them that I had spoken to many people about the water project—to the missionary in Saclepea, Mr. Carson; to some Peace Corps Volunteers, and to a water expert in Monrovia. I explained that based on the recommendations I received, I'd concluded that draw-bucket wells would be the best project to undertake—*at this time*—for Kpaytuo. Whatever type of wells was constructed, the wells would have to be built on the outskirts of town, where the water level was relatively high, in order to ensure a plentiful supply of water.

With Tado translating, Tuazama (father of Paul, my ex-student who was now a police major in Monrovia) asked if I had decided against a generator-driven water system—one in which the water would be transmitted from the well through pipes to the town—because of the problem of maintaining a generator-driven system or because of its cost. If my reluctance was related to maintaining the system, Tuazama assured me the citizens of Kpaytuo could—and indeed would—keep the system in perfect working order.

And we'll all live to one hundred and twenty-five, I felt like responding. Nothing was more typical of tribal Liberians than to talk about grandiose schemes, which

Tuazama, a village elder and father of Major Paul Tuazama, circa 1967. Tuazama was one of the few elders who devoted time to improving education, such as it was, in the village.

rarely came to pass. And if the schemes did become reality, they faltered quickly. This, I had no doubt, would be the fate of a generator-powered water system in Kpaytuo.

I reminded the elders, including Tuazama, a vocal, ornery, but well-meaning town elder whom I knew from my time living there, that kerosene was not always available in the interior. If kerosene wasn't available to operate a generator at a sawmill, what made him—or anyone else—think kerosene would be available to operate a generator in Kpaytuo?

"Imagine what will happen during the rainy season," I said. "You know how the country man thinks. Someone will come to him and say he has to pay his part to buy kerosene for the generator that brings water into the village. He will say to that man, 'Don't humbug me, my friend. I can get my water from the sky. It can come to me with the rain, and fill my buckets one-one, one-one. And fill the barrel next to my house. I don't need to go to the Lebanese or Mandingo man for my kerosene for a generator.' Is this not the way the country man would talk the kerosene palaver?"

As for maintaining the generator, I pointed out that companies in Liberia, with their own maintenance men and vast resources, and towns much larger and wealthier than Kpaytuo, had difficulty keeping their generators operating.

"Who in Kpaytuo knows how to fix a generator?" I asked. No one, was the answer, but that they wouldn't acknowledge. The townspeople actually believed they could afford to operate a generator-driven water system. And of course they knew how impressive it would appear to the world that little Kpaytuo had an electric water system. Think how envious the other villages and towns would be. Never mind that the system would be inoperable in about three months.

The tribal Liberian's greatest joy is to impress others, if only for the moment. In his classic account, *Tribes of the Liberian Hinterland*, George Schwab recounted the story of a chief who craved a motorcycle, bought one for cash, and, not knowing how to stop it once in operation, proceeded to smash it up almost immediately. When regrets were expressed to the chief, he replied that it didn't matter, for everyone knew he once had owned a motorcycle and that was enough.

After discussing the issue for a couple of hours, it finally dawned on Tuazama that I was not going to give any of my hard-earned money toward building a "white elephant." He then told a long, involved parable—often the way tribal Liberians make points in their generally democratic discussions. At the conclusion of Tuazama's parable, everyone was resolved to their not getting a generator for the wells. They all thanked me for my generosity, and said they looked forward to having new draw-bucket wells built. Then the chief invited us to his house for cassava leaf soup with bush hog and rice.

"Old Man" (and "Old Ma") are terms of respect and affection in Liberian culture. The distinguished man pictured here is "Old Man" Gbon, the father of some of my ex-students. During my 1982 visit I often sat in the shade of a tree near his home, there finding some relief from the scorching midday sun.

Chapter 23

Naturally, when I returned to Kpaytuo, I was curious about the state of education, for teaching, after all, was my job during the time I lived there. Everything else—the hikes into the forest with my favorite students, learning about tribal ways, taking thousands of photographs, the many pleasant relationships I developed in the village, listening to tribal songs and watching, even participating, in their dances—was the cherry on top of the sundae, so to speak. (And a tasty cherry it was.)

Until 1960, six years before I arrived, there had never been a school in Kpaytuo. And once the school was established, it was not worthy of the name in the sense most citizens from a developed country think of as a school. The school was housed in a building that, some years back, had been the home of a paramount chief. The principal lived in one of the rooms with his baby brother. In a second room we stored the food donated by that wonderful humanitarian organization, CARE—cans of beans and vegetable oil, cartons of corn meal, bulgur wheat, and boxes of powdered milk. We served the food to the students at recess, from around 10 to 10:30 A.M., and for many of them it was their only meal until the evening, maybe the only meal that day. And in the front room of the "school" was my classroom.

Prior to my arrival, Tado Jackson, the former principal who would soon leave to upgrade his education, had, with the help of the students, built a rectangular mud-walled structure about sixty feet long and thirty feet wide, with a cement floor and a zinc roof. During my time, the principal who replaced Tado and the one other Liberian teacher taught in the newly constructed "building," which was more like a shed, with each one using half of it for his classes. Both of these structures—the ramshackle home where my classes were held and the rectangular "school"—had cement floors and plaster on the mud walls but little else: no desks, no places for the students to sit (until we commissioned a carpenter to build benches), and no blackboards (until we made them ourselves by painting insulating tiles black), and a few outdated American textbooks circa 1955, with stories about Tommy and Jimmy and Susie and Sandy wondering what they would wear for Halloween or stories about kids going to a pajama party. The books had no doubt been donated to Liberia through an American philanthropic or religious organization, in time finding their way to the villages and towns of the Liberian interior. Not surprisingly, the stories were about life in America.

Our school offered classes in kindergarten through grade four. (Forget about a middle or high school; Kpaytuo wasn't large enough to have one. The few residents who reached those grades had to live and attend school in another, larger town, usually an hour or two away.) Because there were only three teachers—the principal, another teacher and I—each of us taught more than one grade at a time.

The school week was five days, but as noted earlier, I considered it a successful week if we had four days of school. Something invariably arose that prevented us from having five days of school: maybe the absence of one or both of the other teachers, out of town trying to charm his way into or pay his way out of a love (read lust) affair; or the morning someone spotted a snake in a tree about twenty yards from the school. Everyone bolted from the classrooms, the better to enjoy the ensuing action. The students threw rocks and sticks at the snake until one of them knocked it out of the tree, where it was promptly beaten to death with sticks. Of course everyone was too excited to return to school, as they were the day a particularly nasty argument between two women over a man interrupted classes: we all ran out to watch the show.

We also had to contend with the rainy season, when the sky poured forth buckets on some days. Kpaytuo receives about 120 inches of rain a year (New York averages about 44 inches); and in some months during the rainy season the village can be inundated with 5 inches a day. Some of the students lived in hamlets two or more miles from Kpaytuo; they would have been drenched walking to school that time of year. None of them (or their families) could afford the "luxury" of an umbrella. I don't want to give the impression it rained all day, every day: there were times in the rainy season when it was dry, though damp and cool in the morning; warmer, even some sunshine, in the afternoon but by 5:00 P.M. the sky darkened and we could expect—and got—one to two hours of steady rain in the evening.

Then there were "work days" during which the students cleaned the grass and debris around the school compound. And, finally, there were the days the students spent eight hours at someone's farm, harvesting the new-grown rice. From the money they earned we chartered two money buses, which carried us to nearby villages or towns to play soccer. Soccer—or as most of the world refers to it, "football"—is Liberia's national sport and, as it is in much of the world, a passion. The male students played it many afternoons around 4:00 P.M., once they had finished chores and the sun had begun its descent. They didn't need expensive equipment or manicured grass on which to play. Cut down a tree, then shape and nail it and you have two goal posts; cut the

Kpaytuo's older students harvesting rice during a "work day" at someone's farm. With the money they earned the student body chartered two money buses in which we traveled to a nearby town for a football match.

grass on a relatively flat piece of ground near the school compound and you have a field. The students' feet were calloused from a life walking shoeless, so they didn't need soccer shoes—which most couldn't afford— although of course they would have played better with them. Most of the players on the village team were the older male students, ages sixteen to twenty, many of whom lived and attended school in other, nearby towns but returned home for the occasional soccer match.

Bragging rights in soccer were important, especially if a village like Kpaytuo beat a larger town, as would have been the case in just about any place on earth. A soccer match was also a big social event—like a Friday night football game in a Texas town. Everyone turned out when we hosted a game, always scheduled on a Saturday. The younger school girls (eight to fourteen) and their older sisters (fifteen to twenty-five) wore new *lappas* and even the homeliest among them looked terrific. The older girl students cooked rice and, after the game, everyone celebrated (that included me). There was a battery-operated record player with a large speaker—how it got there, whose it was, I can't remember. We danced in the large cement-floor structure next to the main school building until around 1:00 A.M. and you could hear the music from far, far away.

During my Peace Corps years I was the language arts teacher in our school, instructing the children in penmanship, reading, speaking, listening, spelling and grammar. I had 35 students in the first and second grades, and I taught them, together, from around 8:00 A.M. to 10:00 A.M. Then I taught the third graders from 10:30 to 11:30, and the fourth graders from 11:30 to around 12:30.

With my first and second graders, I almost always started the day off with "sharing" or "show and tell," both exercises designed to teach listening and speaking skills. Then I read traditional fairy tales such as *Aesop's Fables* and stories by the Brothers Grimm. Eventually I acquired a text that actually had some relevance to their lives—a book of Liberian folk tales. I would've liked to have the students read these books, except that they, especially the younger ones, did not read well enough to do so. After I obtained from the Peace Corps a hand-operated mimeograph machine, I also developed and distributed exercises that helped students in each grade improve their ability to speak, read and print English.

Village women and girls dressed up—and dressed to kill—watching a football (soccer) game in Kpaytuo. Afterwards we ate and everyone danced through the night. And, dare I speculate, some did more than dance.

The Liberian teachers were responsible for teaching kindergarten classes and the subjects of history, science and mathematics to grades one through four. They were ill-prepared and ill-trained. I think the other teacher, Charles Mongrou, had only attended school to grade seven or eight, not uncommon for tribal teachers in the interior in those years. The Liberian teachers devoted most of their time to teaching religious songs to the students.

Liberian teachers relied almost exclusively on rote "learning," mostly because it was the easiest way of "teaching" and because it was the way they had been "taught." They didn't care, or perhaps never

Kpaytuo's football team, circa 1967.

considered, that this method didn't teach students how to think. And sadly, the students liked nothing better than to memorize a list, the more arcane the subject the better. It hardly entered their minds, either, that they didn't understand what they were memorizing. The principal assigned his second grade science class—most of whose members did not know the earth was round—the following definition to memorize: "The medulla is the base of the brain where it joins the spinal cord for its automatic action such as breathing and heart beat."

I tried to pry my students away from rote learning, hoping in the process I might teach them, among other things, to comprehend what

My third grade class, circa 1967. That's Betty Leeleh on the far right, with the bandage on her right foot; and Sammy Dahngbae, my houseboy, second row, third boy from the right. Most of the children in the interior started school at age 11 or 12, some later.

they read and to draw inferences from it. But it wasn't always easy, given their unfamiliarity with the approach and with the English language. We were reading a story one day and I asked my second grade class when George and Teddy had left for the hayfield. (Of course having children in a Liberian village in the rain forest read about a hayfield when they had never seen, but for a photo, a horse or hay was ridiculous, but we had no other books at that point.) The answer to when George and Teddy left for the hayfield was "after breakfast," plainly stated in the text of the story. Yet none of my students could furnish me with the correct answer. One boy said they left before breakfast so I asked him to show me where in the story it said as much. He didn't know what I was talking about. Nor, on that occasion, did any of his classmates. My next question was, "Why did Mr. Gray and the boy go for a wagon and horse?" One of the students gave as his answer, "jumped on the horse," which happened to be the next line of dialogue in the story. The student wasn't thinking about what he had read or what I had asked. He was more interested in mechanically supplying me with an answer. In time they grasped my point.

Maybe my students didn't write Oxford or Harvard English, but they were able to express themselves. I cite two examples, both written to me soon after I arrived in the village. The first was from a sixteen-year-old student in the fourth grade, with his punctuation intact:

Dear Teacher:
   I take this great opportunity to write you this letter. Please excuse me today. is because my father sends me to Saclepea for something. again I didn't really know when will be back. so please excuse me for today and tomorrow. if God will agree I will be back to.

The next letter, with his punctuation intact, was written by a fourth-grade student:

Dear teacher Cherry:
   I am respectfully asking you to please offer me a job in your yard. such a washing close, or any king of job that will be capable to give me.
   I'm your student, my grade is fine, I'm 20 years old of age, for reference in general conduct I beg to refer you to Edwin [a fellow student who worked for me at one time].
   If my letter is take into cansideration I promise to be a serviceable employee in your yard.
   I am anticipating at your early responses."
   Thanks,
   Very Truly your student
   Wallace L. Bleeton

Most students learned something, especially the brighter ones, else no tribal students—from Kpaytuo and scores of other villages and towns and cities—would ever have passed the standardized national examination, the arduous test one had to pass to advance from sixth grade to seventh grade.

The most important "lesson" I taught my students over almost a two-year period, by both deed and word, was that they should ask questions. Tribal society did not place much value on questioning; in fact, in olden days, it was frowned upon and you might be poisoned by a high official in the secret society for prying. Western culture, to its great credit and benefit, encourages independent thinking.

By way of explaining why they believed something, time and time again my students said to me: "Because they said so."

I would ask: "Who is 'they'?"

I knew who "they" were. "They" were the people who had taught them tribal customs. I wanted my students to decide things for themselves after they weighed the empirical evidence. I wanted to prepare them for life in a changing world, for as the German philosopher Johann Wolfgang von Goethe said, "Life belongs to the living and he who lives must be prepared for change."

◆　◆　◆

Upon my return to Kpaytuo in 1982, I usually bathed after the sun had set, but before dinner, which Tado and I ate around 7:30. (Due to Liberia's position near the equator, the sun sets at the same time year round—approximately seven o'clock, with little twilight.) On my way to the bathhouse for my evening bath, I'd pass Tado's wife, Mary, and Mellay, the teenage girl I had hired to help Mary during my stay. Each day they had engaged in back-breaking work from the minute they got up, which was around 5:00 A.M., to that moment, fourteen hours later— yet their work was not finished. There they sat on twelve-inch-high chairs before the fire, surrounded by pots and pans, the ever-present children crying and grabbing at them, engulfed by smoke. Besides preparing dinner for Tado and me and themselves and the family by the dim glow of a hurricane lantern, in an effort to "know book," they were often reciting the times table—three times three is nine; three times four is twelve; three times five is fifteen. On and on they practiced.

Mary Jackson in a familiar milieu, surrounded by pots and pans; the only "ingredients" missing are young children, who normally outnumber the pots and pans.

After dinner one night I walked into town and saw gathered around a lantern four schoolboys, ages fifteen or sixteen, studying their sixth-grade African history notes. When I taught in Kpaytuo, we didn't teach African history, nor did the school go to sixth grade, so on the face of it there had been progress. On the other hand Kpaytuo's school—a modern, six-room school—still lacked an adequate supply of textbooks, so the boys were studying from the notes they had copied from the blackboard. (It took me about a year to lay the groundwork for the new school, which was built by USAID funds, and material that had been donated by Sammy Cooper, Kpaytuo's wealthy Americo-Liberian. Kpaytuo's male citizens provided the labor for the school, which from the time I lobbied for it to completion was five years. I was pleased it was completed within the twentieth century.)

I asked one of the boys, who was about sixteen, to read for me. He tried to read, with little success, the following sentence: "African institutions were usually socialistic in nature." He could not pronounce the words "institutions," "socialistic," and "nature," so I was hardly surprised when it became apparent he had absolutely no idea what the sentence meant. I explained the sentence to them. Their eyes and faces lit up. He next labored over the sentence "Polygamy is an acceptable practice in Africa." Being unable to pronounce "polygamy," "acceptable" or "practice," little wonder he had no idea what the sentence meant, although he might very well have been the issue of a polygamous relationship.

The interior of Kpaytuo's new school, March 1982. Note that the students have a surface on which to write, which they never had in my time teaching there; and the 1982 students, here pictured, look to me as if they've grown up on a more nutritious diet, and are better clothed, than the students I taught fourteen years earlier: progress of sorts.

My after-dinner stroll next carried me to the little shop that sold cane juice—not because I wanted to drink any of the vile stuff, but because I heard enticing African music coming from within, which turned out to be from a tape recorder. During my time living in Kpaytuo, no one, except me, owned a tape recorder. Four boys, around eighteen to twenty, were playing cards by the light of a lantern. The boy minding the shop was around sixteen, and while the others played cards, he served the occasional patron and studied his fifth-grade science notes. (Yes, he was sixteen years old in the fifth grade, having begun school late as had most students when I lived there. No progress on that front, sadly.) I asked if I might look at his notebooks. Of course he agreed.

His science notes, with his punctuation and spelling intact, read as follows: "neurtrons have no charge. proton have positive charge. Electron which orbit the protons and neurtrons have negative charge. the number of protons and neurtons at the necleus is mass number. There are 92 natureal elements and 11 artificial elements. there are 103 elements in the world. matter that contain only one kind of atom is element."

He had no idea what any of it meant. How sad to see how little Liberian education, at least at the village level, had progressed in fourteen years: the modus operandi was still learning by rote.

❖   ❖   ❖

Reading the boy's notes and observing how the students had copied words they would later regurgitate without understanding took me back to my time teaching in Kpaytuo and to the bane of my existence—Otto Whern.

Whern had been the school's principal. But in a school as small as ours, with only about one hundred and seventy students, he had few duties as principal. So he was expected to teach kindergarten and science and history. I didn't know which was better: his presence or his absence. At least when he was out of town on his frequent and extended visits to friends, family or girlfriends, he was not extorting money from the students or disrupting my state of mind.

When I met and worked with him, Otto Whern, who also went by the first name Arthur, was about twenty-seven. He was of average height for a Liberian—around five feet, five inches; slim, coal-black skin color, neither handsome nor ugly, with an air of mendacity and fraudulence. He sported large gold fillings in his front teeth, which flashed when the tropical sun shone on them. He was flamboyant, mercurial, demagogic and intelligent. Much as it pains me to write the words, at times his rakish charm even made him likeable. But mostly he was a son of a bitch, Liberian style, indifferent to his job and with a diabolical approach to everything.

During his weekly fulminations in school assembly, he loved to drone on and hear his own bombast (the latter an all-too-typical Liberian trait). Principal Whern was fond of telling the student body, "If you want to be an outside man, think like an outside man; but if you are a schoolboy, act like one. Respect your parents, your teachers and your God. President Tubman gave us [the school's teachers] power to be here. You think because Wally changed schools, he'll know book. Never. And with all my principalities I make this statement."

And with "all his principalities" Otto Whern extorted money from the schoolchildren by fining them the equivalent of 50¢ or $1 for alleged misdemeanors—fines many of the youngest students in his kindergarten class could ill afford to pay, as many walked to school barefoot; and their family's annual income from subsistence farming was about $300 annually. He also made up national holidays, cancelled school on the flimsiest of pretexts, and rarely stepped into the classroom. When he did, he taught nothing of value to his charges. In this, he was like far-too-many Liberian teachers of that day, I am sorry to report. This indictment of most Liberian teachers—at that time—wasn't just my belief or opinion—based on experience—but an evaluation seconded by many Peace Corps colleagues, who encountered their own versions of Otto Whern.

Sadly, the tribal people were cowed by Principal Whern's imperious style and didn't take action to address his irresponsible approach to his job. Because he was a government employee, and because the Liberian government—at the local or national level—was no friend of theirs, the citizens of Kpaytuo assumed that Whern could not—or would not—be reprimanded for his errant behavior, much less replaced. And, except for the most egregious conduct by a Liberian principal in upcountry Liberia in my time, the townspeople were correct in their assumption.

One day the principal and I were chatting in my house. We each felt an unusual camaraderie, and thus spoke more cordially and frankly to each other than we would have normally. Trying to maintain a veneer of being a "professional," the principal always addressed me as "Mr. Cherry," so I addressed him as "Mr. Whern." On that day, I told Principal Whern I realized he would prefer to live and teach in a larger place than Kpaytuo. I said I sympathized with his problems, appreciated that it must be difficult to live and teach when someone in the government, for no valid reason, sometimes withheld and often embezzled his salary. (In addition to someone frequently stealing their money, government teachers were required to "donate" a month's salary for President Tubman's birthday celebration each November. One year, it would be the teachers in Nimba County, the next year the teachers in Grand Bassa County and so on. The money was always used for useful purposes, such as buying the President his eleventh or twelfth automobile. As part of the birthday festivities, which lasted for days, the President celebrated his birthday in that county whose teachers had "donated" a month's salary.)

Feeling close to the principal that day in my home, I said to him that I recognized how much easier it was for me to perform my job, since I sat in the village confident that my monthly check would always be deposited into my bank account in Monrovia. I was also able to call on the Peace Corps and CARE to supply me with chalk, crayons, paper, books, rulers, a mimeograph machine, etc. How different, I acknowledged, was the fate of a Liberian teacher, who had access to nothing and no one. He received nothing in the way of supplies from his government, not even a pen to mark tests. (Tests, it should be noted, that Otto Whern, in his capacity as one of the school's teachers, never showed an inclination to give.)

Not long after this conversation, Whern and I had an argument, one of many we had while we worked together. He had conducted fewer classes than normal and, fed up with his indifference and callousness, I brought him before three town elders who functioned as our school board, one of whom—the most dedicated, influential and vocal—was Old Man Tuazama, Paul's father. Tuazama was probably in his late-thirties at this time, but to my twenty-three-year-old eyes, he was "old." Unfortunately the school board had no real authority over the principal, so all Tuazama could do was try to harmonize the situation between Whern and me. While defending his behavior to them, the principal used my sympathetic words against me. Whern told the board: "This white man doesn't understand us black men. He doesn't know my problems as a Liberian teacher. Everything is easy for him. He knows he'll be paid every month. The Peace Corps gives him everything he wants—chalk, papers, crayons, books, pens and pencils."

In May of my second year in Kpaytuo I became ill, ending up in a private clinic in Monrovia to which sick Westerners and wealthy Americo-Liberians went for medical care, the only decent medical facility in Monrovia. I had been diagnosed with mononucleosis, but the Peace Corps doctors told me their lab didn't have a pig's bladder to conduct the test that would have given them a definitive diagnosis. I was so debilitated from my illness that, in its early stages, I had a hard time holding a spoon, never mind having an appetite to eat. I was in the clinic for three weeks and spent another three weeks recuperating at a Peace Corps doctor's house. I recovered, but it would take two years, by which time I was back in America, before my spleen stopped aching and I regained my normal energy.

During the six weeks I was away from the village, Principal Whern held only three days of school. At one point he told the students there was no chalk so he couldn't teach. They collected money for him to buy chalk and when he returned he told them he had "eaten the money." When he wasn't teaching, he drank lots of palm wine, so he was often drunk. While intoxicated, he insulted many villagers, including respected town elders. He dared the suffering citizens of Kpaytuo to report him, which they wouldn't do because I wasn't there to stand up to him and because they didn't believe I was coming back, though I had gotten word to them, via a letter, that I would be returning.

Whern's behavior was unacceptable even for a Liberian principal. After I returned from my six-week absence, I wrote a letter to Whern's superior on behalf of the villagers, detailing his wanton behavior during my absence. The Liberian official came to Kpaytuo and, after an inquest in which Whern offended one and all, he was reprimanded. The official also assured the citizens of Kpaytuo that Whern would not be their principal the following school year. By the next year I had returned to America, but the official followed through on his promise: Otto Whern was transferred to another town. (Better to have transferred him to another planet; let the Martians deal with him.)

If I hadn't had to work with Whern, I might have enjoyed his company more, for, scoundrel that he was, there was something charming about this outrageous man. He was like a character out of a Dickens novel right down to his name and gold front teeth.

Every day after flag raising, Principal Whern uttered words to me that I have adopted as my personal mantra: "Ah, life, Mr. Cherry. Ah, Life." The words have stuck with me wherever I've worked—first in a Philadelphia inner city school the year after my Peace Corps experience ended, then in various newspaper offices, a college classroom, and lastly, running a food manufacturing business in the heart of Philadelphia's ghetto. Whenever I have been particularly struck by the vanities and follies and absurdities of human nature (including my own) or when, on or off the job, the shit has hit the fan, I have turned to my co-workers or friends—even to myself—and said, "Ah, Life, Mr. Cherry. Ah, Life." Learning of its origin, my co-workers and friends have been amused.

When I returned to Kpaytuo, I asked Tado about Otto Whern. Tado did not know his whereabouts. But Tado recalled that sometime in the 1970s Whern had finagled a scholarship to the United States, but did not remain long: becoming embroiled in a love affair with a married American woman (and probably guilty of more serious legal infractions), Whern had been ordered to leave the country. Tado had last heard that Whern was teaching in one of Firestone's schools in Liberia. Tado had seen him a year before and remembered the moment well, for on that sweltering Liberian day, Whern had worn a full-length imitation fur coat and a cowboy hat with a long feather in it, souvenirs of his brief stay in the United States.

"Ah, Life, Mr. Whern. Ah, Life."

Chapter 24

We were sitting on the patio after dinner when Tado asked me if it is true that in America a person can be hated because he is black.

Although I qualified the matter by saying not all of the time and not by every white person, I said yes, it was true.

Tado was visibly disheartened by my answer. He succeeded more than most of us in obeying the moral teachings of the Judeo-Christian culture, to which he was exposed by white American and Canadian missionaries; in particular by Tom Jackson, whose last name, out of respect for his spiritual mentor, Tado Jackson adopted legally as his own. The missionaries and the Bible taught Tado to "Love thy neighbor as thyself," not "Love thy neighbor as thyself, so long as he is white." Tado wondered aloud how benevolent, wise, educated America, who had come to the aid of Liberia—and, as he was aware, the world—countless times and in countless ways (World War II, the Marshall Plan, the Cold War), could behave so irrationally and cruelly.

"Let me try to explain the black and white palaver in America," I said. "In the United States, beginning with slavery time, we couldn't agree for the black man to learn book and make business; just like the Americo-Liberians did to the tribal people. So while white people were going to school and going up, most blacks were not. Some black people were, though small-small. This was wrong, but that is the way it happened.

"If you tell a man he is dumb and inferior—even that he is no better than a farm animal—and treat him like he is inferior or worse, eventually he will come to believe it is so. Worse, he will act like it is so. That was the situation in America, particularly in the Southern part, with many black Americans. They didn't go to school in the olden times and when they were permitted to attend schools, their schools were inferior. And during slavery time, their women were taken from the black man,

170

even his children. So, when free, most blacks couldn't find good jobs. Some became criminals. But in the early 1960s, during the time of Martin Luther King, Jr. and President Kennedy, many white Americans realized we had done bad to the black people and we changed But you can't change in twenty years what happened over two hundred.

"Today" I added, "millions of black people have jobs and nice homes in America. And most white people do not hate black people or wish them bad times. But *some* white people still look at black people and see only *groana boys*." (That is the Liberian term for the wild youths who roamed Monrovia, committing petty and increasingly violent crimes.)

The reader should bear in mind that this conversation between Tado and me took place in 1982, twenty-six years before America elected, and four years later reelected, a black President. No one outside of Barack Obama's family would have been happier about it than my dear African friend, Tado Jackson.

❖   ❖   ❖

Skin color has played a pernicious role in Liberia's history, too, mocking its *raison d'être*. Would that more of the former slaves and free black men from America who founded Liberia in the nineteenth century were like Lott Carey, who said: "I am an African. I wish to go to a country where I shall be estimated by my merits, not by my complexion; and I feel bound to labor for my suffering race." In fact, rarely have people been judged by their merit in Liberia—maybe in Heaven, but not in Liberia.

In the early years of the Republic's history, the criterion for status was the color of your skin—the lighter the better. Liberia's early rulers were mulattoes, usually the free-born, illegitimate children of American slave owners. Most of them were well-educated and cultured. Pure-blooded blacks were found among the lower strata of Americo-Liberian society, those being the illiterate freed slaves who had been repatriated from America; and also among the approximately five thousand African captives (many from the Congo) taken from slave ships, bound for America, by the United States Navy after the importation of slaves was declared illegal in the United States in 1808. And, finally, of course, one found pure blacks among the indigenous tribal people, whom the Americo-Liberians warred with and eventually dominated.

It wasn't until the election of 1869, almost fifty years after the colony was established and twenty-two years after independence, that Liberia had a full-blooded black, Edward Roye—though still an Americo-Liberian—as president. It boggles the mind, at least my mind, that in a country founded by freed slaves and free-born blacks, the ruling class—composed of these same freed slaves, and in time, their descendants—employed race as a criterion for anything, much less citizenship and political and social power.

Eventually through intermarriage between the upper and lower strata of Americo-Liberian society and between the Americo-Liberians and the tribal people, the obsession with, and thus the importance of, color diminished. But it was replaced by an equally repellent caste system, with the Americo-Liberians, who represented about three to five percent of the population, on top; and the indigenous tribal people on the bottom. (That is until the 1980 coup overthrew the Americo-Liberians, who have never regained—and I would add never will regain—power.) To their credit—or was it just genetics at work?—by the middle of the twentieth century many of the Americo-Liberian elite were pitch black, conspicuously among them President William Tubman, who, until his death in 1971, reigned for twenty-eight years.

The obsession with color may have dissipated, but hardly vanished: powerful Americo-Liberian males often chose lighter-skinned tribal girls as their mistresses, fathering children with many of them. I cite Sammy Cooper, the *pater familias* of the Cooper clan in Kpaytuo, owner of the sawmill, the village's Rockefeller, so to speak. He selected the caramel-colored Galonpoo for one of his lovers, by whom he had two children. But, a man of good taste, he also bedded the beautiful Mariah Howard, whose skin was the color of a Hershey chocolate bar, and with whom he had at least one child that I know of.

I cast no stones at Sammy Cooper, for like everyone—even I daresay the cultivated and discerning readers of these words—I am not without sin. Nor can I forget, or wish to, that Sammy Cooper was instrumental in helping me set in motion the process by which a modern, new school was eventually constructed in Kpaytuo—the new school that I saw for the first time when I returned for my visit. (More about Sammy Cooper and his family later in our story.)

It was also incredible—but true—that until the 1950s (and perhaps even later), the Americo-Liberians referred to themselves as "white men"—this to distinguish themselves from the indigenous tribal population; even more pathetic, this was how the tribal people often referred to the Americo-Liberians. (Talk about brainwashing!) It was disillusioning, to say the least, for the handful of black Peace Corps Volunteers in Liberia during my time to realize that, far from thinking of them as "brothers and sisters" from America, the tribal Liberians considered, and often called them, "white."

In this matter of color, the tribal people weren't without guilt, either. The tribal people, men and women alike, thought that the lighter the skin, the more attractive the woman. Mary Pratt, a comely village girl with whom I was friendly during my Peace Corps years, once told me that she wasn't as pretty as any Peace Corps (read white) women. No disrespect to my female Peace Corps colleagues, but that observation was demonstrably untrue. And this wrong-headed belief by people of color was—and, I am sorry to report, still is to a degree—prevalent among American blacks, notwithstanding decades of slogans—like "Black Is Beautiful"—and a proliferation of beautiful black models, singers and actresses as role models: a friend's daughter, the offspring of a marriage between her pretty Haitian mother and an African man, confided to me that she, a model and drop-dead gorgeous at nineteen, wished that she were white skinned.

❖   ❖   ❖

Because of their ill treatment by the Americo-Liberians (and conversely the good deeds performed on their behalf by many dedicated white missionaries), and because they were never colonized by a European (read "white") power, Liberians harbored little animosity toward white people, far less, if I may generalize, than other black Africans, who were colonized by the French and British, the Portuguese and the Belgians —often benignly and wisely but at other times brutally and stupidly.

173

Liberians have always looked—and still look, too much for their own good—to white men and women (particularly North Americans) for guidance and help. In so doing the tribal people exaggerate the abilities and power of whites, while denigrating those of blacks. "God make you white people like himself," was an expression I heard countless times when I lived there in 1966–67 and again during my visit in 1982. "Your part is too smart," many a tribal person said to me, by which they meant us white folk and our astonishing technological and medical discoveries and advancements. Though it was less likely to occur in 1982 than years before, many of the less sophisticated tribal people during my time in Liberia believed the two races even ended up in different places after death.

Small wonder that Sammy, my thirteen-year-old houseboy, had the following take in 1967 on the respective history of white and black people: God had two boxes—one shiny and new; the other, shabby and old. God gave the shiny, new box to a black man, the shabby, old box to a white man. Opening his box, the black man found a cutlass, a hoe and a palm tree. And the white man's box? It contained, in Sammy's words, "iron, an automobile and electric."

Chapter 25

From the moment I got up I felt lethargic, a sign that, five weeks in, I had still not acclimated to the debilitating heat and humidity. To make matters worse, I had a sty on my right eyelid and, since it was nearly impossible to keep my groin dry in Liberia's ninety percent humidity—no matter how much talcum powder I applied—a rash was developing between my legs. Rashes are part of everyday life in Liberia: three days after arriving on this trip a rash appeared on my left wrist under my watch band. After I removed the watch, the rash disappeared in a day.

Hoping to lift my spirits and escape the heat for a couple of hours, I decided to hike into the high bush. There, if fortune were with me, I might spot a colony of driver ants. Arthur Wonyou, my ex-student who ran the Kpaytuo clinic, was my guide. About twenty minutes into our journey, we came across a woman heading back to Kpaytuo from her farm. Arthur asked if she had seen any driver ants. Yes, she had, a fair distance from where we were then standing. She must have found the question among the strangest ever put to her: who in his right mind ever sought out driver ants?

So named because they drive away every creature that has the misfortune to be in their path, driver ants—also called army or soldier ants—range the Liberian jungle in huge colonies, often twenty million strong. According to Sir Harry Hamilton Johnston, they, not the mighty elephant or the fierce leopard, were the lords of the Liberian jungle in those yonder years of the nineteenth and early twentieth century. Driver ants are continually on the march, soon exhausting the food supply in any given area. S.H. Skaife, in *African Insect Life*, described them thusly: "Marauding columns radiate, hunting for any living thing they can overcome, cut up and carry back to their nest as food. When the surrounding area has been thoroughly searched for all available food, when there are no more victims to be caught, the order to move on is given, by some means or other, and the great throng treks in orderly fashion to seek fresh hunting grounds." Julian Huxley compared their destructive instincts and nomadic habits to Huns and Tartars. However, as he pointed out, "The most restless of the Mongols were capable of settling down to a stable and civilized life. But the driver ants are forever limited to their way of life by the iron hand. Their nomadism and their ferocity are permanent; their wanderings are barbarous invasions that never end."

Drivers prefer to travel in the night, as ten minutes of direct sunlight can kill them, but if they have to, they'll migrate during the day. Their ideal terrain is the rain forest—forever damp, cool and dim, where their columns, stretching for miles, pass under logs, leaves, branches and stones, and through holes, crannies and hollows. When the natural elements don't provide cover, they throw up dirt to form an archway less than a half-inch high through which they pass silently. They march in a disciplined formation (probably another reason they are also known as soldier ants), five or six abreast. The workers, often carrying tiny white eggs laid by their bloated queen—who is capable of producing three to four million eggs a month—occupy the center lanes; the soldiers or sentries, almost a half-inch long and equipped with mandibles, guard the flanks. Unlike the garden variety ant, drivers are carnivores. They feast on earthworms and insects, but will consume anything in sight, including small animals. And they share a trait with that exalted specie Man: being one of the few organisms that go to war.

◆ ◆ ◆

One night, not long after my arrival in Kpaytuo in 1966, as I was ready for bed, I noticed about a dozen driver ants coming under the back door of my house. As there was at least a half-inch space between the bottom of every door in the house and the floor, including the one in my bedroom, it was easy for insects to crawl into the house. As I stood there gazing and confounded as to what to do, more and more drivers entered. I got a can of insect repellent and doused them with it, which turned out to be every bit as effective as trying to put out a forest fire with a water pistol. I quickly used up the repellent, but the ants were still coming—about five hundred already were in the back room. Thankfully they had not passed into any other room. Someone had told me driver ants could be repelled by kerosene, so next I took the five-gallon can always on hand in the house (to power my stove and refrigerator) and poured some of the precious liquid on the floor in front of all the doorways. The kerosene deterred additional ants from entering through the back door (and, I soon realized, would keep those in from getting out), but what was I going to do when the kerosene dried and presumably more ants could again enter at will? I kept telling myself to remain calm, though it was becoming increasingly difficult. I was exhausted from a long day. My hands and face—nay my whole body—were covered with sweat and reeked of insect repellent and kerosene. My bladder, which I was on my way outside to empty when I discovered the blasted ants, was about to burst. I was unwilling to go to my outhouse, assuming hundreds of thousands, possibly even millions, of ants were prowling about. Of greatest concern, I feared that if I went to bed I'd be eaten alive.

Scores of nights returning from my latrine, I'd felt the bite of a few driver ants that had crawled up my leg. Instinctively, I'd brush them off and, once in the house, by the light of a lantern, might have picked off one of two. The bite or sting felt like a pin prick. In small numbers I knew that the drivers were not dangerous. Not so when there are thousands—make that tens of thousands, nay two hundred thousand or more—of them. Many a tethered goat, caged or sick animal has been picked clean in a night by these dauntless hordes, their pincers and shearing "jaws" tearing at flesh. And pity the bed-ridden elderly or sick person with thousands of driver ants swarming over his face, stinging and eating his eyes; eventually the drivers fall or lodge into his mouth and nose and the victim dies by suffocation.

When they entered my home that first night, what I ought to have done was run out the front door for help. For reasons I have long since forgotten (more likely stupidity or pride than bravery), I remained in my house. I urinated in an empty can, relieving some of the pressure I was under. Next, I poured more kerosene onto the floor in front of each doorway. Then—and this I considered my most brilliant tactic— I placed each of the four legs of my bed in a bucket of water, so even if the ants invaded my bedroom, they could not pass over the water to the bed posts and up onto the bed, where I was safely ensconced. As added protection, I stuffed towels in the space between the bottom of my bedroom door and the floor.

I managed to fall asleep. I have no idea what went on in the rest of the house that night. I must assume the drivers never entered my room, possibly intending to return when I had fattened up. My brilliant idea of placing the bed posts in buckets of water, I later learned, may not have been so brilliant, for by linking their mandibles, the soldiers, in a suicidal gesture, form a living bridge over which the colony marches. I also made it a point to learn the next morning what the drivers fear—fire. The citizens of Kpaytuo tied palm fronds together and lit the torch on those rare occasions when drivers invaded the village proper. From that night on, I also kept unlit torches in my house.

Drivers don't like to pass over clear earth, so the children and women, as I observed during the dry months in my almost two years in Kpaytuo, regularly cleaned and scraped the grass around their huts. What remained was the reddish-brown dirt, baked hard by the tropical sun. But my house, about forty yards from the nearest hut, was surrounded by grass—and one side was not more than 20 yards from where the bush (read the forest) began. Also, as I discovered, my house lay on one of the drivers' migration routes from the bush on one side of Kpaytuo to the bush on the other side. So they were very much a part of my life during the rainy season; thankfully, most of the time, they kept at a manageable and safe distance during my Peace Corps tenure.

I remember one Saturday when Sammy, my houseboy, as was his custom most mornings, woke me up with a knock on my bedroom door and the words, "Teacher, the driver is here." How strange, I remember saying to myself, that John Vonleh, the Liberian employed by the Peace Corps to deliver our mail by jeep every other week, should be at my house at 6:30 in the morning. John never arrived at that early hour; even stranger, he was not due for many days. As my head cleared, it dawned on me what Sammy had meant: driver ants were in my house, possibly rampaging through it. The realization got me up and out of bed quickly. I gingerly made my way with Sammy to the middle room, which served as my dining room, and there I saw a throbbing black blob about twelve feet wide by six feet long: every square inch of the far left white-washed wall—and part of the ceiling above it—was covered by, and humming with, tens of thousands of swarming driver ants. Without trying to be melodramatic, it occurs to me now that had I ever woken up to such a sight—a palpitating, buzzing, menacing, enormous black blob—my heart, young and strong though it was at age twenty-three, might have burst.

Sammy saw that a mass of drivers had enveloped a bottle full of palm oil on the shelf. The sweet cooking oil apparently appealed to them. Valiantly he ran into the room, grabbed the bottle and carried it outside, where he threw it on the ground. He and I brushed and picked the drivers off his body. Within twenty minutes, the drivers crawled down from ceiling and wall, departed by the side door and, *in formation*, marched back into the jungle.

❖   ❖   ❖

On that day many years after the incidents just described, Arthur Wonyou and I eventually spotted a colony of driver ants, but even that didn't perk me up, so we returned to the village, where I discovered that there was no safe water to drink, for neither Mary nor Mellay had boiled any the day before or that morning. Even if one of them started a fire out back the moment I arrived back in the village, and then let the water boil in the pot for twenty minutes, it would have taken a couple hours before it would be tepid enough to drink. I was peeved at their oversight, more so on a day when I already felt weak and slightly dehydrated. I forced myself to eat a couple sardines with stale crackers for lunch, after I had flicked ants (of the non-dangerous variety) off the crackers.

I finally found a way to cool off, if only temporarily: I asked little Martha Gweh, who must have thought I was daft, to dump a bucket of water over my head. It took at least forty-five minutes for my hair—of which in those years I still had a fair amount—to dry completely and while it did, for the first time in days, I felt comfortable. But I was still dragging, so I went to the bench in front of Old Man Gbon's house and, shaded by a tree, lay down to sleep. About thirty minutes later

Arthur Wonyou, my guide that morning, woke me and insisted I join him in eating some food one of his girlfriends had prepared.

Whenever I visited any family in Kpaytuo I was usually offered food, for that is the Liberian way, but most of the time I politely declined the offer, as much because I couldn't tolerate the inordinate amount of peppers with which the Liberians lace their food as from my fear of picking up something. Because I had eaten so little for lunch and hoped the food might revive my flagging spirits, I accepted Arthur's invitation. We ate lukewarm, reheated rice with a greasy collard greens soup (really gravy but the Liberians call it "soup"), with some indeterminable meat, which could have been anything from dried monkey to bush hog. None of it tasted fresh, so I ate little. Through most of the afternoon I remained under the tree on the bench, trying to read, but with little concentration. Then someone announced that the girls would soon be coming from the Bush school, that place and institution where tribal girls were initiated into the secret society called the *Sande*.

Until the changes wrought by the post-World War Two years, the most important institutions in tribal life had been secret societies: the *Poro Society* of the men, and, less so but still influential, the *Sande Society* of the women. Much of what the world knows of these secret societies—certainly what little I know—derives from the writings of Dr. George Way Harley, a medical missionary who in the late 1920s established and ran the hospital in Ganta. Dr. Harley and his wife, Winifred, a botanist, lived in Liberia for 35 years, during which period he found time to also construct and run the Ganta Mission and a leprosarium. He also studied and recorded and—through his work with Harvard's Peabody Museum—became an authority on the ways of the all-male *Poro Society* in Northeastern Liberia, where not incidentally Kpaytuo is located, a mere thirty-seven miles from Ganta. (In about half of Liberia's sixteen tribes the male *Poro* and the female *Sande Societies* flourished, but their influence was strongest in Northeastern Liberia—Mano and Gio tribal territory.)

The initiation process by which tribal children became members of the tribe lasted three to four years, with the instruction taking place in secret, off-limits groves near the village called Bush schools. Tribal boys and girls entered the Bush school as children and departed, symbolically reborn with bodily markings and new names, as full-fledged members of the tribe. But the influence of the *Poro* and *Sande Societies* extended far beyond the initiation rites. The *Poro* was an educational, political, judicial, religious and cultural organization and those in its upper degrees and inner circles controlled tribal politics, even, in those far-off days of the early twentieth century, inter-tribal relationships. The most powerful men in tribal society, more powerful than tribal and clan chiefs, were the leaders of the societies, referred to as "Devils." They supposedly had supernatural powers, derived from ancestral spirits. And they scared the hell out of the tribal people: crossing the "Devils" or breaking the taboos of the secret societies could mean death.

Discipline was strict in the Bush schools and many a young boy or girl saw a friend executed for committing some unforgivable offense, like revealing a secret of the society to an uninitiated person. It was in the Bush school that boys received instruction in tribal history and tradition, in hunting and fishing, and in matters of sex, religion, medicine and law. And where girls learned their roles, responsibilities and privileges, including how to use herbs, spices, medicines and poisons, and how to please their husbands, both in the kitchen and in sexual matters.

Years ago initiates remained in the Bush schools, segregated from family and friends, for as long as four years, but as the way of life for so many Liberians began to change after the Second World War, the length of the schools got shorter and shorter. By the time I lived in Liberia—and up to my return in 1982—Bush schools ran for six to eight weeks. In spite of the shorter length, young Gio boys and girls still considered the initiation ritual one of the most important events in their lives.

From the time I arrived back in Kpaytuo I knew that the Bush school was in session, for Zoelay Retty had mentioned that one of her daughters was there, and Sammy had told me his sister, Anna, was "a so-so important" woman in the school. I had never seen the girls come out of the Bush school during my twenty-three months in Liberia, so I felt fortunate to be in the village, purely by chance, on the day the girls were coming out.

The girls appeared around 5:00 P.M., the hour when villagers trickled back on foot to the village from a long day's work on their farms. There were ten initiates, ranging in age from about nine to fourteen. They wore headbands, raffia skirts and brass anklets. All save four were topless; and those four wore bras more from a sense of fashion than modesty. A few girls wore plastic curlers in their hair, once again as a fashion and style statement. Some of the girls wore cowry-shell or leopard-teeth necklaces. Their foreheads and eyelids were streaked with white clay, a symbol of the spirit world.

Escorting the girls were many village women, both young and old, exuberantly shouting, singing, chanting and laughing. The initiates and their escorts danced down Kpaytuo's only road and then weaved through Kpaytuo's quarters, with about a hundred young boys and girls tagging along behind. When they had passed through the various quar-

Five girls resting during their "coming out" celebration in April 1982. They and other young girls had been initiated into the Sande Society, a secretive women's organization once all-powerful in Liberian tribal life. One of its rituals has in recent decades been condemned the world over, the practice of female circumcision—better known as FGM, female genital mutilation.

Two girls celebrating their initiation into the Sande Society.

ters, the group shuffled back down the road and stopped near Zoelay
Retty's home. There the initiates individually performed dances of the
most sensual nature, and the residents of Kpaytuo, who had gathered
in jubilation to observe them, *dashed* each of the girls five cents after
her solo dance. The mothers, aunts and sisters of the girls also paid
homage, in the form of rice or cloth, to the high officials of the *Sande
Society*, old ladies who sat solemnly under a temporary bamboo shelter,
shielded from the sun by palm fronds. I kept my camera in its case, lest
I offend anyone, but, much to my surprise, someone asked Arthur
Wonyou, my ex-student who was explaining to me what was going on,
why I hadn't taken photographs of the girls. I was more than willing to
oblige. The initiates were serious, even intense—intensity being an
expression one rarely sees on the face of a Liberian. And throughout
the ceremony none of them smiled, an even rarer occurrence for a
Liberian. They appeared exhausted—and no doubt they were, having
been up singing and dancing for twenty-four hours.

One aspect of the Secret Society initiation that hasn't changed for hundreds, maybe thousands of years, is circumcision for the boys, clitoridectomy for the girls—or as the latter's many critics now refer to it, FGM—Female Genital Mutilation.

No one is unduly concerned with male circumcision, probably because there are fewer post-operative complications and it is accepted as a hygienic measure, but female circumcision has been condemned—justifiably—the world over for at least 30 years, especially and increasingly by the more educated women (and men) in Europe, the United States and Africa. (I can't speak for the Middle East.) These critics—including in recent years Liberia's government, which has condemned but to date has not banned female circumcision—consider the procedure barbaric, dangerous and a male plot to deprive already downtrodden Third World women of sexual gratification. As do I. As should any sensible person. Given that the procedure was—and probably still is—often performed in less than hospital-like conditions, and that a razor or knife, sometimes sterile, but just as often not, was used to make the cut, infections and hemorrhaging were not uncommon. When a fatality occurred in the old days, at least among the Liberian tribes, the parents of the victim were told that their child had been born a witch. Infection and excessive bleeding aside, critics of female circumcision point out that the procedure, especially if the cut is clumsy or "too generous," also may—and often does—lead to long-term complications, including pain during urination, menstruation, intercourse and childbirth. (Statistics vary and are hard to verify, but by 2017 only about a third of Liberia's women underwent the procedure, compared to two-thirds or more in the 1980s. The days of the ghastly custom are numbered, but I write about a time when it was prevalent.)

Exactly where and when clitoridectomy arose has never been established, though I find it interesting that it was—and still is—practiced among African animists (who worship nature or sprits) *and* devout Middle East and African Muslims. The justifications for it vary: one explanation is that excision keeps the woman cleaner, the same justification, among Liberians, for circumcising the male. A second is that it prepares a woman for marriage and childbirth—never mind that it can lead to complications in childbirth. Another hypothesis is that men want to dampen the sexual ardor of their women—"keep them cool" in the words of one Liberian. And this will discourage female promiscuity. Therefore, Liberians—and presumably men throughout Africa and the Middle East—devised a rite that would surgically remove the most sexually sensitive and responsive part of a female. If this were the reason for the custom—to keep the women faithful—let me record its epic failure in Liberia. I can't speak to other African and Middle Eastern cultures, but in Liberia, women were (and I assume still are) active sexually, in fact every bit as much as Liberian men. It's probably apocryphal, but asked about the fidelity of Liberian women in 1928, an American anthropologist supposedly answered, "There is no such woman in the country."

The theory that makes the most sense to me is that clitoridectomy *in Liberia* was—and is—part of a fertility rite, enabling women, so the tribal people believe, to conceive children and propagate the tribe.

Whatever the reason or reasons, millions of women believed that a clitoridectomy was one of the most important religious-cultural rites of their lives. Indeed, when I lived in Liberia, and upon my return, numerous women friends in Kpaytuo, told me, in their rudimentary English, that they believed they were not "whole women" unless they had been cut.

How ironic and how sad. How very sad.

❖   ❖   ❖

After watching the new initiates and the hoopla surrounding their coming out of the Bush school, I returned to Tado's house, feeling queasy. By dinnertime, I knew something was wrong. I had indigestion and, as I had no appetite, I mixed water with baking soda, hoping the bicarbonate of soda might settle my stomach; it didn't. By this time I was also slightly dizzy and nauseous. The best antidote for my symptoms was to induce vomiting, thus discharging from my system whatever was making me sick, most likely the food prepared earlier in the day by Arthur Wonyou's girlfriend. This I did, continuing to throw up behind Tado's house until I developed the dry heaves. I had also by this point developed diarrhea. The following two hours do not rank among my most pleasant in Liberia. I crawled into bed around 10:30 P.M.—limp, nauseous, feverish and reeking of sweat and vomit.

I slept intermittently. It began to thunder and rain, the kind of tropical storm I normally enjoyed, more so at night during the dry season, as we were then in, because it cooled Tado's house and made it fun to snuggle up in bed and go back to sleep. But because of my condition, I was shivering from the "cold." I also had to go to the bathroom again, which under normal circumstances, when I was not sick and it was not pouring, I found unpleasant to undertake in the village in the middle of the night. And these were hardly normal circumstances. So heavy was the rain I dared not go outside, lest I be soaked in seconds. An hour later the rain ceased, by which time I was dizzy, doubled over with stomach cramps, and from all the liquid I had lost in the past eight hours, close to dehydration.

Donning my clothes and shining my flashlight, I picked my way to the latrine, only to discover the door ajar and a huge puddle of water about eight inches deep in front of the door. By taking a running start, I leaped over the puddle into the latrine, landing on the concrete floor in four inches of water. Water covered all but one side of the interior. The latrine was built on a slope, like the home, which explains why one area of the floor remained dry. Praying that a snake or scorpion wasn't lurking in the pool of water inside the latrine, I lifted the wooden cover, giving the many cockroaches under it time to scamper either farther in or out of the hole. Sitting sideways (I couldn't face the door as there was at least four inches of water on the floor where normally my feet would have been placed), a roll of toilet paper tucked under my chin, there being no dry place to put it, I went about my business.

No sooner had I returned to my bed than I felt the need to use the latrine again, so I repeated the laborious procedure. When I came out of the latrine the second time, I noticed the 55-gallon drums under the eave of the house filled with water—cool, no-need-to-boil-it-for-twenty-minutes, safe-to-drink rainwater. I drank three cups, my first cool water in days, all the more refreshing and delicious since my body had lost so much water. I climbed into bed once again. My stomach having finally settled down, wrung out but at peace in the manner of the sick, I fell asleep.

186

Chapter 26

I arose feeling much better, but then it would be difficult to feel much worse than I had the night before. As my body needed liquid and my stomach was tender, I ate nothing during the day except a bowl of Campbell's chicken with rice soup, which I had brought up from Monrovia, but, until getting sick, had no taste for in the heat. My bowels seemed to have calmed down. I hoped that I had expunged from my system whatever it was that had made me so ill.

Tado, who usually spent every day, save Sunday, at his rice farm or vegetable garden, returned to the house in the afternoon as he was not feeling well himself. He asked if he could continue reading an article I had written for a Philadelphia newspaper about my life in Kpaytuo (photocopies of which I had brought along to show people). In the article, I had mentioned Duna, a Kpaytuo resident with the reputation as a powerful medicine man.

"You know, Bob, many *kwi* Liberians, who can own cars, came to Duna for medicine. Even some of these fine girls slept with Duna for his medicine." (To appreciate the full import of that statement, you have to know how unattractive Duna, who waddled like a duck and had eyes like a fish, was.) Duna had fallen on hard times, according to Tado, and no longer had the power to produce powerful medicine for himself, much less others. His downfall began, it seems, when he offended a relative in another village during the mourning period for one of their kin.

Tado remained amazed, and not a little disappointed, at the number of Liberians who studied in the United States for years, many of them acquiring degrees in the sciences and other technical fields, only to come back to Liberia still believing in, and practicing, what most Westerners would call black magic. He said this included cabinet ministers and other high government officials.

To substantiate Tado's point, herewith an excerpt from a 1982 memo by the principal of the Booker Washington Institute, Mr. Daniel

Jappah, who said, "Individuals involved in making human sacrifice to win positions and social recognition have been warned to stop such habits."

I also quote in its entirety an article from Liberia's *Daily Observer*, March 13, 1982, datelined Maryland County, Liberia:

"Mr. B.E. Pettiquoi, former administrative assistant to the Grand Cape Mount county superintendent, has been arrested and detained here along with three others, for his alleged involvement in the recent death of a four-year-old boy, Varney Rogers.

The four-year-old boy was found dead in the Londeji Creek here early last February, with the tongue, ears, upper lips, testicles and other parts of the body missing.

Following the incident, a team of CID agents [*Liberian law officials*] from Monrovia came to Robertsport to conduct an investigation into the circumstances surrounding the death of the boy.

During preliminary investigation, the father of the deceased admitted offering his son to Mr. Pettiquoi for slaughter in a sacrificial right aimed at inducing the head of State to appoint him (Pettiquoi) as an ambassador, and his son, J. Ebenezer Pettiquoi, as deputy internal affairs minister.

In his voluntary statement to CID agents, Abraham Rogers [the father of the deceased] further revealed that Pettiquoi promised to reward him by naming him as his secretary or sending him to the US for studies, if he (Pettiquoi) were appointed ambassador.

Rogers discussed that the 'medicine man' who performed the rights lives in Kono, Sierra Leone."

Does this article mean that it was common practice for all Liberian parents—father or mother—to sacrifice their children or to partake in weird rituals involving their child's body parts? Of course not. But it happened on rare occasions, given the same parents' belief in magic and spirts, witchcraft and medicine men. Most Liberians condemned it and tried to rid the country of it. And the law considered it a crime. Before we in the West get on our high horses, remember that less than one hundred years ago one of the most advanced countries in the Western World, Germany, destroyed millions of humans, including babies, in ovens.

◆ ◆ ◆

Marie Sonyah, the eighteen-year-old I had met the first time I sought shade under the tree in front of Old Man Gbon's house, visited me at Tado's house. It's worth noting that an eighteen-year-old tribal woman, in life experience—usually a mother by sixteen and used to working hard most of her life—was more like a twenty-five-year-old Western woman. Marie was fun and flirtatious and I enjoyed teasing and flirting with her—mindful to keep matters on the right side of probity. Marie asked questions like, "In your country, can you have bush?" or "Can people make rice farm in America?" I once told her I could make limes appear from the sky. She smiled, knowing that I was joking.

On this occasion I told her I would use medicine—or as a Westerner might say, magic—to produce a pineapple. I took an empty box of wooden matches—the only kind one uses in Liberia, since paper matches wilt and don't ignite in the country's humidity. In the box I placed two grains of rice, chanted an incantation of Spanish and Yiddish words, and, waving my hands to the right and left of the box, raising my eyes toward heaven, I reverentially placed the tiny matchbox inside a compartment of the old kitchen cupboard and closed the door. Twenty seconds later I repeated the Spanish-Yiddish incantation, reached into the dark compartment of the cupboard, and, like a man pulling a rabbit from a hat, produced a pineapple. Marie, who enjoyed my playfulness, chuckled appreciatively. I offered her a slice of the pineapple, but she refused. "It can make me cold-oh," she explained. "I can only eat the thing when the sun can be high in the sky."

I used to see Marie with her mother or nursing her child, playing and singing with Mellay, Placid or Martha or plaiting the hair of one of the village girls. Never with any of the young men in the village, which surprised me, for she was young (age eighteen), attractive and available—the father of her child, she told me, was somewhere behind Monrovia. But then it dawned on me: she wasn't available, at least not while she was breast-feeding her infant. It was a taboo to have intercourse with a woman nursing her child. If one broke this taboo, the Liberians believed, the man's sperm ended up in the woman's breasts, there turning her milk sour; by drinking the sour milk, the infant became ill. The taboo serves as an effective method of birth control, as the Liberians breast-feed their children for at least one and sometimes as long as two years. So instead of giving birth every year, a Liberian woman usually gives birth every two or two and a half years. Because of this taboo, Sir Harry Hamilton Johnston saw polygamy as a necessary institution in tribal culture. Sir Harry held those views early in the twentieth century. Were he living today, I wonder if he'd expound such a view. If so, feminists would have his head.

◆　◆　◆

When I lived in Kpaytuo, one of my sources of information on matters like the aforementioned taboo was Josiah Peye, a handsome, well-built man about my age from the Kpelle tribe who circa 1967 had been the boyfriend of one of Andrew Karma's sisters and was employed tending Tado's garden while Tado was away upgrading his teaching skills. Not that my and Josiah's conversations were very profound. We were more like two schoolboys, groping in the dark, comparing notes and trying to understand life, usually life having to do with the mystery and wonders of sex. For example, Josiah asked me if it were true, as a Lebanese man once warned him, that if an African loved to a white woman, he'd turn into a snake. Of course not, I answered. That's good, Josiah said, because if he loved to a white woman, then, as a result of his conquest, he could have any free woman in Kpaytuo. He once asked me if white women can make blood once a month, and after three days the blood ceases, at which time sex can resume. Intercourse during menstruation is another taboo in the Gio tribe, the violation of which in the minds of the people can lead to catastrophe—anything from a crop failure to a death in the family. (Maybe the Gio are one of the wandering tribes of Israel. I jest, because under rabbinical law Orthodox Jews are prohibited from close contact, never mind sex, during a woman's menstruation period and for seven days afterwards.)

Ever the romantic, I asked Josiah if he thought it fair—I certainly did not—that a girl was forced to marry a rich man, even though she loved a poor one. Josiah said that if he were the girl's father, he would make sure she loved the man who could help her (and thus the family) the most. He was forever urging me to make love to the village girls, enviously pointing out that if he were caught loving to another man's wife, there would be a $10 fine (about $75 today) and "a helluva palaver," but how could the man blame his wife for wanting to love to a rich and powerful white man like myself? Besides, Josiah said, "The girl can know the white man 'knows book.' You can bring bad medicine on her head if she confessed she was loving to you. She cannot talk your name, for true-oh." All well and good but I had no intention, or inclination, to play around with another man's wife.

❖   ❖   ❖

That night I visited Marie Sonyah, who lived in her father's house on same side of the village, but in a different quarter, than Tado. Walking into the house, which was never locked when people were inside or close by, I heard singing and dancing. As I peered into the faintly lit room to see who was present, Marie, with her unmistakably raspy voice, said, "Yes, your daughter is here." She was referring to Mellay, the girl hired to help Tado's wife Mary with the cooking and washing during my stay. Mellay was not, of course, my biological daughter, but while helping to take care of me, she was called that by the Liberians. Also present were Marie's other constant companions, Martha and Placid, both age fourteen. Nothing promised more pleasure than to come upon four Liberian teenage girls who might start singing and dancing.

The Gio people sang when they worked, they sang when they played, when you came into the tribal world there were songs, and when you departed. Teenagers sang the most often, the longest and the loudest, having the time and energy; but women and men in their twenties and thirties also sang at night, usually in groups of four or five, segregated by sex. Invariably the women sang about present, past and, they hoped, future loves; the men, likewise. There were also the many occasions the villagers danced and sang together—men and women, young and old. Knowing how much I enjoyed listening to their music and watching their dances, my students often came to my house in the evening and sang and danced for me, some of which songs I taped and still own. Or I'd go into the village proper, there to watch, and often participate in, the merrymaking.

Their music was wonderful for me to behold when I lived there or during my brief visit. They danced in their bare feet, sliding them across and patting them against the hard brown earth. The drums beat, the flutes and rattles played on. The villagers danced and sang for two or three hours, sometimes four or five. I've never seen anyone move with their joy and—in the case of the post-pubescent girls and women—their sensuality and seductiveness. Especially when the moon was out, the village exploded in song and dance and laughter. More than any others, these were my favorite times in Kpaytuo.

◆　◆　◆

Much as I enjoyed Kpaytuo, it was trying to remain there for long stretches during my return trip. Life was difficult there under the best of circumstances. Sharing Tado's tiny home most of the time with a half-dozen people, accommodating and pleasant though they were, and living without many of the basic amenities, weren't the best of circumstances. It was a constant struggle to make certain there was boiled water and adequate food on hand. It was difficult going to sleep in a room that at midnight was sweltering, when outside there was a delightful breeze. And I was fed up with the mosquitoes, who must have taken me for a huge sugar cube, for nothing else can explain the zest with which they attacked my body every night, leaving scores of red welts on my legs. I was also tired of getting up in a puddle of sweat, awakened by flies walking on my face. Matters would have been different if I had had my own house and staff. Then I could have lived the way I wanted. But I was a guest in Tado's house, so I could not. I needed a respite from Kpaytuo.

Now that we had agreed on constructing draw-bucket wells, there remained a few details to iron out in Monrovia. But first my thoughts turned from contaminated water and wells to the lovely Betty Leeleh, my favorite ex-student only two hours away in Ganta, the town conveniently situated on the route to Monrovia. I had become infatuated with Betty. What about Zoelay Retty, my Kpaytuo girlfriend? With the lack of privacy at Tado's house and Zoelay Retty being away at her family farm for much of the time, we had seen little of each other after those first few days of my return. I still held—and always would—affection for Zoelay Retty, but Betty was now the one. Though it was unlikely, I hoped she did not have a boyfriend and that, if fortune smiled upon me, Betty and I might become intimate. There was only one way to find out: by visiting her in Ganta, which is where my journey—and my heart—next took me.

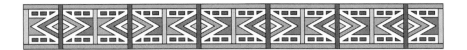

GANTA

Two Ganta students coming from school, their notebooks expertly balanced on their heads.

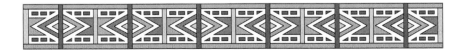

Chapter 27

Located at the intersection of an old trade route to Guinea in the north and the Ivory Coast to the east, Ganta is one of Liberia's largest cities. Its population circa 1982 was about 15,000, which besides native Liberians included many Mandingoes from Guinea, whose border is little more than a mile away; a smattering of Lebanese merchants, whose dozen general stores lined either side of the main street—all selling essentially the same household items; a handful of Peace Corps Volunteers; and, last but certainly not least, Betty Leeleh. With its dirt roads and bustling commercial activity, Ganta resembled a town in the American Wild West of a hundred and fifty years ago, with an African tang of course.

I arrived in Ganta around noon, thirsty and covered with red dust. I walked down the main street, passing sidewalk vendors hawking food and clothing and pirated tapes; schoolchildren in their colorful uniforms, some returning from school and others on their way to begin the second shift; and tall, stately, coal-black Mandingoes, the men garbed in flowing gowns, the women in *lappas* and loose-fitting tops.

I came to a sign that said, "John Bashir and Sons." John Bashir was the Lebanese merchant who owned a small general store in Kpaytuo until he decided, two months after I arrived in 1966, that little money was to be made in a village as small and impoverished as Kpaytuo. Upon my return to Liberia, I learned that John Bashir lived in Ganta, where, with a change of fortune, he owned not one, but two, large stores.

Lebanese merchants ran the retail and wholesale establishments throughout Liberia. Their goal was to earn enough money after fifteen or twenty years in Liberia to retire to Lebanon, where they usually had wives and children. The men, usually minus their families, were in their 30s and 40s when I lived in Liberia and many had tribal girlfriends, by whom they fathered children. They had always been congenial to me and introduced me to Middle Eastern food. While it is easy to criticize

197

them as interlopers, they also provided jobs to many young tribal Liberians, as well as reasonably-priced essential goods to the population.

Entering the store, I asked the young Lebanese man behind the counter if the owner was the John Bashir who had once lived in Kpaytuo.

"Yes, he can be so," the boy answered. "But he is not here. He can be in Monrovia."

"I am an old friend of his from Kpaytuo. I used to be in the Peace Corps there."

"We can have many Peace Corpse friends," he replied, mispronouncing the word 'corps' in the accent of a Middle Easterner speaking English, Liberian-accented English at that. "They [the Volunteers] can come here to take drinks with us. You are welcome back. I am Nazem Bashir, John's son. Can I get you something to drink? I know Mr. Scott too good. He is the Peace Corpse man in Ganta. Do you know him?"

"No, but I would like to meet him. Do you know where he lives?"

"Let me call the boy. He will show you. Let us eat first. Then you go with the boy."

These were words I had hoped to hear, for when I left Kpaytuo I'd had no idea where I would eat lunch or dinner. I asked John's son, who was about twenty-two, where I might wash before eating. He led me past the glass counter through the back of the store into a courtyard, where I saw a Liberian ironing clothes. John and his family lived in the house one entered from the courtyard. Two pre-teenagers, each of them with olive-colored skin like Nazem's, sat eating at a table under a canopy. I was led to a shed off the courtyard with a sink and faucets (the water came from the barrels hooked up near them), and an old but functioning toilet, which one flushed by dumping a bucket of water into the bowl. I returned to the front of the store, sitting behind the counter in a wicker chair and there, while Nazem waited on customers, ate rice and lamb in tomato gravy with pita bread.

So the talk in Kpaytuo was correct: John Bashir had done well, with a store whose shelves were stocked with biscuits, Quaker Oats cereal, vegetable oil, canned corned beef and sardines, Marlboro cigarettes, soap, margarine, Tide detergent, Clorox bleach, Dr. Monroe's worm elixir, boxes of wooden matches, aerosol cans of disinfectant, hurricane lanterns, kerosene lamps, small kerosene burners, and tin pots. It was a far cry from the understocked store he owned in Kpaytuo sixteen years before. The tinned goods came from Europe, much of them from Poland and the then Czechoslovakia (the Czech Republic as I write this); while the manufactured items—the pots and pans and the burners—were made in China. Only a poor country like China, whose workers circa 1982 earned only pennies an hour, could manufacture a pot or pan that sold for $4 or $5 in Liberia. John could have stocked stainless steel pots from America or England, costing $30 to $50, but who in up-country Liberia was going to buy one? Sheets of the ubiquitous thin-gauge corrugated metal roofing material were piled four feet high. Near the sheets lay bags of cement, a box of cutlasses, and metal buckets nested one inside the other. Off to the right was a bed with a mattress, for sale to that Liberian rich enough to afford such a luxury. The counter ran around the inside of the entire store.

During lunch I kept an eye out for Betty Leeleh, whom I suspected passed by the store on her way to and from school. Within thirty minutes I saw her coming from school, looking adorable in her school uniform, a navy blue skirt and a pink blouse.

Betty and I walked to the house on the outskirts of Ganta in which she rented a room. Students from all over Nimba County attended junior and senior high school in Ganta, as the villages and towns of their birth—places like Kpaytuo, for example—were too small to have secondary schools. Unless they were fortunate enough to have a relative with whom they stayed for free, many of Ganta's students rented rooms, like Betty.

Betty introduced me to two young male students who also lived in the house and the wife of the man who owned it. The owner's wife lived there without him, and was out back cooking rice for the household. There was no furniture in the house, save two chairs. Each of the four inhabitants, including the wife of the owner, herself a student in the tenth grade, lived in his or her own sparsely furnished room.

After Betty ate a plateful of rice, we walked back to the town's commercial center, for I wanted to track down Scott Lewis, a Peace Corps Volunteer stationed in Ganta. Assuming he had room and was amenable to the idea, I hoped to stay at Scott's. We returned to John Bashir's store and I asked Nazem if he had seen Scott. Yes, he said, only minutes before. He added that Scott was his "so-so good friend."

Nazem commented on the delight Scott derived from working with his hands, no matter how menial the task. The Lebanese and the Liberians found it incomprehensible that an American like Scott, who in Liberia didn't have to, got his hands dirty constructing a biology exhibit at the school, where he taught. They, especially the Liberians, believed once you were a "so-so big man"—and all representatives of the United States government were, even a twenty-two-year-old Peace Corps Volunteer—you needn't ever do manual labor: indeed, the sign of being a "big man" was not working with your hands, but having someone else follow your orders. One finds this attitude in all countries, but where I've encountered it the most—tragically so—was in the then-developing countries; and in no place was it more virulent and pernicious than in Liberia.

Liberians admire Americans; pity they don't realize that long before our fancy technology, what made us excel was a willingness to work with our hands, dirtying them in the process.

Betty and I walked about the main street of Ganta until we spotted Scott, which was not too difficult as he was the only white face among hundreds of black ones. He stood about five feet, five inches, with dirty blond hair, a sandy-colored beard and a muscular build. I was not surprised to learn he wrestled when a student. Scott made me feel immediately welcome, and said I could stay with him for as long as I wished. He enjoyed telling corny jokes and making even cornier puns. By the manner in which Scott engaged in repartee with the Liberians, I knew he was my kind of person.

We carried my bags to Scott's home, where I met William and Mack, his Liberian "play brothers." The term, which was new to me, meant they were like brothers, but were not biologically related. Mack and William were eighteen and lived with Scott. The three of them shared the duties of the household. In exchange for their cleaning the house, though not very well, and some cooking, Scott provided them with room and board and helped with their school fees and the like. William came to work for Scott after writing the following letter, which follows with the punctuation and spelling intact:

200

Dear Mr. Lewis:

It happen that where I live there are lots of work to be done before going to school, so for this reason there is hard time on my part. I am facing National Exam this year. I will like for you to help me so as to live with you in the house. If you and myself live here I will do the cooking, do any work. As you know I'm strong working man. Kindly sympathy with me and do it as possible you can. You can write Don [whom I assume was also a PCV] and ask him, he will tell you more about me, how he and myself use to live together in Negbeh. Scott, I think you know the kind of friendship that existed between Don and myself, and is still existing. I hope you will do it for me. Thanks— your best friend.

William Kokeh

Also staying at Scott's until she found her own place was a Volunteer named Beverly Silver, who had arrived in Liberia a month before. She, like many new Volunteers, was frazzled and depressed— the technical term is culture shock. I urged Beverly to remember that it takes at least two to four months, for some Volunteers longer, to adjust to Liberia. And for some, an eternity wouldn't suffice. I well remember culture shock, even though in Peace Corps training I vowed it would never happen to me. Not for the first time in my life had I been wrong.

Scott, Beverly, William (Scott's Liberian play brother) and I ate dinner on Scott's

Scott Lewis, the Peace Corps Volunteer stationed in Ganta in 1982, in whose home I stayed. My kind of guy, Scott was a great host, corny jokes and all.

front porch, with the Guinea Mountains standing watch in the background. Scott and William ate country-style, that is to say from the same large pan of rice. But whereas the tribal Liberians eat communally from a large pot with their hands—rolling the rice into a ball, dipping it into the gravy and then into their mouths—Scott and William used forks. Beverly and I ate from our own plates, with forks—New York and Philadelphia style, respectively.

After dinner Scott and I walked about town, ending up at a tiny outdoor cafe where we drank cold beers and listened to reggae music, which in the last few years had become popular in Liberia. Scott told me that twice the citizens of Ganta had forked over $10 each as an assessment for a generator that the town was to purchase, and twice there had been ground-breaking ceremonies at the site of the power plant. To date, however, not one pail of dirt had been dug, not one kilowatt of electricity generated. No one knew who ate the money, but it was gone. Was it any wonder, Scott asked, that the citizens of Ganta, having been burned twice, were reluctant to give money a third time?

Returning to Scott's about eight o'clock, we encountered a distraught Volunteer named Steve Katz. Steve had cut his wrist badly while opening a coconut with a penknife. It had taken three hours to get from Kpain, where he was stationed, to Ganta, a distance of twelve miles, for the only vehicle in the village had run out of gas en route. Steve, probably in mild shock, was forced to walk the last two miles in the dark.

On foot we accompanied Steve to the Ganta Hospital, which was about three quarters of a mile from Scott's home. Scores of old women slept on mats on the ground outside the hospital ward, the mothers and grandmothers of young patients inside. Thousands of dead moths and other insects were piled up under the electric lights. The Mission compound, consisting of the mission, the hospital and the leprosarium, had its own generator. Entering the hospital from outside, where everything was pitch dark, I had to shield my eyes from the glare of the light. Once everything came into focus I saw and heard patients, mostly children, groaning and screaming, lying amid the filth and stench of their dressings.

As the Liberian doctor on call was away, though he was not supposed to be, Scott led us to the nearby home of two women who worked at the Ganta Leprosy Center. One of them was a nurse, the other a doctor. It must have been common for people to show up in need of medical attention at nine o'clock at night, for the two of them seemed not the least perturbed. Theresa Hicks, the nurse, was a member of the Society of African Missions; in her early thirties, Nurse Hicks reminded me, in looks and disposition, of the English actress Julie Andrews. She decided that "butterfly" bandages rather than sutures would suffice for Steve's cut, and ordered him to go to the hospital in the morning for a tetanus booster, reminding him that cuts take abnormally long to heal in Liberia's humid climate, and, as such, easily become infected.

While Theresa went for the bandages and penicillin ointment, I chatted with Dr. Margaret Chambers, the sixty-year-old Irish nun who had been the director of leprosy control in Liberia until the coup, when she was replaced by a Liberian. Transferred to Ganta, she headed the leprosarium. Scott later told me she was a crotchety, brilliant, hardworking, world-renowned leprologist.

Speaking with an I-don't-give-a-hoot-whom-I-offend frankness, Dr. Chambers, a sister of the Medical Mission of Mary, said the People's Redemption Council had allowed the country to crumble. She said the government had taken over the operation of former President Tolbert's vast estate, which produced eggs, rice and pigs, and in no time had run the businesses into the ground.

"Liberia is a mess," she said.

Chapter 28

I remained at Scott's house in the morning while the others went to school—Scott and Beverly to teach, Scott's Liberian "play brothers," William and Mack, to learn. There was more than the usual traffic on the dirt road in front of Scott's home, for this was "Guinea Market Day." Women from Guinea, whose border is a mile away, cross over into Liberia, carrying on their heads baskets and buckets of food, cloth, pots, charcoal, meat and fish, which they sell to the Liberians who come from miles in all directions for the weekly market.

With Scott's permission, I read some of the letters hand-delivered to him from his students, similar to the kind every Volunteer received. I reprint a sample of them with the spelling and punctuation intact:

Dear Mr. Lewis:
   I wish to inform you that the 5th this month will be my birthday. So as a sponsor of our class I just like to inform you about that.
   I hope that my birthday to be a success once. It is just a special information for you, therefore let pray God for me.
   Sincerely yours,
   Edward K. Dahn 10A

Dear Mr. Scott:
   This is to inform you that I am suffering of yellow fever which in fact, I am not able to come to school. Accordingly I would like for you to remit me for my abscene.
   Your student, Josephine Flomo

To All Instructors Concerned:
   When I came here for weekend I met one of my brother's dead. Kindly consider me for this matter.
   I do hope you will take this into consideration.
   Unsigned

Mr. Scott:

Kindly excuse me for today cause I am feeling very sick. My eye is turning and I could hardly walk.

Unsigned

As I had time to kill (perhaps not the best choice of words for what follows) I browsed through one of Scott's books, *When There Is No Doctor*. Once again I was aware of the considerable health hazards Volunteers faced in Liberia, particularly those of us stationed in out-of-the-way villages. Had I ever needed immediate medical attention when I lived in Kpaytuo—if, for example, I had been stricken with appendicitis or severely cut myself or broken an ankle—it would have taken, at best, two hours, on the bumpiest of roads, to reach the nearest medical facility (the Ganta Hospital), assuming that a bus or, much rarer, a car had arrived in Kpaytuo the moment I took ill or was injured. More likely, it would have taken three to five hours to reach medical help or, were it the middle of the night, five to eight hours.

I next read about snake bites, which we Volunteers in the interior had reason to worry about, for some of the deadliest snakes in the world are indigenous to Liberia's rain forest, among them the green mamba, the puff adder and the Gaboon viper, the latter about four feet long, weighing as much as nineteen pounds, with fangs as long as two inches. Many persons have died from the bite of a Gaboon viper, but a few quick-thinking souls have saved themselves from death by quickly amputating a bitten finger.

In the twenty-two months I lived in Kpaytuo I saw four snakes. On the first occasion I was behind my house, talking with the mason constructing my latrine. He saw a thin, green snake—the highly venomous green mamba—slithering through the thatch on Tado's rice kitchen. Knocking it to the ground, the mason chopped it in half. The next snake was discovered by my houseboy Sammy in my bathhouse and that, too, was summarily destroyed. The third one was spotted in a tree and I have already described its fate (students threw stones at it and, when it fell, beat it to death). The fourth snake, as thick as a professional football player's calf, was already dead when I gazed upon all twelve feet of it. Four boys carried the monster on their shoulders; they had slain the beast in a nearby creek.

During my Peace Corps years, if a snake had sought a good spot in which to hide or browse close to the village, it would have been the area around my house. It was impractical to clear all the grass around it, but I kept the grass short. Thank God no snake ever got into my home. I had flies, ants, worms, lizards, beetles, wasps, frogs, chickens, goats and rats in my house, but never, to my knowledge, a snake.

My fun read finished, I walked over to the J.W. Pearson High School to observe the new Volunteer Beverly Silver teach her tenth-grade mathematics class, mainly because among the one hundred students in the class was Betty Leeleh. Since there were not enough benches for a hundred or more students, many carried their own chairs to school. Those who did not and arrived late stood in the back. Beverly seemed to me to know mathematics well. She wrote a few problems on the board and then randomly checked the students' work. I wished I had brought my camera with me, for the sight of petite, pale Beverly enveloped by a sea of eager, large, and mostly male students would have made quite a picture. Beverly was not, of course, able to check each student's work, for that would have taken most of the hour, but by wading through them, looking right and left at every paper attached to an outstretched arm, she was able to check the work of a good number. The brighter students solved the problems, the less bright copied the answers from the bright ones. With so many students in the classroom, the ones in the back, where I was standing, barely heard Beverly. So education, such as it is, "progresses" in a typically understaffed, overcrowded high school in Liberia.

I hung around until school was over and then walked with Betty back to where she lived. The landlord's children were playing out back, where their mother was preparing the midday meal over an open fire.

I had never been in the situation where I had known someone as a child and now found myself attracted to the mature woman. Of course I had enjoyed Betty's company and personality when she had been my student. But because she had been a child around twelve and I twenty-two, there had been absolutely no sexual aspect to our relationship. Not so now, leastwise on my part: I, age thirty-nine, was attracted to Betty, age about twenty-eight. I knew Betty enjoyed my company: she was always telling me how happy she was that I had returned and hadn't forgotten Kpaytuo. I didn't know the degree of her affection. But I intended to find out soon enough, for we agreed to meet the following week in Monrovia.

❖ ❖ ❖

In my time, there was no typical situation in which a Peace Corps Volunteer lived. I lived alone, most have roommates. Some were assigned to rural villages, others to urban areas. The quality of housing depended on what was available. Compared to the home I lived in as a Volunteer, Scott's, with three large bedrooms, a living room, kitchen and an indoor bathhouse, was palatial. And his indoor bathhouse beat going outside, especially in the dark, when who knew what was going to turn up (Hello, Mr. Green Mamba); or during the rainy season, when it was wet and chilly (Hi there, Mr. Scorpion). Scott's toilet, however, was in an outhouse—a two-foot high mound of concrete with a hole: it reminded me of a scale model of a volcano. His water came from a well in the front yard, a luxury few Volunteers enjoyed. Everyone in the vicinity used the well until Scott noticed the Liberians and Mandingoes made no effort to keep it clean. Because of this, coupled with the possibility that in the dry season all this use might have caused the well to go dry, Scott reluctantly restricted access to his immediate neighbors.

When I served, one of the myths about the Peace Corps the American public (and the congressmen who funded it) wanted to believe was that we Volunteers lived like the natives. This image, cultivated by the Peace Corps, added to the romance and the excitement of the Peace Corps experience. And that was good for recruitment and funding. But in fact, we Liberian Volunteers didn't live exactly like a country person. It is accurate to say that we lived more modestly than almost all other Americans and Westerners—missionaries excepted—who lived and worked in Africa. Government and business people from the West lived grandly in huge homes often guarded and staffed by servants; moved about in air-conditioned, chauffeur-driven automobiles; and many expected to be treated like pashas or panjandrums.

I didn't want to live exactly like the tribal people, even if that had been possible—and it really wasn't. There is no more ridiculous figure to my eyes than a Westerner who tries to "go native" in the Third World. I make no apologies for having a refrigerator that ran on kerosene or a houseboy and a cook. Or for wearing shoes, boiling my drinking water and owning a kerosene stove and a desk. I could have tried to live like the tribal people—except I'd have been sick a good deal of the time; and when not sick, I'd have been fetching water and wood. What I would not have had was the time, the health or the energy to perform the job I'd been sent there to do: to teach school. Tribal people don't cook on an open fire because they think it is quaint or more efficient; they can't afford a stove or a refrigerator, which all of them desire. What do tribal Liberians think of a Volunteer who lives in a hut and tries, as near as possible, to live like a country man? That he is a fool. And so do I.

Chapter 29

Most of the Volunteers in the Ganta area knew of Walter Barron, there not being many sixty-two-year-old white Americans, who weren't missionaries, living in up-country Liberia. Some Volunteers, young enough to be his grandsons or granddaughters, said they had heard rumors about Walter being addicted to alcohol and drugs; others believed he was living in squalor, on the verge of madness, a human wreck to whom Volunteers, out of pity, occasionally gave money.

Walter had joined the Peace Corps when I did, but following his two-year stint he remained in Liberia with a tribal woman whom he married. While most Volunteers enter the Peace Corps in their early twenties, Walter joined at the age of forty-three. And while few of us had worked at anything but summer and vacation jobs, Walter had worked in the real world, as a minister. Then he had left the church and had married, only to see his wife die not long thereafter. I considered him one of the brighter people in our Peace Corps group. Though we had never been close, Walter and I had had an amicable relationship. He was very close to a friend of mine, Bill Fickling. If only to pass along Bill's regards, I'd have visited Walter. But of course I was also curious to see how he was getting on after living life in the interior for so many years.

Soon enough I'd see for myself, for I journeyed from Ganta to nearby Palala and asked two men standing on the road for the home of Walter Barron. They pointed me in its direction. I walked along a dirt road until I came to an unplastered and unpainted home whose owner apparently had run out of money before he completed building it. There, in the hallway, his silhouette unmistakable, stood Walter Barron.

He didn't recognize me, but once I said my name, he was flabbergasted and happy to see me, since I was only the second person in the

Walter Barron, the former Peace Corps Volunteer, and his Liberian wife, Musu. Walter taught in a Liberian school and of his meager salary observed: "The government is in arrears."

last fourteen years he had seen from among the group with whom he trained for the Peace Corps. And I was happy to see him. His shoulder-length, yellow-whitish hair and his eight-inch straggly beard made him look like Robinson Crusoe. He was quite thin and sallow, looking not at all well. It was difficult to think of him as sixty-two: not because he looked young and vital, for he looked anything but; rather, because there was always something youthful in his manner and voice.

He introduced me to Musu, his wife, a shrunken country woman dressed in a *lappa*. She, in turn, proudly introduced me to their children—all seven of them. His children were dark except one, a beautiful mulatto whom they'd called Old Lady. Her face was freckled and she had sparkling eyes. Old Lady was about thirteen. She was also a brat, refusing to pose in the family picture until I promised her and her older sister I would take their pictures alone. Being light-skinned and half-American, Old Lady would have already been aware that Liberians considered her special and beautiful, not least for her skin tone as for her

Walter and Musu Barron's seven children.

attractive features. Perhaps that is why she acted like a spoiled princess, at least on the day of my visit. Judging by Walter's home and his children's shabby clothes and footwear or, in the case of the youngest children, their lack of footwear, it was obvious Walter was not living high on the hog.

Walter and I strolled into town for a drink at the one little shop with a refrigerator, where each of us ordered a soft drink. Whatever truth lay in the stories of his alcoholism, he was off the bottle now. His life had been pleasant but lately had become more difficult, mostly because of the strains on the Liberian economy. Though he lived with a country woman, he didn't affect the bearing and pose of one who has "gone native." I think that is a "disease" that strikes mostly young Westerners temporarily living in undeveloped countries like Liberia.

Walter taught school and was a salaried employee of the Liberian government. Like most of the civil servants in the country, he had not been paid in two months. "The government is in arrears," he said.

I was struck by the phrase, which wasn't spoken ironically or sarcastically. Its understated eloquence and reassuring tone was in stark contrast to the chaotic, festering situation to which it referred. For the first time since living in Liberia, he had been forced recently to borrow money, and at the exorbitant rate of twenty percent interest. The most incredible assertion Walter made in our two hours together was that he had recently discovered mission schools were superior to government schools—indeed, by observing his younger children, he had reluctantly concluded they had not learned much of value at the government schools. It had taken him sixteen years in Liberia to discover that!

He spoke deliberately and softly, groping for and measuring each word. He seemed to me to think and react slowly, almost as if he had suffered slight brain damage. He was beyond mellow, in a state I'd describe as passive and lethargic. Through his early years in Liberia his health had been good, marred by two incidents of kidney stones, but in the last few years he had weathered a few bouts of malaria, which had taken their toll. When I asked him if he took the malaria prophylactic Chloroquine regularly, he said no. Big mistake, that. We Peace Corps Volunteers, and visitors like myself, took one weekly. I wondered if

Walter were lax or if he could no longer afford the tablets. I asked if he would consider moving back to the States. At his age, he said, it would be difficult securing a job and were he to find one, it would only be a few years until his retirement, a shocking reminder to me that, indeed, Walter was sixty-two. Happy as I was to see him, I wished he might have given me more insight into his life, though perhaps I was expecting too much from a brief conversation.

We returned to the house so I might say goodbye. His wife Musu, clearly the dominant member in the marriage, was disappointed I was not staying the night, for she was visibly pleased that someone from Walter's past, however tenuous the connection had been, had appeared. She implored me to inform Walter's brother, whom I did not know, that they were suffering, and that he should send them money.

"I will bury Walter or he will bury me," she said. "I can't leave him."

When I asked if I might take their pictures, Musu directed Walter to change into something a bit nicer, which he did. And there he is in the photograph with a decent pair of pants, a faded shirt, his shoulder-length hair, his unkempt beard and mustache, and tinted glasses. And he is wearing boots, which he put on for the occasion, forgetting to lace them up.

◆　◆　◆

Back in Ganta, I met Nancy Keeler, another new Volunteer staying with Scott Lewis until she found suitable lodging in the nearby village to which she was assigned. She had recently arrived from Monrovia, where she had gone to see a doctor. Since arriving in Liberia the previous month, Nancy hadn't spent seven consecutive days in Ganta, having developed a cough that the medical staff speculated was an allergic reaction—to just what they had no idea. Confiding in me, the Volunteer Beverly Silver said she had heard that if Nancy's health problem didn't clear up soon, reluctantly the staff was going to send Nancy home.

Nancy had come to Liberia to teach agriculture, even though she hadn't studied it in college. Her knowledge of agriculture was practical. She had been raised on a Kansas farm, so she knew more than enough to help the Liberians. While teaching them how to grow vegetables more efficiently, among other things, she treasured the opportunity to study her real loves—wildlife and birds.

Much remained to be learned about the fauna, flora, birds, reptiles and insects of Liberia. Even as of 1982, there had been relatively few efforts to study them. Given that it was never a colonial possession and the restriction placed on European travelers by the Americo-Liberians, Liberia had not attracted as many explorers and naturalists as other regions of Africa, most notably British and German East and Central Africa, the area that now encompasses Kenya, Uganda and Tanzania, and Sudan. In fact, during the nineteenth century—the great age of African exploration—those few European explorers and naturalists who ventured into the Liberian interior—and then not far—usually became ill or died and had done very little in terms of collecting and categorizing specimens.

The first, and still the most outstanding, naturalists associated with Liberia was the Swiss taxidermist (and later director of the Rotterdam Zoo), Johann Buttikofer, who visited the country from 1880 to 1882. During that visit, Buttikofer's assistant died of fever and Buttikofer, too, fell ill and was forced to sail back to Europe, only to return again from 1886 to 1887. From his two journeys, Buttikofer published *Reisebilder aus Liberia* (*Picture Journey from Liberia*) in 1890, the first detailed account of Liberia's diverse wildlife. (An annotated edition of this classic work is now entitled *Travel Sketches from Liberia*.)

Buttikofer's work provides a fascinating glimpse into nineteenth-century Liberia and its wildlife. He describes collecting many rare species of chimpanzee, bongo, zebra duiker and pygmy hippopotamus. By the time of my own visit in 1982, the rare animals Buttikofer referred to in his book—as well as leopards and other species unique to Liberia and its adjacent neighbors, the Ivory Coast, Sierra Leone and Guinea, like the forest buffalo, the forest elephant, Jentink's duiker—had become much more rare, some extinct or nearly so.

The Liberian government—pre-and post-coup—ever incompetent and corrupt, had allowed foreign concessions to plunder the country's resources without regard to the future. Because government officials were too dense and paranoid to grant the logging companies ownership of the parts of the forest they harvested, the companies had had no incentive—as similar companies had in Europe and in the United States—to reforest the land. Granted, foreign-owned logging companies had, like foreign-owned mining companies, provided jobs for many tribal Liberians, but they also had stripped and gouged and burned and scarred the great forest, upsetting the delicate ecological balance and driving game from its natural habitat.

I remember my conversation in Monrovia with Ross Dickerson, a twenty-five-year-old Peace Corps Volunteer who worked in forestry in Grand Gedeh County, southeast of Nimba County. (Being that much farther from Monrovia, Grand Gedeh County was even more isolated, less developed and poorer than Nimba County.) Ross told me that unless the logging companies were restrained and there was some kind of central planning in Monrovia, the future would be dire: that Grand Gedeh (one of Liberia's then nine counties) would be logged out in a short time, as had already happened in much of Nimba County (where Kpaytuo and Ganta are located).

Ross said, "If I close a concession for illegally cutting down trees in an area they aren't supposed to be in, they [the concessionaires] just come down to Monrovia and bribe someone to open them up again. And if I close down a logging company, I put hundreds of Liberians out of work. They need the work. I feel guilty as hell about that. I could make thousands of dollars a month if I accepted bribes from the concessions."

Rather than shut down a logging company, knowing it would be back in business in a couple of weeks, or accepting a bribe from it, Ross often agreed not to report violations if the logging company donated medicine and books to villages and towns in that part of Grand Gedeh County.

The Liberian government had never prohibited the killing of rare animals, mainly because it never had the inclination or the manpower to enforce whatever regulations existed against exploiting the environment. It was not until 1983 that the government established its first national park, theoretically protecting a large tract of virgin forest in southeastern Liberia from commercial exploitation and from cultivation and allowing the fauna and flora to exist there in peace.

Subsistence agriculture—the method used by the tribal people to grow rice—has also contributed to the decimation of the natural land-scape. The slash-and-burn method quickly exhausts land already low in fertility. The tribal people must continually move to new patches to allow the old land to lie fallow. That wasn't a problem in the old days, when the land seemed to be unlimited and there for the clearing. But decades of such practices led to a steady diminution of the primary for-est, more so after the tribal farmers gained access, thanks to roads bull-dozed by the mining and logging companies, to hitherto inaccessible regions. Once there, they burned everything in sight, destroying valu-able timber lands, (thus depleting a perpetuating resource) and driving the game from its home.

Tribal Liberians also indiscriminately trapped, shot, skinned, ate and sold any animal without regard to rarity or breeding season, trag-ically unaware that they were rapidly killing off one of their few sources of animal protein. Indeed, as all these factors converged—commercial exploitation, expanded agriculture, a larger population—bush meat had become scarcer, to a point where it was, in 1982, unavailable in many regions of the country where fourteen years before it had been plentiful.

Animal husbandry can't replace the wild meat, because there is not much grazing land in Liberia, and most cattle quickly are killed off by the tsetse fly. Therefore, eating meat regularly is often restricted to the wealthiest Liberians in Monrovia, who can afford to buy beef trucked in from nearby countries.

Even we in the West, with our abundance of money and resources, and our stable, mostly responsive, political systems, haven't solved the problem of balancing the good done by technological advances with the bad caused by those advances as they degrade—or even poison—our water and air. The poor countries of the developing world suffer even more in this regard. Though ultimately it is their responsibility to amend the situation, we in the West need to help the developing world before the rare creatures of the earth and the majestic rain forests and grasslands and fertile fields they inhabit fade away and become nothing more than distant memories.

Chapter 30

On my last day in Ganta I decided to visit the Ganta Leprosy Center. So after the members of the household had left for school and I had typed up the previous day's events in my journal, boiled three teapots of water for twenty minutes each—the household always being low on drinking water, this was the least I could do to repay Scott for his hospitality—ate bananas and grapefruit for breakfast, and washed up, I set off for the Center.

The leprosarium was located little more than a mile from Scott's house in a well-manicured, secluded area off Ganta's main road. On the walk over, children, seeing my camera, yelled to me, "Take my picture." And when I called their bluff, they squealed in delight, saying, "You must carry my picture-oh."

Carry it where? To America, of course.

I had mixed feelings about visiting a leprosarium, even as I reminded myself that I had spent almost two years in Liberia without contracting leprosy. It was therefore unlikely I would become infected by one morning's visit. But try as I might, I still felt anxious about entering the grounds.

Lining the only road of the Center were palm trees and tiny homes, no more than 15 feet by 15 feet, inhabited by former patients who had nowhere else to go. Next I came upon a circular open-sided thatched hut, about fifteen yards in diameter, from which some of the lepers sold wood carvings they had made: there were sculptures of zebras, antelopes and elephants and various masks and bracelets, all fashioned from local mahogany and palm wood. When I got to the dispensary I learned that Dr. Chambers and Nurse Hicks—whom I had met the night I accompanied the bleeding Volunteer, Steve Katz, to their home—had driven down to Monrovia for supplies. However, Paul Steinwachs, a Peace Corps Volunteer whom I had met briefly at Scott's, was there. As Paul was a new Volunteer—his group had arrived only a few months before—I would have preferred being shown around by Dr. Chambers or Nurse Hicks, both long-time residents of Liberia and intimately involved with the operation of the leprosarium. But as they were absent, I had no choice but to rely on Paul Steinwachs' good graces. While someone went for him, I sat in the dispensary, there watching the patients, many without toes or fingers, hobble in to receive their morning medicine, two pills dispensed in a tiny paper cup, or to have their ulcers bandaged. Having obtained their medicine, the patients milled about, as did a few Liberian medical personnel dressed in white. A few patients were in wheelchairs—"iron toes" as one man called them.

When Paul Steinwachs appeared, I asked him if I might walk about the facility. By all means, he said, and as he had the time, he guided me on the tour.

First we visited the men's ward, where I saw scores of patients swaddled in bandages, some in bed, others limping about. Then we were off to the women's ward. In every room that we visited, the patients' eyes and faces (and, for some, what was left of their faces) lit up as we entered, so delighted were they by visitors and attention. Paul shook or touched every deformed hand or stump in sight. I was queasy about doing likewise but after he assured me there was no danger, as the patients were all on medication—and thus not capable of transmitting the disease—I joined him. The patients were particularly grateful, for by visiting them and shaking their hands we were treating them as humans—not as horrible creatures to be scorned.

In a short while, I realized I could not have chosen a more enthusiastic guide than Paul. If he wasn't as knowledgeable as Dr. Chambers or Nurse Hicks, he knew much more about leprosy than I, and was an able and willing teacher.

Leprosy is caused by a bacteria—to which most people have a natural immunity—that attacks the peripheral nerves of the arms and legs. If neglected, it will frequently destroy the nerves that control and move our muscles. With the nerves dead, the muscles can no longer move, so they atrophy and become fibrous tissue. Since the afflicted person can't feel anything in the affected areas, as the sensory component of the nerve has also been destroyed, a trivial injury to the "dead" fingers or toes, like a cut or burn, quickly becomes infected. (In a more ghastly, though in Liberia not uncommon, scenario, a rat gnaws on the "dead" fingers or toes while the victim sleeps.) The infection turns into an abscess, which ends up as osteomyelitis, an infection of the bone. The way the body deals with the infected bone is to get rid of it: in the process of doing so, the cartilage is absorbed into the body and the fingers or toes shorten or they may be lost altogether—thus the mistaken impression that leprosy directly causes fingers or toes to "fall off." This process may occur in an amazingly quick time—as little as four weeks from cut to infection to loss of a finger.

To my astonishment, I learned that most forms of leprosy are curable. There is no reason its victims should suffer disfigurement and immobilization, provided the disease is diagnosed and treatment commences in its early stages. But at the time of my visit this rarely occurred because of myths that surrounded the ancient disease. Another contributing factor in Liberia, and I assume in most of the poorer nations, was the lack of treatment centers.

Indeed, when many Liberians noticed the lesions and discolored patches on their skin, the only early symptoms of the disease, there was no sense that something was wrong, save for what they mistakenly believed was a minor rash—and rashes, as I wrote earlier, are commonplace in Liberia's climate. Even if in time that person thought something was amiss, many, though not all, lepers were reluctant to seek medical help, fearing they'd be ostracized by their family and community. And, lastly, if a Liberian wanted to see a doctor, the chances were slim he or she would have access to qualified personnel; for the Liberian Health Department did not have the funds or enough competent and dependable personnel to staff its leprosy clinics. Nor did it have the dependable personnel—and the money to pay them—to send tribal clinicians into the more inaccessible regions of the country so that stricken Liberians could be diagnosed and treated in the disease's earliest stages. To venture into remote rural areas to diagnose and treat suffering Liberians was to be one of Paul Steinwachs' jobs; the other was to train tribal Liberians, who could then perform the task without Westerners supervising them.

Leprosy also attacks the facial nerve that controls the muscle that

Paul Steinwachs, my guide around the Ganta Leprosy Center. Next to Paul is a man with leprosy, wearing the "rocker shoes" that enable the disease's victims to ambulate better.

allows us to close our eyelids. The eyelids of many lepers droop over their eyes, for the muscle has locked up and atrophied, with the result that vision is impeded. As if this isn't bad enough, because lepers can't keep their corneas moist, by opening and closing their eyelids, their corneas dry out. And because lepers can't close their eyelids, their eyes are constantly exposed to air, dirt, dust and bacteria. It isn't long before the eyes get infected and then ulceration of the cornea sets in. Scarring results and, in time, blindness. Surgery can restore the ability to close the eyelids if it is performed in time.

Paul and I next visited a ward of patients who had benefited from this surgery. The surgery involved removing a tendon from the patient's leg and attaching it to the temporal muscle in the face (one of the closing muscles of the jaw). By practicing the motion of biting, these Liberians were learning how to close their eyelids—thus avoiding possibly going blind and, for the first time in years, seeing clearly.

We also visited the room in which the patients underwent rudimentary physical therapy, designed to bring back as much flexibility as possible to stricken toes and fingers. And we visited the section of the leprosarium where former patients—all of them cured and in no danger of re-contracting the disease so long as they took their medication—made artificial limbs and "rocker shoes," the latter a specially designed shoe that makes it easier for a toeless person, who would have difficulty in regular shoes, to walk.

Everywhere we went the patients, save for the very ill, were anxious to show off their progress, demonstrating the use of a limb that for years had been useless, or scurrying on deformed or artificial limbs to their lockers, hopeful of earning $10 or $15 by selling us a wood carving or baskets they had made.

Then we moved outside, where an ex-patient took us on a tour of agricultural projects initiated about a year before. One project consisted of a large swamp in which the cured patients hoped to grow rice; those who labored in it under the glistening midday sun that day whimsically referred to it as "Camp Suffering." There were also two fish farms, both established by Peace Corps Volunteers; a vegetable garden, in which they raised cucumbers, cabbage, eggplant and peppers; and, lastly, a small hog and chicken farm.

The food that was grown and the animals that were raised were eaten by the patients and hospital staff and sold in markets around Ganta. The agricultural projects were a boon to the leprosarium, which was always short of money and unable to meet expenses from its main sources of revenue, the former West German Leprosy Relief Association and the Liberian government. The projects were equally a godsend to the lepers, many of whom were working at a real job for the first time in years. Aside from giving meaning to their otherwise bleak existence—and who is foolish enough to ever underestimate the psychological factor in the recuperative process—the income from the sale of the crops and poultry also helped the patients pay for the food they and their families consumed while they were undergoing treatment at the leprosarium, a process that normally took about six months, but might take as long as two years. (In the not-so-distant past patients had to undergo at least five years of treatment or, for some, a lifetime of medication at the Center, but new medicines had drastically cut the time of treatment.) Those patients unable to work were, of course, not expected to.

In the past, many patients had remained at the leprosarium until they died, since they had no place else to go. The cluster of small homes along the road leading to the clinic was testament to that. However, by the time of my visit the policy had changed and staff now encouraged patients, once they had received treatment and were on medication, to return to their homes and families. (To its credit leprophobia was not as prevalent in Liberia as in many countries where it still flourished.)

I will always remember, and be eternally grateful for, my unforgettable day at the Ganta Leprosy Center. May I never forget to pay homage to anyone associated with it, most especially to the memory of the extraordinary man who founded it—Dr. George Way Harley. He was the missionary-doctor whom I wrote about earlier in the story in connection with his studies of Liberia's secret societies.

Born in Asheville, North Carolina, in 1894, George Way Harley earned a medical degree from Yale University and after his studies at a seminary, he and his wife Winifred in 1925 moved to Liberia, where they would spend thirty-five years in Ganta. There he built a medical dispensary, which would eventually become the Ganta Hospital; the Ganta Leprosy Center (now called the Ganta Rehabilitation Center for

The Ganta church built by, and whose grounds are the eternal resting place of, the legendary Dr. George Way Harley—medical doctor, Christian missionary, renowned anthropologist and author, whose collection of Liberian masks are exhibited in American museums.

Leprosy and Tuberculosis); a village where the lepers lived; a school, sawmill, tile factory and a lovely stone church, which I walked by on my way to the Leprosy Center that memorable day.

Sometimes treating as many as 150 patients a day, Dr. Harley found the time to amass data on, and collect masks carved by, the members of the *Poro Society*, the men's secret society. His mask collections are on display at various American museums and universities, among them the Peabody Museum of Archaeology and Ethnology at Harvard University, which also houses some of his correspondence; and the Anthropology Departments of the College of William & Mary and Duke University. If that isn't impressive enough, he was also a fellow of the Royal Geographic Society and the Royal Society of Tropical Medicine and Hygiene.

He and his wife, Winifred—his partner in all his endeavors and in her own right a botanist and author—had three children in Ganta, the first of whom died at age four, laid low by a tropical fever. In their 60s and due a well-earned retirement, the Harleys left Liberia in 1960 and moved to Virginia, where he continued to write, was affiliated with Harvard and was a consultant to many institutions, including the Peace Corps and the World Health Organization. In 1966, age seventy-two, he died from a heart attack. George Way Harley's ashes were flown to Liberia and buried near the cornerstone of the Ganta Church that he helped build with his own hands—he was a carpenter and mason who had learned blacksmithing. His death was declared a national day of mourning in Liberia.

◆　　◆　　◆

By the time Paul and I returned to Ganta proper we were exhausted from being out in the sun, hatless at that, for more than an hour. We proceeded to one of the few bars in Ganta with a working refrigerator and guzzled two cold soft drinks each. While Paul and I consumed our drinks, an old man approached us. He explained in barely understandable Pidgin English that he was a barber, and asked if either of us wanted a haircut. We did not, but thanked him for the offer. He then withdrew from his pocket a tattered piece of paper on which, in now-faded ink, the following message had been typed:

To Whom It May Concern

The bearer Mr. William Cooper has worked in our employment for a period covering fourteen (14) years, as a Barber strictly employed for Europeans. His last rate was $.40 per hour. During this interim Mr. Cooper was punctual in the discharge of his duties.

He has asked leave of absence to attend the burial ceremonies of his Mother. As we hate to lose Mr. Cooper, we welcome his return to the job after his leave is ended. In the event he does not return, we do not hesitate recommending him to Europeans and on Europeans who might like to engage his services as such."

M. M. Lee

District Accountant, Liberian Mining Company, Bomi Hills

The letter was dated March 1965. He still carried it with him seventeen years later. (Think of the Old Man the next time you hear someone say that blacks are lazy and don't want to work; or think of Tado Jackson, up at 5:00 A.M. to work on his farm or garden and, after ten hours of strenuous work, teaching night school to the adults in Kpaytuo. Or if you want an example of a black American, think of Jacob Morton, who opened the doors of my father's factory at 5:00 A.M., mixed mayonnaise and salad dressing all day, and after leaving work at 4:00 P.M., drove to his second job, cleaning carpets for the next two hours. He didn't need the money for his second job—he liked to keep busy—and never missed a day of work.)

Paul and I then went next door to a chop shop (what we Americans call a greasy spoon), whose food Paul said was safe to eat and ordered— what else—rice with meat and a gravy, washed down with two more sodas each. As Liberian food goes, it was mild. In my time, it was *de rigueur* in most Peace Corps households to provide each guest at dinner with his own quart bottle of water, so fiery was Liberian food. And I never drank as many sodas in my life as during my return trip. When there was not safe drinking water available, soda, as often as not warm, was usually my only alternative.

Even so, I should be grateful for small things: the legendary nineteenth-century African explorers—Burton, Speke, Baker, Livingston, Stanley and Kingsley—had fewer options for keeping hydrated and comfortable. What was inconvenient to me, like riding in a sweltering money bus over dusty, crater-laden roads and going without cool water for days on end, would have been a picnic to them, who *walked* many hundreds of miles through Africa. Nor could they pop into the capital city for cold water, a refreshing shower, and some fine food every few weeks or months to break the monotony of the jungle. They were in the bush, cut off from civilization, for years at a time.

Paul Steinwachs, my guide that day, like most Volunteers, was a recent college graduate in his early twenties. He hoped to enter medical school after his stint in the Peace Corps. I had no doubt he'd be an effective Peace Corps Volunteer, and get the most out of his exposure to Liberian culture, since he had the personality for doing so. He was firm when necessary, but also informal and self-deprecating. As for

225

working in the leprosarium, he was a natural, having a perfect bedside manner, which I saw displayed throughout our tour of the colony.

My visit to Ganta had been delightful. I was heartened to see that idealistic, hard-working middle-class young Americans—also adventurous and not without senses of humor and irony—still joined the Peace Corps. I had taken immediately to Scott Lewis and Paul Steinwachs. They reminded me of myself and my Volunteer friends at their age. Paul said he was encouraged to meet someone my age "who was still enthusiastic and hadn't fallen into the kind of rut most people do, despite saying they won't." He also said that it was nice to hear someone like myself, who actually had some experience in life, espouse values in which he also believed. It is one thing, Paul said, to hold these beliefs at age twenty-two, when one has not really "lived much," quite another to espouse them at thirty-nine, when one has lived some. I thanked him for the compliments.

Scott Lewis, whose house was already temporary headquarters for the Volunteers Beverly and Nancy and home to his Liberian "play brothers," William and Mack, had every reason to be less than thrilled at the prospect of one more guest. But he was nothing if not the perfect host, even including his corny puns. I didn't have to wish Scott success on the job, for that was already his.

And where was fate going to lead me? I hoped into the lovely arms of Betty Leeleh. If that were to occur, it would take place in Monrovia, where in a few days we were scheduled to meet at the Holiday Inn. And so to Monrovia I next repaired.

MONROVIA

Betty Leeleh, whom I taught when she was a child. But in 1982 she was a woman and I wondered if—and hoped that—she would become more than a friend.

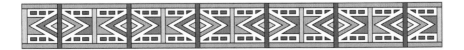

Chapter 31

I didn't recall an immigration checkpoint outside Ganta during my Peace Corps years, but there was one in 1982. When we—myself and those strangers with whom I shared the taxi en route to Monrovia—arrived at the immigration checkpoint upon leaving Ganta, a soldier, standing behind a long bamboo pole that traversed the road, directed the vehicle to pull over and us passengers to report to the officer in charge. We walked over to a small shed, in the shade from which a group of soldiers reposed. Several were slovenly and corpulent, looking as if they had just awakened, which I found to be typical of soldiers at immigration checkpoints: they often appeared to have just emerged from a midday snooze, unless they were playing cards. Whatever the soldiers were doing—or more to the point, not doing—a few young tribal girls, around seventeen, who never spoke, invariably hovered in the background; just as I observed their counterparts, always silent in my presence, in the background in most government offices.

The actual "checking" process varied. Sometimes the soldier in charge barely glanced up at the group of passengers before dismissing them; other times he asked the foreigners—usually citizens from nearby West African countries—to produce their papers. On this occasion, as on the other occasions when I arrived at the checkpoint, I was never asked to produce my visa or passport. My "golden passport" apparently was my white skin; granted that is unfair and undeserved, but it was the reality of such encounters at that time and place. In contrast, the Africans were asked to show their papers. While their documents were being checked, lower-ranking soldiers sniffed around the vans and taxis by now lined up. Half the time the soldiers, after a perfunctory look at the passengers and their cargo, let a vehicle pass without a *dash*. Not that day. They demanded 50¢ from our driver before they would let us proceed.

Scott Lewis, the Ganta Peace Corps Volunteer, told me the going rate for a Lebanese businessman wishing to pass through the checkpoint was a $5 *dash*, coming and going; and as much as $40 (equivalent to $100 in 2017) for the Lebanese businessman's truck ladened with goods from Monrovia. Scott told me of the time the soldiers hassled a Mandingo truck driver with whom Scott had hopped a ride. The Mandingo driver could not afford to pay a bribe. Scott finally said to the soldiers, "Hey, let the guy past. He's done nothing wrong." To which one of the soldiers replied, "Who are you, a member of the CIO?" He meant to say "CIA" but had gotten the initials wrong.

How disheartening that Liberians spoke with such familiarity of the CIA, as if every American abroad was or is employed by that organization. Admittedly in Liberia some were. The CIA station there in the 1960s, so the scuttlebutt went, was at one time the largest in Africa, serving, among its many functions, as a telecommunications monitoring facility from which the United States' government spied, electronically and in other ways, on the rest of Africa. (That Liberia's governments in the post-World War Two years allowed America such entry was part of the payback for all the aid given to Liberia, in those Cold War years by far the highest per capita of any country in Africa.) Even so, the number of CIA spooks in Liberia, compared to the total American population working there, was, I believe, minuscule.

This is a good place to point out that I was never approached before, during or after my Peace Corps service by a representative of any American or foreign intelligence agency; nor, as far as I know, was any other Volunteer. People often asked me when I had returned home from my almost two-year stint if we were surreptitiously gathering intelligence information about the country in which we served. No, no and no. And, while in Liberia, if any Peace Corps or American government official had discovered that we had gone to any intelligence service on our own, we'd have been terminated and sent home in days. Indeed, as my fellow Peace Corps Volunteer, Bill Fickling, recalled—and with which I concur—one couldn't belong to an intelligence agency five years before serving in the Peace Corps or five years after. Both he and I aren't sure if this was a law—or maybe Peace Corps myth—but it was something, we both agreed, we heard expressed many times among Peace Corps Volunteers during our Peace Corps service.

Communications from the outside world were, in those pre-Internet years, scant for the overwhelming number of people in most of the developing world. In my experience, far too many people in these countries believed (and probably still believe) the most outlandish tales and myths about the world beyond their village or town or country. And information printed in government-run or government-subsidized newspapers or broadcast over government-controlled airways was unreliable, if not fabricated. The news was somewhat more accurate, though not without problems, in non-government newspapers, of which Liberia has always had a tradition. As a result, the CIA—which meddled, in some instances, where it probably ought not to have—was blamed for just about everything negative in the world, especially in the underdeveloped countries: government scandals, intra-country power struggles, failures of five-year plans, assassinations and coups, whether successful or unsuccessful, real or imagined. There was an exception to this phenomenon: the countries of the Arab World, where if a toilet failed to flush, let alone a government plan faltered, first to be blamed was Israel and the Zionist Conspiracy—then the CIA.

◆　◆　◆

Besides my forthcoming rendezvous with Betty Leeleh, other business brought me to Monrovia. Having decided to pay for draw-bucket wells to be constructed in Kpaytuo, I wanted to speak to someone at the Nimba County Agricultural Development Project's Monrovia headquarters about possibly receiving some planning or building assistance from them. I also intended to speak to the people at the Chase Manhattan Bank about establishing an account in the name of the Kpaytuo Self-Help Association. And I still hoped to locate a member of the Cooper family, the wealthy Americo-Liberians who had owned the sawmill outside of Kpaytuo.

The driver of the taxi in which I rode to Monrovia from Ganta knew the location of Sammy Cooper's rubber farm outside of Kakata, and was nice enough to go fifteen minutes out of his (and the rest of the passengers') way so I might inquire about Cooper's whereabouts. As we approached the farm, a laborer told us the Old Man (as he referred to Cooper) was in America, but that his son, Ben, was in

Monrovia. Since I did not know the location of Cooper's home in Monrovia nor where his son, Ben, lived or worked, my next tack was to find Charles Cooper, Sammy Cooper's "outside child" with Galonpoo, Tado's niece. The boy, whom I did not know, attended Monrovia Central High School and I hoped he might lead me to his stepbrothers, Ben or John.

After dropping my bags at the Holiday Inn—my third stay at that hotel, where by this time everyone knew me—it was to Monrovia Central High School I headed. Arriving around noon, I met a vice principal, who was sitting on a chair in the courtyard looking at the sky. I introduced myself and told him why I wanted to speak to Charles Cooper. The man confirmed that Charles Cooper, son of the important Americo-Liberian Samuel B. Cooper, attended the school. And of course I was welcome to speak to him. Unfortunately, neither Charles nor any other student was at the school, for that very afternoon there was a faculty-student football game, which I was promptly invited to attend. I was reminded anew of the tradition of little, if any, school on Fridays in Liberia. The vice principal told me he would be leaving Liberia in a few weeks to attend school in the United States; in fact, he had already sent his wife and child ahead. As he would be departing midyear, I asked him what was going to happen to Central High in his absence. "They will manage," he replied.

I noticed a sign posted on a door at the school, dated April 25, 1980—thirteen days after the coup. Part of it read as follows:

"It is hereby decreed by the People's Redemption Council of the Armed Forces of Liberia:

1. That all political activities within the Republic of Liberia are hereby prohibited except in so far as shall be specifically allowed or directed by the People's Redemption Council.

2. That the penalty for violating this decree or any section thereof shall be death by Firing Squad."

And the Liberians referred to April 12, 1980, as Redemption Day.

I skipped the invitation to the football game and instead took a taxi over to the U.S. Agency for International Development (USAID) building and met with Curt Wolters, an economist in the delegation who spoke to me about the Liberian economy. Wolters told me that the price Liberians were paying for a hundred-pound bag of rice, $24, was an artificially low price set by the Liberian government. (In contrast, the price of a hundred-pound bag in the adjacent African countries of Sierra Leone, Guinea and the Ivory Coast was $30 to $35.) The Liberian government was extremely sensitive to the price of rice, the country's staple food, for were the price to rise to its market level, food riots would likely occur. It had been such an increase that had triggered the Rice Riots of April 1979. They, in turn, had triggered a series of events that led, almost a year to the day later, to the coup in which then-President Tolbert was murdered and which spelled the end of Americo-Liberian rule.

At the artificially low price of $24 a bag, the economist pointed out, it did not make sense for a Liberian farmer to grow rice for market, so he grew only enough to feed his family. And as Liberia's citizens abandoned the life of subsistence farming for a salaried job or unemployment, which ran at forty percent in Monrovia, the country had been producing less rice and importing more. The situation was aptly summed up by the then Education Minister, who was quoted in a newspaper article saying, "Liberia is producing what it doesn't eat and eating what it doesn't produce."

Liberia's food problem was too complex to attribute only to the subsidization of rice. The truth was the Liberian government lacked the technical expertise, the money, and the will to help the rural farmer become more productive. I had been told that just by using a better grain of upland rice, which, ironically, had been developed in Liberia, rice production could have risen twenty-five percent. But the rice grain had not been made available to the rural farmers.

If the Liberians had eaten more eggs, fruits and vegetables, they would have been healthier and wouldn't have had to spend scant resources importing rice. Their land was not really suited to growing rice, but to the cultivation of potatoes and other tubers; also mangoes, grapefruits, pineapples (Liberia's are every bit as succulent as Hawaii's) and bananas. At the time of my visit, few pineapples or bananas were cultivated on a large scale, as they were in the neighboring Ivory Coast, which exported pineapples.

But Liberians didn't grow or eat potatoes. As for fruits, when I asked Betty Gbon in Kpaytuo why she didn't eat grapefruit, she said, "It can make my blood thick." Another Liberian told me that eating pineapples gives you high blood pressure. Liberians didn't eat vegetables, except those few leafy green ones they made into the gravies—and those were boiled until the vitamins were long gone. Liberians ate, in tremendous quantities, rice—mounds of it topped with spicy gravies, mixed with tiny portions of chicken, meat or fish when those luxury items were available. They ate rice, hot or cold, day and night: meal after meal, month after month, year after year.

Since it was going to take many years for Liberians to change their diet to include more fruits and vegetables, visiting foreigners had been pressing for a while to at least increase rice production. Experts from the United States, Japan and Taiwan had labored, with little success, to convince Liberians of the advantages of growing wet (or, as it is called, swamp) rice, rather than dry (or upland) rice, the primary one being that swamp rice yielded much more rice per acre than dry rice. Also, growing swamp rice didn't further deplete the already fragile soil, in contrast to the slash-and-burn agricultural approach adopted by Liberian tribesmen.

But Liberians hadn't taken to swamp rice farming in large numbers because they didn't like mucking about in swamps. In a way, one couldn't blame them, since Liberian swamps harbor both the anopheles mosquito, which transmits malaria, and snail-borne flukes, which carry schistosomiasis, another debilitating disease.

An equally compelling reason, I think, for tribal persons' reluctance to take to swamp farming was that the rhythms of village life were calibrated to the cycle of the dry rice crop. Tribal Liberians' very reckoning of time was based on it, with the year commencing at rice-cutting time and ending when that period comes around again. The moon—at least among the Gio tribe—took its names from the cycles of the rice crop, there being the planting moon in April, the hungry-time moon in July, the harvest moon in October.

◆　◆　◆

This was the day Betty Leeleh and I had arranged to meet at the Holiday Inn. I remained around the hotel lobby through most of the evening, but to no avail. There may have been any one of a hundred reasons for her not coming—from losing the paper on which I had written the hotel's name and address, to a member of her family taking sick, to the taxi breaking down on the way to Monrovia. There was no way of contacting her in Ganta to find out what had happened. Maybe she would arrive the next day. I went to my room, read for a while, and turned off the light at what was for me, in Monrovia, the early hour of 11:00 P.M. Fifteen minutes later the phone rang.

"There is a woman down here, a Betty Leeleh."

"Tell her I'll be right down."

I went downstairs to get her. I don't recall whether she explained why she had arrived so late. No matter, was there ever a nicer expression than "Better late than never?"

When we entered the elevator for the trip up to my room, she was astonished and not a little frightened by the contraption, which must have seemed to her like a tiny room with an electric light and a metal door that was mysteriously going to transport us skyward. She had read about elevators, but until that moment had never been in one. As it clanged and banged up to the third floor, she clung to my side. Once inside the room, we sat on the bed and talked. Then she showered. I showed her how to operate the faucets—the force at which the water came out scared her. When she had finished, I again went into the bathroom to turn off the shower. Then, as she had not eaten in more than twelve hours, we went downstairs to the coffee house adjacent to the hotel lobby and she ate, at midnight, a plate of—what else—rice and meat.

Chapter 32

After Betty's late night meal we returned to my room, talked for thirty minutes and, it being around 1:00 A.M. and both of us tired, we went to sleep. Even though we were not lovers—indeed, had yet to even kiss—I felt completely at ease sharing the room, even a Queen bed, with Betty. I felt the same familiarity in the morning, as if we had spent hundreds of nights, not just one, together in the same bed. It is difficult to feel self-conscious about one's body and physical functions around Liberians, for they, bless them, never do.

Coming out of the bathroom after a shower, I found Betty making the bed. I told her she didn't have to, as someone was paid to make it and also to clean the room, which she thought strange, another bewildering practice of the white world. Once more she showered. Liberians are very clean and often bathed twice a day in the village. And once more I turned on and off the faucets for her, though in time of course she'd become accustomed to them.

We took the elevator downstairs, with her standing closer to me than she ordinarily would have, tensing slightly, and not quite certain that the marvelous *kwi* invention was going to work. Waiting for us in the lobby was Sammy, who had guessed, correctly, that I might be in Monrovia. I thought, probably incorrectly, that Betty might be embarrassed with Sammy, and thus in time all Kpaytuo, knowing we had been together in Monrovia. When was it finally going to register with me that Liberians were casual, to say the least, in regard to these matters?

The three of us went into the coffee shop, the same place where Betty had eaten her late-night meal, and we ordered breakfast—Betty and I eggs, Sammy rice. The woman behind the counter reported there were not enough eggs for the two orders, but if we didn't mind waiting, she would send the boy to the supermarket a few doors away.

I had spent a good deal of time in the restaurant. I knew that the owner, a Liberian, made little money, had no credit, and thus couldn't stock much inventory. But as so few tribal Liberians entered the retail trade, I admired his gumption and tried to give him some business. All the more reason I should not have, but did, berate the cook for the delay in our being fed. I complained about the service throughout the meal. I was miffed, more, truth be known, at Sammy unexpectedly showing up than at the restaurant being out of eggs. Call me selfish, but I wanted to be alone with Betty. No doubt my boorish behavior embarrassed Betty and Sammy. It was not one of my finer moments in Liberia.

Our breakfast over, we went to the post office so I could mail to America the carbon copies (from which people used to make copies of documents before the advent of photocopier machines, to say nothing of flash drives and the like, rendered them as obsolete as a buggy whip) of the journal I kept and letters I wrote during my return visit; this way if anything happened to the originals—if they were lost or destroyed or confiscated (fortunately they were not)—I'd still have the raw material from which to construct this book. I also recorded observations and experiences in a marbled black and white composition book, of the kind schoolchildren used in America when I was in elementary school in the 1950s; and carried a pocket notebook—and I'm not talking about a "notebook computer," but a lined three by four inch book with a spiral binding—in which I also made observations and noted the names or, in Monrovia, the phone numbers, of people whom I met in my travels.

Because of Liberia's year-round high humidity, the sealant on envelopes evaporated. The post office staff provided glue in jars from which, using a brush, one swabbed the glue onto the envelope to seal it. There was also a sign at the post office, imploring its customers not to wipe their sticky hands (from the glue) on the wall.

Walking down Tubman Boulevard after the trip to the post office, we three ran into Mary Pratt, an old friend from Kpaytuo living in Monrovia. Both Sammy and Betty referred to her as "Sister" Mary, an endearment since she wasn't the sister of either of them. Mary was bringing food (a dish called *foo-foo*) she had prepared for "Uncle" Joseph Young, another of Kpaytuo's more successful sons.

I remembered Joseph Young from my Peace Corps days in Kpaytuo, even though, a registered nurse in 1967, he had been living in Sanniquellie, the county headquarters. He'd come home to Kpaytuo

237

on holidays, always like most Liberians who have made it, a bit too os-
tentatious and boastful for my taste—and, also, again like many tribesmen who had made it, full of hot air. (Maybe these were some of the
attributes required of any tribal Liberian who "made it" in those years.)
"Uncle" Joseph, Mary told us, was at the home of a Mandingo woman
whom he was treating. Joseph was not a doctor, but what did that have
to do with anything?

We trekked to the Mandingo woman's home and in due time were
joined by Joseph—a small, well-fed, jolly man with a healthy milk-
chocolate complexion, in his early-to-mid-forties. Sammy and Betty
greeted him and treated him with the kind of respect his position and,
more important, his age, vis-a-vis theirs, entitled him to in their culture.
Then "Uncle" Joseph, "Sister" Mary, Sammy and Betty (I was invited
but declined) sat down at a table next to the Mandingo woman's house
and ate the foo-foo, a doughy, and to me, tasteless, dish made from cassava and served with a slimy, fishy, peppery gravy. The Liberians ate it
on those rare occasions they didn't eat rice. My friends, on this day, ate
it "country style"—each of them tearing off a piece from the doughy
cassava, rolling it into a ball, dipping the ball into the slimy sauce, and
popping it into his or her mouth.

Remembering my interest in the health of Kpaytuo's citizens, and
not a little jealous that a younger man, Sammy Wowah, had been the
first person to open a clinic in Kpaytuo (when all these years it had been
assumed that he would), Joseph told me that Samuel K. Doe himself,
the Head of State, had personally approved a government clinic to be
established in Kpaytuo. When, Joseph did not specify, meaning it could
be one month or ten years. Joseph claimed to have diagnosed and then
successfully treated Samuel K. Doe's sister for a uterine tumor, this long
before Doe became the most important person in Liberia. At that time,
Doe had been just another obscure, poor tribal soldier in the Liberian
Armed Forces. Come the coup, Samuel K. Doe, now Head of State,
visited his sister at Bong Mine, in whose hospital Joseph worked as a
nurse. Learning of the care, dedication and skill with which Joseph had
so effectively looked after his sister, Head of State Doe summoned
Joseph, inquiring what it was, above all else in the world, Joseph's heart
desired. According to Joseph, he pleaded for a government clinic in

Kpaytuo. The Head of State granted his request. Though it may have been true, I was skeptical of Joseph's story.

After our time with Joseph, Mary Pratt went home and Sammy, Betty and I were off to Diana's, my favorite Monrovia restaurant, where I ate and they had sodas. I advised Sammy that he ought to finish high school and then become a nurse. Lunch over, we walked around and I bought Betty her first watch, a Timex. Though I had hardly exerted myself, I was tired. I returned to the hotel to rest, Sammy returned to his army base and Betty, with some money I gave her, walked down to Waterside market, where she bought an inexpensive handbag and some inexpensive shoes.

Later that day, in our hotel room, Betty told me she had had trouble going to the bathroom. Her problem had been diagnosed as schistoso-miasis, a disease that afflicts "the poorest people of the poorest nations." Schistosomiasis, a debilitating malady, is spread when people infected with it defecate in the local streams and lakes. A parasitic worm, trans-mitted to humans by fresh-water snails, penetrates the skin of anyone who enters the polluted water and migrates to the veins surrounding the bladder, harming the kidneys, liver and bladder, and making urina-tion painful and often bloody. The disease's symptoms manifest them-selves during the early teens of the infected host, and so common was bloody urine in Liberia that it was considered to be a kind of male men-struation. Though rarely fatal, schistosomiasis took its toll on hundreds of millions in the developing world, ranking next to malaria as the most energy-sapping of tropical diseases.

I hoped Betty did not have schistosomiasis, for under the best of circumstances treatment was painful, expensive and not without side effects. Where and by whom, I asked, had she been diagnosed? At the Ganta Drug Store, she answered.

No one was going to confuse the Ganta Drug Store with the Lon-don Hospital for Tropical Diseases, so it was possible Betty was suffer-ing from any number of ailments, none of them especially desirable but all less serious than schistosomiasis. After assuring her I'd pay the bill, I made her promise to visit the Ganta Hospital, where she stood a better chance of receiving an accurate diagnosis and maybe, if the hospital had not run out of funds or medicine, the appropriate treatment.

Our time in Monrovia had to have seemed like a dream to Betty: all the hot running water her heart desired, without walking to a well to fetch; a big, firm bed with a mattress. (She had a bed in the room she rented in Ganta, but no mattress; and for most of her life had slept in a hut on a "bed" of hardened mud.) And she ate two, and often three meals each day, which she didn't have to cook; no dishes to wash, no water to gather, no wood to cut, no charcoal to buy. Compared to her simple, Spartan, impecunious existence—her Monrovia stay had to feel like Paradise. I enjoyed our time together, too, as did she, in addition to the amenities.

Of course I wanted to become intimate with Betty but that evening, when we returned to the hotel from a dreadful movie (*The Jaguar Lives*), she was very tired, and, much to my disappointment, we (or at any rate she) went to sleep soon after getting into bed.

Not wishing to disturb her, so, in time, did I.

Chapter 33

Thunder and a torrential tropical rain storm woke us at 6:00 A.M. We lay next to one another in silence as the day began to break. I found the scene of the two of us lying there naked, covered only by blankets, erotic. Betty lay on her side, with her back to me. I did not know what her reaction would be if I put my arm around her. Suppose she were offended? Suppose she said, "Look, Buster, I'm trying to sleep. Buzz off." Talk about an awkward scene. Surely if she had agreed to stay with me in a hotel she knew what was on my mind. Not necessarily, I argued with myself. She might have come down for the excitement of being in Monrovia, a city she visits, if she is lucky, once a year.

As I have told myself on so many occasions—and not only involving the courting of women—if I didn't try, I'd never know. As if by accident while turning in my sleep, I let my arm fall on her shoulder. Five minutes later, I began to caress her shoulder. In time, she responded, and one thing led to another.

It was pleasurable becoming intimate with Betty. Like most Liberian women in that time, Betty was quiet during lovemaking; also like the few I had been with, she squeezed rather than caressed. But I had no complaints, for I felt so much affection for her. During the past two days together whenever she'd made an observation it had produced a tender, tingling, warm feeling in the pit of my stomach.

Betty and I spent the next couple of hours lolling around in bed—laughing, talking, touching, teasing one another, and kissing—the last an activity circa 1982 foreign to many tribal Liberians and, as such, one they were not accomplished at; but Betty was willing to learn and, to paraphrase Chaucer, gladly would I teach.

She was fascinated with my hair, telling me that we whites are blessed to have naturally soft hair. She also enjoyed playing with the tuft of hair on my chest. And I asked her if Liberian men could kiss a woman's breast and she said not country men, but *kwi* [or modern] men, yes, they did. (Then, as I said to myself, let me be known as Mr. *Kwi*.) And she asked me why I couldn't come back to Liberia to marry her, a fair enough question to which I answered, truthfully, "Let's see what happens in the future."

As I wanted to hear her lovely, lilting accent and voice when I returned to America, unbeknownst to her, and long past our amorous moments and after we had been talking a while, I had slipped a blank tape into the tape recorder, which earlier had been serenading us with African music, and recorded our conversation. Having had trouble with her eyes, she was telling me that she had recently gotten glasses. A portion of that conversation follows:

"After I carry it [the glasses] home then the whole family say I shouldn't use it," she said. "Because when you are using glasses, it can be hard for you to see without it. It can make your condition worse."

"So this time you can't wear glasses?" I asked.

"Oh! I didn't wear it when I carried it. I'm still having it-oh. But I didn't wear it one day."

"But do you still have the condition?"

"No."

"Tell me again what the condition was?"

"Farsightedness."

"But what happened?"

"When the sun be shining, then I didn't used to see far. Sometimes then my tears can run."

"Only when the sun is shining?"

"Yes."

"What about in the rainy season?"

"Oh! I can see-oh. It is the sun that can affect me-oh."

"Sounds like sun blindness," I said.

"Oh! They have certain complaint like that? Eh! They call it sun blindness."

"Maybe," I said, smiling.

"Oh! That you giving that name to me? Or that the doctor?"

"That me," I said, both of us laughing at my silly joke.

"Easter vacation is Friday," I said.

"Yes," she answered. "This is what the principal says."

"So the vacation runs from April 2 until when?"

"Maybe until the tenth. Like that. Because Easter is only one week."

"So you get the next week off?"

"Yes."

"I hear. But you are not a Christian, so you shouldn't have Easter vacation."

She laughed. "You are talking about me in particular."

"Yes."

"But not the whole school?"

"Well, the people who aren't Christians."

"Oh!"

"If you're not a Christian, you should not have the vacation," I said with a mock seriousness.

"Of course. But this is how the Liberian government made the schedule."

Betty was on her stomach. I straddled her and began to give her a massage. I explained that in America people pay other people to give them a massage, something she found incomprehensible. I really con-fused her by saying that a man can go to a man for a mas-sage, a woman to a woman. But if the person wants to have sex, then they might go to a person of the opposite sex for a massage.

Whatever her thoughts on the subject, she told me she enjoyed what I was doing to her.

However, when I told her that I had been taping our conversation, she was miffed, even as I explained that I wanted to carry a record of our talking.

Betty Leeleh, lovely and radiant, in Monrovia.

243

"You call what I said important?"

Try as I might, she could not comprehend why in the world I would want a tape recording of our talking about "Sun blindness," "Easter Vacation," "Being a Christian," and "Massages." Of course she did not realize the joy I expected to derive each time I played the tape. For when I did, I would be transported back to Liberia, in that room with her.

◆　◆　◆

We got out of bed around ten o'clock, though I would have been content to lie there touching and talking and laughing all day. Possibly because of our conversation in which I teased her about not being a Christian (though I knew she considered herself one), Betty wanted to attend church. She even knew of one—The Faith Healing Temple, better known to most everyone in Monrovia as Mother Dukuly's Church.

The facility was not a church but in, by Monrovia standards, a well-preserved building in the small industrial section on Bushrod Island, which is across the People's Bridge from Monrovia. We arrived as the eleven o'clock service was about to begin. The congregation members were distinguished from visitors, like Betty and myself, by their dress: every man, woman and child was dressed in white—the men in white leisure suits or white sports jackets with white shoes and white socks; the younger women in white skirts, dresses or *lappas*, the elder in white gowns. Upon entering the church, women were expected to cover their heads, which they did with white scarves. In addition, the elders and trustees, all of them males, wore over their white jackets blue or burgundy collars.

About five hundred people were present, most looking lovely and angelic, their innocent and generally handsome black and brown faces offset against their white clothes. After we were in our seats—visitors, elders, trustees and members of the congregation—the service commenced with the entry of the choir: marching in from the back of the church, their right hands raised to God, dressed in white gowns with red collars, shoeless but with feet covered with white socks, they sang *Go Down Moses*. They were accompanied by a guitar, tambourine, piano and a drum. There followed more songs by the choir, readings by the congregation, announcements of church projects and classes. On two occasions the entire congregation rose, walked row by row, beginning from the front, down the aisle to the alter, gave a tithe, and returned to their seats.

Two hours after the service began (I was conscious of the time, as we hadn't eaten all day), we were graced with the appearance of the star of the event, Mother Dukuly herself. A light-skinned woman in her fifties, she was adorned in a white gown and draped with a scarlet robe. Perched on her head was a huge red mitre, like a bishop wears. She wielded a jeweled cross about a foot and a half long with a circular glass or gem at the intersection of the bars, and this she thrust at the assembled as she spoke, the light reflecting off it, probably scaring the wits out of more than a few of the people in attendance.

Mother Dukuly was spellbinding and she mesmerized her audience with a powerful, if to me fraudulent, sermon. Among the many subjects of her rambling, impassioned, one-hour harangue, she related the story of a woman who, under the influence of the Devil, planned to assassinate Mother Dukuly. As the woman reached under her blouse for the poisonous knife with which to perform the deed, the woman's hand, we were told, froze inside the blouse—paralyzed. The audience gasped. "And that night," Mother Dukuly said, "the evil woman who wanted to kill the good Mother Dukuly died by the wrath of the Lord."

During the more hair-raising parts of her sermon, members of the congregation popped out of their seats, jumped up and down throwing their hands to the sky in orgasmic spasms and exclaimed, "Praise Jesus, praise Jesus. I feel you, Jesus." No sooner had a congregant erupted into this frenzied state than a female or male attendant festooned with tiny red crosses would walk up and stand behind the by-now-gyrating believer, ready to take action lest he or she fall down and injure him or herself.

Two more times (making four in all) did we rise, proceed slowly and in an orderly fashion to the altar and back to our seats—the last time for Holy Communion, of which Betty, but not I, partook. (I was, incidentally, the only white person in the church, and was made to feel extremely welcome.) It was now 2:30 P.M., three and a half hours since the service had begun. I was exhausted from the heat in the non-air-conditioned church and from not having eaten, yet the climax of the service remained. For thirty minutes, with everyone standing, the better to clap, shout and rock, the parishioners, louder and more enthusiastically with each rendition, sang four lines over and over and over:

> "Just a closer walk with Thee,
> Grant it, Jesus is my plea,
> Daily walking close to Thee,
> Let it be, dear Lord, let it be."

To behold, even better to participate, in the moment, palpably feeling the warmth and piety of the congregation, enchanted by the rhythm and repetition of the four lines, was worth the heat, my growling, empty stomach, the preaching, and the four long hours.

The service over, we ate for the first time that day. And then—to use the Liberian vernacular—I carried Betty to the Nimba County Parking Station. Sharing a taxi with other passengers, Betty left for Ganta around 6:00 P.M.—though not before we arranged to meet again in Monrovia prior my departure to America, where some day I hoped she would come visit me.

Chapter 34

Sammy Dahngbae, my ex-houseboy, wanted to discuss his future, specifically what he would do when his army service was over. He also wanted me to meet his younger brother, Hastings. Sammy and Hastings had the "same Ma, same Pa," but different last names. Sammy and Hastings' father had two wives—his head wife and his second wife, who was Sammy and Hastings' mother. The daughter of the head wife married Old Man Tarpeh, who lived and worked on the Firestone plantation at Harbell. She wanted to educate Hastings, so she asked her people to send Hastings to her at the Firestone plantation. The Firestone schools rank among the best in the country; likewise the general living conditions there. Aware of the situation, Firestone officials limit attendance at the schools only to the children of their employees. To circumvent the regulation, children like Hastings take the last name of the person, usually a close relative, with whom they stay at Firestone: thus his name is Hastings Tarpeh rather than Hastings Dahngbae.

Hastings was in his mid-twenties, a couple of years younger than Sammy. A high school graduate, he worked in an office of a European logging company. He desperately wanted to attend the University of Liberia. It was that or probably remain a clerk for the rest of his life— that is, as long as his foreign employers were able to make a profit exporting logs from the Liberian forests to build homes in Europe.

Thousands of students took the entrance examination to the University of Liberia, the only university in the country. The applicants were not permitted to see their completed tests or their scores, according to Hastings. All they saw was a posted list announcing which students had been accepted. Hastings said that not a few students, the lucky ones with funds, bribed their way in.

Regarding Sammy's post-Army career, I suggested he consider nursing, but as Sammy and Hastings spoke, it became clear to me that

Sammy, though clever, was not much of a student (then again, neither was I). Short of coming to America, his first choice, Sammy thought he might want to operate a small retail shop in Monrovia. I could see him succeeding at that. In the practical matters of daily living he had a good head and got along well with people. He was the kind of person everyone likes immediately upon meeting. We all agreed he could not do anything while his obligation to the army remained—and that was three more years.

◆　◆　◆

I can't imagine anything conveying the bizarre nature, *at times*, of life in Liberia better than the following newspaper story, which ran in the *Daily Observer*.

> Moses Weeks, 33, a former chief of Security at the National Port Authority, Harper, who admitted last Friday that he poisoned and killed Alfred Dupley and Harold Fredericks, both of Harper, gave the police no reason for his move.
>
> Recounting the events that led to the confession, Major Benedict Williams, commander of Maryland County Police Detachment, said that Weeks was arrested on February 15 at his home, following widespread rumors about his alleged involvement in the murder case.
>
> During the investigation, Weeks reportedly told the police that he had been to the church of a spiritual prophetess, Mother Phebee Nyema at Gbasp, to find out who had poisoned his friends because he too had become ill after the party they had all attended.
>
> Meanwhile, two other friends of Weeks from the party were receiving treatment at Mother Phebee's Church. They are Paul Hammon and A.B. Thompson.
>
> In addition to this, Weeks said he also visited a witchdoctor called Plo at Gedetarbo, Cavalla Firestone, in his attempt to discover the cause of death of the two men.
>
> Plo said he told Weeks that he (Weeks) was the murderer of the two men and added that this was not Weeks' first nor fifth killing in Maryland County. Plo disclosed that the suspect possessed a bottle of poison, but Weeks denied all these.

It was after Plo's revelation that they decided to go to Mother Phebee's church to get a statement from the two sick men there as well as prayers, Major William said.

Major William said during the prayers, Weeks stood up and admitted putting poison into his friends' drinks. Weeks said during the night of the party last December, he had hid the poison dust in his nails and had sprinkled it into their drinks before serving them.

Another witch doctor, Lawrence Chea, 22, hearing about the search and murder case, offered his services to the police. Chea unearthed the bottle at the back of Weeks' house and explained that only those with "eyes" could have discovered its hiding place.

Moses Weeks then admitted that the bottle belonged to him. He said he had it since his school days but could not remember who had given it to him.

Having confessed, Moses Weeks then wrote out his will, dividing his possessions among his children and his girlfriend.

During a brief interview with the Daily Observer's Sando Moore, Weeks explained that the bottle of powder was actually a love potion which he blew into the air whenever he wanted a particular woman to fall under his spell.

He however added that the powder is extremely harmful if taken orally. He also said that since he possessed the powder he had only been successful in getting four women in the last 16 years.

Chapter 35

The phone rang and, as we had arranged the previous day, Ben Cooper was in the lobby of my hotel. We had met, quite by accident, in the Chase Manhattan Bank where I had gone to inquire about establishing a bank account for the people of Kpaytuo. Ben, whom I had not seen in 14 years, and I had agreed to meet for breakfast.

The Coopers were the Americo-Liberian family who owned the sawmill on the outskirts of Kpaytuo. I knew three of them—the father, Samuel B., a burly, handsome businessman then in his mid-forties; and his two sons, Ben and John, then in their early twenties; both reserved, well-mannered, and not without charm and senses of humor. The Coopers were members of the political and social caste that had ruled Liberia until their recent ouster. Members of the many branches of the Cooper family in general—and Sammy Cooper in particular—were well-known, well-off and well-connected.

When I was a Peace Corps Volunteer living alone in Kpaytuo, I was bewildered by the new culture during my first few months there. I even considered the possibility of transferring to another site where I wouldn't be alone. Initially I sought out the only people in the village with whom I shared a scintilla of common experience—the Coopers, educated and culturally much more "American" or "Western" than tribal Liberians. But though we were always pleasant to one another and never had cross words, I was never buddies with any of them: surely not with Sammy Cooper, who was closer to my father's age than mine. His sons Ben and John each alternated one-month stays in the village with their father, so I didn't have that many opportunities to see them, either. And once I began to feel at home with, and enjoy, the tribal people, the less time I spent with the Coopers.

The Coopers were the richest and most powerful Liberians in Kpaytuo—indeed, the only wealthy ones. They were treated like royalty by the villagers, who especially venerated—but also feared crossing—the Old Man, the sobriquet by which everyone, including his sons, referred to the formidable and impressive Sammy Copper.

These many years later—aided by my Peace Corps journal and letters to my family during those years—I can picture Sammy Cooper holding court in front of his stately house which was located on the outskirts of the village, at least fifty yards from the nearest hut. It was constructed of cement bricks with a slate roof, the only structure of its kind in Kpaytuo circa 1967.

Sammy Cooper rarely walked the hundred yards from his home to the town, preferring to let the "town" come to him. After a long, hard day at the sawmill, he sat many evenings in front of his home, relaxed and courtly, dressed in slacks and a bright, freshly laundered and immaculately ironed white undershirt—all the brighter against his rich, dark chocolate skin. His long-time cook, a tribal man named Robert, had prepared a sumptuous meal. Afterward, around 7:30 P.M., the "Lord" of Kpaytuo, holding court, summoned the town chief or elders to share a Liberian-brewed beer or Guinness stout while they discussed a tribal or sawmill problem. Or maybe they gossiped about village and Liberian matters, as he also liked to tease and banter with them.

Sammy Cooper's after-work hours were not all sawmill and village business. Usually one or two pretty young village girls, in the sixteen-to twenty-year-old range, accompanied by their mothers or grandmothers were in attendance. Always the gallant gentleman, Cooper offered Johnny Walker Red Label Scotch whiskey to the young girls' mothers and grandmothers, who were as likely, in their daily lives, to taste Johnny Walker Red as walk on the moon. And having his pick, Sammy Cooper bedded some of the prettiest girls in Kpaytuo, fathering children with at least two of them.

To his credit, Sammy Cooper supported—with his time, prestige, employees, and wood from his sawmill—my efforts to construct a desperately-needed new school building in Kpaytuo. Without his support—and additional money and material from CARE and USAID—the project would have never been completed years after my departure.

It was my impression that the Coopers avoided Liberian national politics, the vehicle through which most America-Liberians acquired wealth. Instead—again to their credit—the Coopers earned money by real and hard work—not by pushing papers and taking kickbacks and bribes or skimming money from the work of others. Only after President Tubman informed Sammy Cooper that he had no choice had he reluctantly accepted an appointment as Secretary of the Interior. Appointing their fellow America-Liberians to government posts was, incidentally, the technique employed by the America-Liberian establishment to pull potentially rebellious members into the fold. Let it be stated, however, that such rebels were few and far between.

◆　◆　◆

During my return visit in 1982 I had asked about and searched for the Coopers—without success until the day before when, serendipitously, I had run into Ben Cooper in the bank where I had gone to inquire about the steps to set up an account for the people of Kpaytuo.

I went down to the lobby to greet Ben. Physically he had changed remarkably little in the intervening fourteen years, except that there were flecks of gray in his hair and mustache. His figure was svelte, his face still round, the chin still weak.

He struck me as phlegmatic as he filled me in on his life since last we had seen each other. He had spent the late 1960s in New York, and had married a graduate of Mount Holyoke, an America-Liberian. He claimed to have been accepted to Columbia Law School in 1970, but the Old Man, as he referred to his father, could not afford to send him to law school, having eight other children, including his illegitimate brood, to support. Sammy Cooper told Benedict, as the Old Man always called him, to return to Liberia, manage the family logging business, and save his money. In three years, the Old Man said, Ben would have enough to pay for law school. So Ben and his wife returned to Liberia, beginning a family and becoming involved in the logging business. Imperceptibly, he said, he had lost his desire to attend law school and intended to remain in Liberia for the rest of his life. Then came the coup in April of 1980 and, fearing for their lives, the Coopers fled Liberia for New York City.

Most of the Cooper clan that I knew were still in New York—Ben's wife and children; his father and mother; his brother John and his Puerto Rican-born wife and family. No one actually knew (or, if so, was saying publicly) how many Americo-Liberians had fled Liberia after the coup. The estimates ranged from one- to two-thirds of the 25,000 to 35,000 Americo-Liberians. Most of them were among the relatively few skilled and educated Liberians. The country's new rulers, Samuel K. Doe and the People's Redemption Council, had repeatedly urged the Americo-Liberians to return, proffering amnesty to those in government and guaranteeing the safety and property of all. Obviously Ben had believed them, else he'd never have come back.

Ben said the family had over-expanded the sawmill in Kpaytuo during the 1970s and they had been forced to close it. By 1982 they owned a sawmill in the Liberian coastal city of Buchanan, at one time, he claimed, one of the largest in West Africa. Now, he said, the family was exploring the possibility of importing kitchen cabinets from America (manufactured by the Amish in my home state of Pennsylvania) to sell in England.

Lowering his voice and looking around the hotel's dining room before he spoke, Ben asked me the impression in America of what had happened in Liberia, hoping to derive from me the answer to the question that will haunt him and other Americo-Liberians for the rest of their days: how was it that the most entrenched ruling elite in Africa—indeed, also one of the most stable, successful and longest-serving oligarchies in the world—had been ousted by a handful of near-illiterate, tribal soldiers in hours?

I said that those Americans who knew anything about Liberia, not a very large group I daresay, were stupefied by the coup. More than that I did not know, I told Ben.

Glancing around again to make sure he was not overheard, he said in a barely audible voice: "There was something behind this coup. The actual mechanics were easy enough to explain—their bursting into the mansion and killing President Tolbert. But who motivated them? Who put the idea into their heads?"

I was tempted to tell him there was no "who," but there was a "what": that being the pent up rage that had been building for one hundred and thirty years over the misrule and mistreatment by his class of the tribal population. But I kept my peace. And soon thereafter—neither of us probably finding all the answers that we sought from our meeting—Ben and I had an amicable parting.

◆　◆　◆

The freed American slaves and free-born blacks—hence the name Americo-Liberians—who founded the Republic of Liberia in 1847 may have proclaimed their desire to help the oppressed children of Africa. But their actions spoke otherwise: they fought, conquered and then dominated the indigenous people in the nineteenth century, though this was hardly the first or last instance of an indigenous population subjugated by a stronger, outside force. (See the history of the human race for more examples.)

By the early decades of the twentieth century the Americo-Liberians forced the tribal people to work on their plantations and government work projects without remuneration. In the 1920s government soldiers abducted many tribal people in the middle of the night, shipping them, against their will, to the then-Spanish-owned island of Fernando Po (now Bioko) in the Gulf of Biafra to pick cocoa. Responding to rumors of these abuses, the League of Nations conducted an inquiry in 1930, eventually condemning the Liberian government for practices "hardly distinguishable from slave-raiding and slave-trading"—this in the country founded by and for former slaves; whose name comes from the Latin *liber*, meaning free; and whose national motto is *The Love of Liberty Brought Us Here*. In the aftermath of the League findings, Liberia's president and vice president resigned.

The Americo-Liberians didn't give the indigenous tribal people the right to vote until the middle of the twentieth century, even though they, the Americo-Liberians, numbered only 25,000 to 35,000 out of a population circa 1967 of about one and a quarter million. Granted, tribal people could vote by the 1960s, but so what when the only candidate on the ballot was chosen by, and represented the interest of, the Americo-Liberians, who owned sixty to seventy percent of the country's wealth? I can verify from firsthand observation that just about anyone in Kpaytuo could, and indeed did, vote in the presidential election of 1967, among them my cook, Kamah, then about fourteen: she voted *five* times. It was a festive day in the village, with no school but plenty of dancing and, for the men before or after voting and dancing, cane juice or palm wine. Each time Kamah dropped her ballot into the box she added to President Tubman's and Vice President Tolbert's landslide—theirs being the only names on the ballot. And magazines like *Time* and *Newsweek* and *The Economist* and other reputable international journals reported on Tubman's landslide victory, included in which were my fourteen-year-old cook's five votes.

By the late 1960s about fifteen to twenty Americo-Liberian families ruled Liberia, and through intermarriage perpetuated their reign. Nepotism ran riot. In 1968, members of President William Tubman's extended family held a stunning number of key political positions. Among his cousins were the ambassadors to Israel and the United Nations, the Chief Justice of the Liberian Supreme Court, and a representative from Maryland County. His wife's cousins also had plenty of clout. Among them were the Director General of the National Public Health Service, the Secretary of State and the Under Secretary of State. The President's wife's brother was Ambassador at Large. And demonstrating that among Liberia's ruling clique politics didn't make for strange bedfellows, in 1965 President Tubman's son, Shad Junior, married Vice President Tolbert's daughter, Roslyn. And, of course, President Tubman, after a reign of twenty-eight years, was succeeded upon his death in 1971, by Vice President Tolbert.

The relationship between the Americo-Liberians and the tribal people could be described, at best, as colonial in nature. At worst, especially in the years prior to the Second World War, it was akin to that between the white Afrikaners and the blacks in South Africa during the Apartheid era.

But, to keep matters in perspective without condoning them, even during the Americo-Liberians' long reign, the country was never a totalitarian state like Hitler's Germany or Stalin's Russia, or, today, Kim Jong-un's North Korea: by which I mean a government that tried or tries to control what its citizens see, hear and think. Liberians are too ornery, unruly and independent for that. No, Liberia was never

255

totalitarian, just a typical one-party authoritarian state.

And while President Tubman hardly rose—or more properly sank—to the butcheries of prodigious mass murderers like Stalin or Hitler, Tubman ruled absolutely for twenty-eight years and, whether it was banning opposition parties or having his way in smaller matters, his word was law. In the Tubman era (1944–71), one didn't criticize the government too vociferously, especially not President Tubman personally, for if you were vocal enough you'd end up in Liberia's notorious prison, Bella Yella.

It was even unwise to ignore a Presidential "request," as illustrated by an incident told to me by my friend and fellow Peace Corps Volunteer, Bill Fickling. When Bill and I lived in Liberia, the owners of a European-style café—the only one of its kind in Monrovia—were a married couple from Vienna, whose popular establishment carried their names, *Heinz & Maria*. Summoned to the Executive Mansion, Heinz was told by President Tubman that he had to cater a Presidential affair, to be held in a day or two. Heinz said that on such short notice, he didn't have the time and couldn't ignore his own thriving business. Then, so the story goes, he dared asked President Tubman, "Don't you have a kitchen staff, Mr. President, for such affairs?" Heinz soon thereafter was declared a *persona non grata* and was given 72 hours to leave the country. (Maria stayed for a month or so and then closed the shop and joined her husband in Europe.)

Bill Fickling was stationed near Monrovia and spent most weekends there—much more time than I ever did. He recalled the many occasions he observed Americo-Liberians bullying and berating waiters. Bill imitated their arrogant and haughty manner: "You boy, I still don't have water. You, boy, bring me the check." And there was an occasion when Bill found himself sharing a taxi in Monrovia with an Americo-Liberian. At the Americo-Liberian's destination, the man got out and walked away. The taxi driver, a tribal Liberian, said to the Americo-Liberian, "Sir, you forgot to pay." The Americo-Liberian stopped, turned around, looked at him disdainfully and sneered, "Pay? I don't pay." And walked away. No police officer would have dared given the taxi driver redress, of that you could be certain. It is not an exaggeration to say that the Americo-Liberians were above the law on matters large and small.

Maybe that's why circa 1967 Ben Cooper told me that he never bothered to obtain a Liberian driver's license, although he drove all over the country and in Monrovia regularly. What lowly-paid policeman was going to give Sammy Cooper's son a ticket?

And then it all ended in the wee hours of April 12, 1980, when tribal soldiers stormed the Executive Mansion, killing President Tolbert—and, in the days that followed, executed thirteen members of his cabinet, thereby terminating one hundred and thirty years of Americo-Liberian rule. That, Ben Cooper, was the "who" and the "what" behind the 1980 coup, which in reality was a Revolution; for it was no less thorough and transformative—for good or ill—in rooting out the Old Regime for the New than the more famous (and consequential) French or Russian Revolutions.

I give the final word on the Americo-Liberians to Sir Harry Hamilton Johnston, who in 1906 wrote presciently: "They [the Americo-Liberians] must turn their backs on America and their faces towards Africa, or they will dwindle to nothing, leave no heirs, and implant no permanent civilization on those whom they have come to redeem."

Chapter 36

As it was Good Friday, with most of the city closed down, I accepted an invitation to spend the afternoon at the beach with Dr. Steve Robinson, who had come to Liberia under the auspices of CARE to design a training program for village health workers; and his girlfriend, Janet, an English teacher at the American Cooperative School.

When United States government employees are assigned overseas, their primary concerns are how much they will earn, where they'll live, and where their children, if they have any, will attend school. They want their children, not surprisingly, to attend English-speaking schools, but they don't want them, particularly in Liberia, to attend, or go anywhere near, government schools. Wealthy citizens of Third World Countries feel the same way about *their* public schools, so *they* send their children abroad to be educated—with London, Paris and New York being the most popular choices. But United States Embassy personnel—whose number in 1982 might have included the Harvard-educated preppy in the political section to the good ol' boy from Oklahoma who operated the communications equipment to the divorced secretary from Sandusky, Ohio—rarely sent their young children abroad to be educated. Thus the existence of schools like the American Cooperative School, a private institution with grades one through twelve. (Not all of Liberia's wealthy elite sent their children abroad, for many of them enrolled them in the American Cooperative School, where they mingled with the children of the diplomatic corps posted to Liberia and the children of the above-named United States Embassy personnel.)

Dr. Robinson and I got to talking about health, a subject very much on one's mind in the tropics. He observed that "there are three kinds of country medicine—the kind that helps; the kind that doesn't cause harm; and the kind that is harmful." In the category of the kind that helps, he said, he would put cures for snakebites, and the extract from papaya, which kills some hookworm. "Liberians are great with bones," he said. "I believe they have special techniques to increase the healing of bones. I've heard story after story of people walking just two weeks after breaking bones in their leg or foot."

◆　　◆　　◆

Excusing myself, I strolled along the beach. It was deserted, save for a few Liberian children, who from their sun-bleached hair and copper-colored skin looked as if they lived on it year-round.

I followed the various bends in the beach, long since out of sight of Dr. Robinson and Janet. Coming around one bend, I saw in the distance a group of about thirty people, all of them dressed in white, except one: he (or was it a she?) was dressed in purple. I've always wanted to see a mirage and thought, for a moment, my wish had been granted. But as I drew closer, I discerned the particulars of the scene: the people in white were women—elderly, mostly hefty, black Africans wearing white dresses with white scarves. There were a few men among the group, also dressed in white. The person in purple was, I assumed, their leader.

"Welcome," he said. "I am Bishop Sunday M. T. Saydee, founder of the New Jerusalem Faith Healing Church." He and his followers, he said, had come to the beach as part of their celebration of Good Friday. I assume to show me the power he had over his acolytes, Bishop Saydee turned to them and shouted: "Kneel for Jesus," which his followers promptly did. "Clap for Jesus," he commanded, which they also did. "Laugh for Jesus," and laughed they did. "You with problems, go down to the water." The group arose from their knees, and walked towards the ocean.

Radiating warmth and good cheer, if not piety, Bishop Saydee turned to me and, waving his hand towards the ocean, said, "This is our River Jordan." Then he shouted to his flock, who were standing with their backs to us, about thirty yards away: "Raise up your hands to Jesus! Raise up your hands to Jesus!" And the group raised their hands.

"Jesus, lose your people! Jesus, lose your people! I rebuke the stumbling blocks before you—you who can't born child, you who can't find man, you who have job palaver! Jesus, New Jerusalem has come!"

Bishop Saydee then commanded the group to walk back to him, where they formed a semicircle around him. He was holding a palm frond in his hand. One by one, stepping forward and kneeling before him, his followers recounted their dreams, which Bishop Saydee interpreted. It was at this point I left them on the beach—with the rocks, the sand, the sun, the glare and the ocean.

Experiencing Bishop Saydee was almost as good as seeing a mirage.

Chapter 37

I had diarrhea, but then, according to the lead story in the *Daily Observer*—"Diarrhea Epidemic Hits Monrovia"—so did a good deal of the population of Monrovia.

I spent part of that day with my ex-houseboy, Sammy, and my ex-cook, Kamah, the only time during my return visit the three of us were together. Sammy was on night duty at the Camp Schieffelin clinic that week, so he was able to come into Monrovia during the day. Kamah asked for the day off, telling her employer—she called him her "boss man"—that since my time in Liberia was short she wanted to spend an afternoon with me.

I took them to Diana's, my favorite Monrovia restaurant, for lunch, during which Sammy advised me to marry: "Suppose you die, teacher? Who will bury you?" he asked.

I asked Sammy what he looked for in a woman and he said: "Her ways must be good. She must give respect to my people. She must not give my children bad things to eat."

"Does she have to be beautiful?" I asked.

"No," he said. "That one not so special. Suppose you are nice looking but you don't have good ways, then no one will like to speak to you." He asked me if I saw anything wrong in whites and blacks being together.

"No," I answered.

"Then why can't you take a Liberian wife?"

"Maybe I will," I responded.

Sammy wanted to give me his son to raise, an offer repeated, in due course, by Kamah. And both of them wanted to work for me again, either in Liberia or, even better, in the United States. I said maybe someday they could visit me in the United States; but as I was single, it would be difficult to raise and adequately care for their children.

The author with Sammy Dahngbae, my ex-houseboy, and Kamah Fendahn, my ex-cook, in Monrovia, April 1982—the only time during my return visit that the three of us would spend together.

I drank mineral water with my hamburger, Kamah an orange soda with hers, and Sammy a cherry-flavored soft drink with his. He drank it, he told me, because he believed the red soft drink was good for his blood. He also said that drinking beer gives you malaria. I smiled. I could see that he had learned a good deal about medicine from his experiences at the Camp Schieffelin clinic.

Even though he knew his three-year-old son was not ready for school, Sammy told us that nevertheless he had tried to enroll him in one. The person administering the admittance test printed the letters A, B, C, and D on a piece of paper and asked Sammy's son what he had written. "Blue ink," the child answered. Sammy obviously enjoyed telling the anecdote as much as I had enjoyed hearing it.

"You may please not to forget about looking for my late father's picture," Sammy reminded me at one point.

Sammy hoped that among the more than two thousand photographs I had taken during my Peace Corps years in Kpaytuo, one might be of his father. I was fairly certain, to Sammy's ill luck, none was. I remembered the circumstances of almost taking a picture of Sammy's father, but soon afterwards thanked my stars I had not. I was on my way back to Kpaytuo one afternoon from a long hike in the bush when I passed through the Old Man's farm. I stopped and snapped some pictures. I wanted one of Sammy's father, but the Old Man, like most of the older people in Kpaytuo in those days, would have nothing to do with a camera: he thought it was medicine, bad medicine at that. So I never got to take his picture that day. One week later the Old Man died, rather suddenly. Had I taken his picture, I might very well have been accused of witching him. But I didn't say any of this to Sammy during our lunch at the restaurant; I just promised to look through my photographs.

After lunch I told Kamah I wanted to buy her a present. Having already given Sammy money and a gift since my return, there was no reason for him to feel slighted. I bought Kamah a pair of jeans, a T-shirt, and her first wrist watch. She instructed the salesman to leave the price tag on the watch, explaining to me that she wanted her people to see what I had done for her. She was almost speechless at her good fortune.

I was amazed to see girdles for sale in the shop. I couldn't imagine any apparel more uncomfortable in Liberia's climate. But Sammy said many women wore them. "They can have too much flesh, so they buy it." He also said that Kamah would be "zoot" that night and that her husband would go crazy when he saw her in her new clothes.

Our few hours together reminded me of those wonderful days and nights in Kpaytuo years before. Kamah was still shy, Sammy still teased yet protected her, and he amused us all with his stories. Our chemistry was as potent as ever, and I still enjoyed them both. Years before I had hoped Sammy would attend trade school and become an electrician. I'd even sent him the tuition, but he had failed to attend. And I was disappointed and angry. Upon my return to Liberia I wanted to find him happily married and prosperous, conveniently forgetting that few people, in or out of Liberia, are. I cared too much about Sammy to re-main angry at him. Maybe someday, I thought, I could help him open a shop in Liberia.

Near the end of my time with Sammy and Kamah, we ran into Sam Massaquai, an assistant to the Minister of Rural Development. Paul Tuazama and I had met with him and the Minister of Rural Develop-ment weeks before to discuss the Kpaytuo well project. Massaquai said Mike Greenfield, of the Nimba County Agricultural Development Project (NCADP), was in Monrovia. And so it was to Mike Greenfield's office at the NCADP I headed. He told me there were plans to include Kpaytuo in the next phase of the NCADP's well and latrine project. I was, of course, pleased but concerned about the time frame for com-pleting the project—the estimates ranged from two to three years—and the pre-condition, that a village build latrines *en masse* before the wells would be dug.

Projects like this sound impressive, but they have a way of never coming to pass in Liberia. If the project did begin, who was to say the NCADP, funded mainly by the West German government, would not lose patience with the Liberians and junk it outright? I had the money to build wells in Kpaytuo now, as I told Mike Greenfield. Why wait two or three years for a NCADP project that, if he would forgive my frankness, might never commence; or once begun, might never reach completion? Mike saw my point. And I saw his. He couldn't speed up the project's timetable to accommodate my wishes. He agreed to help me out without violating the NCADP procedures. If Kpaytuo could find someone to dig the wells—which should not be too difficult—he would allow its citizens to buy concrete culverts from the NCADP to line the wells. It sounded like a good idea to me and I left on that note.

Some time before my return trip to Liberia, I had seen a marvelous Masterpiece Theatre presentation on Public Television entitled *A Town Like Alice*, in which a beautiful Englishwoman, befriended by a group of Malayan villagers during the Japanese occupation of Singapore, re-turned to the village after the Second World War. To show her grati-tude to the villagers, she offered to build them a well and a community center.

On television everything progressed smoothly. There was no talk about what kind of well to construct, where to buy the materials necessary, and who might embezzle the money; no need to receive approval from the government, no mention even of the possibility let alone the likelihood that the truck that was going to bring the materials to build the well would be inoperable or be used to move someone's household; that the driver of the truck, instead of reporting for work, would be miles away, visiting one of his girlfriends; no hint that even if the driver were present and the materials arrived, the gasoline to propel the truck might have been sold illegally; that in the unlikely situation the driver reported for work, the materials arrived, the truck was operable and full of gas, then the road would be impassable from heavy rainfall; and no mention, not even a hint, that the community in which the well was to be dug would argue incessantly over its location and who would be responsible for helping to dig and maintain it. There was no reference to any of these matters—just a vote by the village elders whether they wanted the well. In no time we viewers saw fresh water gushing forth from the new well, leaving the impression the project had been completed, from beginning to end, in about one week, maybe two.

Pity that life isn't like a television show, even Public Television.

Chapter 38

I walked to Waterside, site of Monrovia's large open market and the hub of Lebanese- and Indian-owned stores. I intended to buy some cassettes of African music and to take some pictures. After buying a couple of cassettes, I headed back up the hill, stopping at one corner to photograph that most ubiquitous of Liberian scenes—someone sitting on a stool next to a wooden table on which many items for sale are displayed. It turned out the owner of the stand preferred not to be photographed, but a boy, whose precise relationship to the man I couldn't identify, agreed to. Lest the owner of the stand feel exploited, I bought some candy, that being the main item for sale. As I was focusing the camera, a passer-by asked me, in none-too-friendly terms, how much I was paying for the picture. I said to him that unless he was the boy's father, it was none of his business. He said, to no one in particular, that I intended to carry the boy's picture to America to make fun of the boy.

"That is not so," I said. "May God kill me this minute if I intend to use the picture to make fun of the boy."

This wasn't the first time I had heard this sentiment expressed. Many Liberians were unable to conceive that anyone could want nothing more than a visual record of their country, much of which I think is exotic and beautiful. For this reason I preferred to take my photographs up-country, where people are not so suspicious. Best of all I preferred to take them in Kpaytuo, where I had willing, make that eager, subjects, especially the children, who literally begged me, day and night, to photograph them. And as I think Liberians are among the most handsome people in the world, certainly among the most photogenic, it is a photographer's paradise.

Continuing my walk back up the hill, I heard someone say to me, "Take my picture." I turned to see a smiling boy and girl sitting on a ledge, with their market stall of cigarettes, biscuits and packs of Juicy Fruit gum before them. As requested, I took a number of pictures of

A boy and girl at Monrovia's Waterside market, the taking of whose photograph had for me unexpected consequences.

the two, who were both about fifteen. Before, during and after my taking their pictures, we bantered. "Carry me to America," the boy, the more brazen of the two, pleaded.

While the boy and I were talking and joking, a man walked up to me and told me to follow him. I asked why I should do so? He said he had been observing me taking pictures for the past three hours.

That was strange indeed, for at most I had been on the street taking pictures for perhaps an hour. And besides, I thought to myself, what if I had been taking pictures for three hours? What business was it of this guy?

By this time the man, who was dressed smartly in civilian clothes, had walked on, so he was about ten yards ahead of me. Once again, he firmly instructed me to follow him. "I am not going any place," I said, "as I am not through speaking to the children."

He walked back to me. "By whose authority are you taking pictures?"

"On no one's authority," I answered.

"Are you a journalist?"

"Yes." What was apparently beyond his understanding was that one did not have to be a journalist to take photographs in Liberia.

The man reached into his back pocket, opened his wallet and flashed a badge. Liberians, alas, had seen too many American police and spy movies and, for those Liberians in Monrovia with access to television, too many episodes of the then-popular shows from the 1970s, *Kojak, Starsky & Hutch* and the like. They were particularly enamored of removing their wallets from their pockets and flashing their badges. Since after the coup it seemed that every fifth Monrovia resident possessed a badge of one kind or another, people were forever flashing them.

Another man in civilian clothes, who also showed me his badge, joined our conversation. Then two National Police officers and two Liberian soldiers, all of them in uniform, came over. That made six of them, one of me. The four newcomers must have reasoned that I had done something wrong, else why were two undercover policemen questioning me?

The senior of the National Police officers asked the plainclothesman who had instigated the charade by asking me on whose authority I was taking the boy and girl's photograph, what the problem was. The plainclothesman said he was trying to determine if I had asked, and received, the children's permission to photograph them. He lied. He had asked them no such thing. The young boy who—it should not be forgotten—asked me to take his picture had fled at the first appearance of trouble. He must have seen or experienced first-hand the ways of Liberia's law enforcement personnel, so who can blame him for skedaddling out of there? The girl, visibly frightened of the police, the detectives and the soldiers, murmured that I had, indeed, asked her and the boy if I could take their pictures and that they had agreed.

By now, fifteen minutes into this farce, I raised my voice and pointed out that I had committed no crime, I had disturbed no one, I had been taking pictures in the middle of the afternoon, with the permission of my subjects, I was a returned Peace Corps Volunteer, and I was leaving their country soon. And that having been interfered with for no account, I wished now to go about my business.

"Do you have any identification?" one of them asked me.

"No, I do not have my identification," I answered. "It is back in my hotel room, where I was heading before this man stopped me," I said, pointing to the undercover policeman. (This was decades before 9/11 and the proliferation of world-wide Islamic terrorism; it was a very different world than the one in which I write these words, a world where I do not walk about without identification, especially when traveling.)

"You mean to tell us you do not have any identification on your person?" one of them uttered in disbelief.

"Correct. It is not the habit of police in my country to ask citizens, who are minding their business, to produce identification. And since I only left the hotel room to buy some cassettes and take some pictures, I saw no need to take along my wallet."

They were flabbergasted. In modern Liberia, salaried employees carried with them at all times an identity card, in hopes of warding off the irrationality and rascality of the law enforcement system, and also as a means of displaying one's status, such as it was, in the new social pecking order.

I suggested to my interrogators that if they wanted to see my identification they were welcome to follow me back to my hotel, only a ten-minute walk away. There I would produce my documents.

"My job is to protect the country from invasion," the undercover detective who had started the incident said. "How do I know you are not planning to sabotage the country?"

"By taking a photograph of a boy and girl selling chewing gum?" I asked.

More undercover agents and policemen had arrived on the scene. There must have been at least fifteen of them. And at least fifty spectators. Sensing that I was not going to come forth with a *dash* or quietly go anyplace except to my hotel, the plainclothesman who'd started the mess found a way to extricate himself. His way out was in the person of a bumbling and obviously drunk National Policeman, to whom he turned over the "case." And then he went on his way.

The National Policeman "in charge" told me there was a problem in his accompanying me to my hotel. He did not know whether National Police were permitted to do that. Perhaps, he mused out loud, it would be better if he carried me to the police headquarters, where they could try to straighten out the situation.

As soon as I heard that suggestion, I said that I'd be damned before they were going to take me to their police headquarters. I had done nothing wrong; if they carried me to their headquarters, I said, I was going to make a helluva palaver for them all. Before I was finished, I vowed, the palaver was going to reach the American ambassador and Samuel K. Doe himself and they were going to regret humbugging me so. By now another undercover agent had joined the parade. He suggested that we could resolve the matter by going to my hotel and letting me produce identification. I could have sworn I'd made that suggestion thirty minutes earlier.

The drunken National Policeman asked by what authority he made such a suggestion. To which the man responded, "I'm a member of the NSA [National Security Agency]." This prompted the drunken National Policeman to ask the undercover agent to produce identification supporting his claim. The undercover agent refused to do so, referring to the walkie-talkie in his hand as all the identification he needed. There were no fewer than twenty officials gathered around me and they began to argue among themselves over who had jurisdiction over me and, once that was determined, what to do with me.

While they were arguing, I announced that I was going to my hotel and that they could follow me if they wished. I then marched off. My interrogators, all twenty of them, followed about a half block behind. And about fifty spectators, who were having almost as much fun as at a soccer match.

At the hotel, I went to my room, returning in a few minutes with my passport, a press card signed by the police chief of Philadelphia (which official insignia and imprimatur I knew would impress them), and a faculty card with my photographs on it from Temple University where a few years before at night, after work at my fulltime newspaper job, I had taught a journalism course. I threw the documents onto the counter of the hotel.

Sammy, my ex-houseboy, who coincidentally had been waiting for me in the hotel, told the soldiers and police officers they should be ashamed. He told them I was a good friend of Major Paul Tuazama (my ex-student). He told them this was no way to treat a visitor to their country, especially someone who used to live there and had returned, on his own, to help the people in the interior. Though I know that was asking for small miracles, I hoped Sammy's reprimand might jar these guys into feeling a tinge of remorse.

Then, to my delight, the Mandingo manager of the hotel began to berate them for harassing me. "This is why no white people want to come to this country!" he shouted at them. "Because of the way you can humbug this man!"

I told my interrogators I was going to the United States Embassy, hoping that would give them cause to reflect. And to the embassy I went, though not to report the incident. I went to cool off—literally and figuratively—by taking a swim, which in those more innocent pre-9/11 years was an option available to any American citizen in Monrovia, as strange as it might read today.

Chapter 39

In the afternoon of that next day I went to the Peace Corps office, where the nurse informed me that an examination of my stools had revealed I had giardiasis, an annoying though not serious illness caused by the parasite giardia. The symptoms were stomach cramps, indigestion, belching and diarrhea, all of which I had been experiencing the past few days. She said I got it because someone had not washed his hands properly or at all before cooking my food or handling my dishes. I might have picked up the parasite in any one of fifty situations. At first I thought I got it the day in Kpaytuo when I ate a meal prepared by Arthur Wonyou's girlfriend and soon thereafter found myself vomiting and suffering from diarrhea for most of the night. But that incident occurred almost 4 weeks prior, and since I hadn't had the most obvious symptoms (diarrhea) the previous weeks, save for that one night in the village—maybe I hadn't picked up the parasite in Kpaytuo, but rather since coming to Monrovia. In any case, the nurse provided an antibiotic that I was to take every day for a week, at the end of which time I should be cured. And it would be necessary to have my stool checked in the United States to be sure.

The parasite explained my excessive lethargy and irritability of late, particularly the past week. Add to that a cold that had lodged further in my chest, and it was no wonder I had been increasingly peevish toward everyone and everything. Some Westerners can live in the tropics for years without taking a pill, never the victims of serious illness. I am not one of them. Were I to live in Liberia, I have no doubt I'd be dead within two years, certainly five.

◆　◆　◆

My two-month trip almost over, and tired of living out of a suitcase and missing my home, family and friends, there remained only the matter of visiting Kpaytuo once more. There I'd report on the final arrangements for the wells and say my goodbyes. To some, though I could not know it at the time, it would be "goodbye" forever.

KPAYTUO

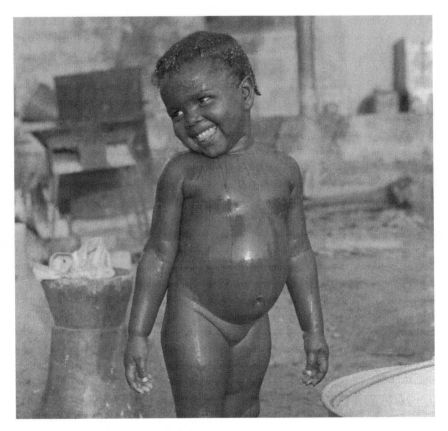

A child after her bucket bath, 1982.

Chapter 40

En route to Kpaytuo, I stopped at Ganta for the night, intending to say goodbye to the Volunteers whom I had met and stayed with there, particularly Scott Lewis. I arrived at 7:00 P.M., just in time for dinner at Scott's. Unfortunately, he and Bev Silver, another Volunteer whom I had met when I stayed with Scott, had gone to Monrovia. I ended up eating at Scott's with three other people: Nancy Keeler, the Volunteer from Kansas who was staying with Scott until she found her own place; a friend of hers, also named Nancy, who taught Liberian teachers how to teach reading (she said she really ought to be teaching them how to read); and Steve Katz, whom I'd last seen the night he'd cut himself opening a coconut. I was enjoying the spaghetti with tomato sauce until one of the Nancys told me that the "meat" in the sauce was snails. No thanks, I said, I wouldn't eat snails in Liberia no matter how long they were cooked: the bloody things in Liberia give people schistosomiasis.

Nancy, the reading specialist from Boston, asked me how Liberia compared to my earlier, much longer stay in the country. I told her that it had changed very little, much as I wished I had concluded otherwise. The same inefficiency, the same lack of planning, the same dependence on foreigners, especially we Americans; the same greediness, the same incessant palavers, the same corruption; and, of course, the same good things were also present in abundance—the friendliness, the beauty, the color, the excitement.

Nancy, the reading specialist, said contemptuously, "Liberians don't want to work for change. They just want to become like America without putting in two hundred years of hard work."

I said I disagreed that *all* Liberians were unwilling to work hard. I cited a day in the life in Kpaytuo of Tado and Mary Jackson, both of whom worked like beasts of burden from about six in the morning to six or later at night. And Tado, a tribal person who admired Western religion and culture, hardly felt and acted the way Nancy described.

Then Nancy Keeler, the Nancy from Kansas, who seemed to possess the tenacity and flexibility to make a success of her tenure in Liberia, described a meeting of the staff at her school. There was $500 in the school treasury; a meeting was called to discuss how to spend the money. The school, Nancy pointed out to us, had no books, no desks, no chalk, no supplies—in other words, a typical up-country school. Nancy, sent to Liberia to teach modern farming techniques, favored spending $100 to buy a hoe and other basic farming equipment the school lacked. With that exasperated tone I had heard myself employ on many occasions, she told us the faculty had voted to spend the entire $500 on football (soccer) uniforms for the boys and girls.

Hardly the first Peace Corps Volunteer or Westerner to be bewildered at and annoyed by the Liberians' behavior, Nancy and the others awaited my response—me, the wise, experienced, old (at thirty-nine about fifteen years their senior) Peace Corps veteran. "This is the way of their culture," I said. "It isn't a question of right or wrong—it is the way they are."

Though I didn't quote him at the time, the noted anthropologist George Schwab recognized this Liberian trait when he wrote in 1928, "They [the Liberians] cannot resist attractive trifles. They will spend days cracking palm nuts and taking out the kernels, walk forty miles to the market carrying sixty to sixty-five pound loads, and buy with the proceeds perfume or perfumed Vaseline and other non-essentials when they need salt and cloth."

I told them that when I was a Volunteer the way I dealt with the frustrations of Liberia—I hasten to add not always successfully—was to focus on what I enjoyed about it—village life, tribal lore, reading, sports, dancing, traveling through the game parks of Kenya on my three-week vacation, visiting other Volunteers, the satisfaction of teaching, learning to type and my relationships with the country people.

Steve Katz was an intense, handsome young man from New York. I wondered whether he possessed the temperament to laugh at life's absurdities so crucial to a Peace Corps Volunteer surviving in Liberia. (For his sake I hoped he had, else his time in Liberia would be unpleasant and unfulfilling.) Steve told us he questioned whether the Peace

Corps was doing any good in Liberia, for it seemed to him we only perpetuated the process by which the Liberians did nothing for themselves.

I said that I thought, on balance, we Volunteers had done well. We had performed no miracles, but then that is best left to God—not young Americans. We had educated thousands of Liberians. Many of these people, for good or ill—and I said I thought for good—were now, or would be soon, in important positions in the country. We had also helped build schools, wells, latrines, science labs, chicken houses, and fish farms. (And some of us—here I was referring to myself—leveled the dirt ground for a basketball court, cut down a palm tree for the "pole," and commissioned the village carpenter to build a mahogany backboard, possibly the only such backboard ever constructed, for most people don't use expensive wood like mahogany to build basketball backboards.)

We Volunteers had also instructed Liberians in health and family care, and in preserving their wildlife and forests. We had also conveyed to some tribal Liberians, however small their number, the American belief in the efficacy of change and of challenging assumptions and, where appropriate, authority. Being conservative, tribal culture not only discouraged individuals from questioning, it often made it dangerous to challenge the status quo.

Lastly, I pointed out, by watching and listening to us young Americans and, for some, living with us, Liberians learned to speak up for their rights and to examine the status quo. So we Peace Corps Volunteers fomented change. We were revolutionaries, though few of us saw ourselves that way.

Chapter 41

After stopping in Saclepea to say goodbye to the Carsons, the missionaries I'd met early in my trip and for whom I had developed esteem and affection, I was back in Kpaytuo. Tado and I were talking on the patio after dinner when we heard singing coming from the far quarter of the town. When a visitor came to the house, he told us the merriment we had heard was the homecoming celebration for Sammy Wowah.

Proud (though envious) of a fellow village dweller who had "made it," Kpaytuo's citizens had been telling me about Sammy Wowah since my return. Though he had lived in Kpaytuo during my Peace Corps years, he was then a young child, so I never got to know him in the way I did the older boys and girls.

He had been educated by the "Swedish people," by which the Liberians meant his employers at LAMCO, the giant Liberian-Swedish-American consortium that mined Liberia's rich iron ore from the Nimba Mountains. Sammy had worked in the LAMCO Hospital near Yekepa. Impressed with his work at the hospital, his employers had rewarded Sammy Wowah with a one-year scholarship to continue his studies in Sweden. Then it was back to Liberia, where he took a job in Monrovia as an X-ray technician at the John F. Kennedy Hospital, the largest—and the best, though the term is relative—hospital in the country.

Realizing a long-time dream, Sammy Wowah had recently opened a private clinic in Kpaytuo—the one situated in the home of the wealthy Americo-Liberian, Sammy Cooper, and through which, in my first days back in Kpaytuo, my ex-student Arthur Wonyou had taken me on a tour. Since Arthur lived in Kpaytuo (while Sammy Wowah lived and worked in Monrovia), Arthur was responsible for the day-to-day operation of the clinic, but Sammy owned it. It was he who had the money and the contacts to buy medicine in Monrovia, neither of which Arthur had.

Soon after my arrival back in Kpaytuo, Sammy Wowah left for Monrovia in a taxi. He had noticed a back tire wobbling, and warned the driver, but the man ignored Sammy's warnings and merrily sped along until the tire flew off. The car rolled over and Sammy lost nine teeth and required sixty-five stitches to close the wounds in his head and mouth. After six weeks in the hospital, he was back in Kpaytuo to show his people he was mending. Thus, the celebration we had heard emanating from the far quarter of the village.

Tado and I went to Sammy Wowah's parents' home to wish him well, there meeting scores of people, most of them his relatives, dancing in one small, hot room. Sammy was in a back room of the unfurnished house, where we conveyed our pleasure to him that he was safe and back in the village.

"Sammy," Tado said, "our people might try to discourage you over this accident business from accomplishing what you have set out to do. Don't let them discourage you." Sammy, whose jaw was wired, mumbled appreciation for our visit and for Tado's pep talk.

I thought I understood what Tado was referring to, but to be certain, I asked him on our walk back to his house. He told me that when Sammy had conceived the idea of opening a private clinic, some people had opposed it. Maybe now, Tado suggested, people would say that those opposed to opening the clinic had witched Sammy. And Sammy, fearing for his life, might be reluctant to continue with the plans.

Sure enough, no sooner had Tado finished his explanation than we ran into Old Man Tuazama, Sammy Wowah's uncle (and Major Paul Tuazama's father). Tuazama was among those who had expressed opposition to opening a private clinic—on what grounds I never did establish. Tuazama was angry, for it seemed that Sammy Wowah's father (Tuazama's brother) was going about none-too-subtly accusing Tuazama of causing the accident. The motive: Tuazama supposedly envied Sammy Wowah's success.

I knew Old Man Tuazama from my time living in Kpaytuo. Though he could be stubborn, he was the only member of the three-person school board who gave a damn about education for the tribal people in Kpaytuo. I found the accusation absurd, but that didn't assuage Tuazama's anger. Such is the darker side of life in Kpaytuo.

Chapter 42

Tado Jackson was trying to mediate a "polygamy palaver" behind his house with two of his relatives, Edwin and James Siaway. Also present were James' and Edwin's wives. The gist of the palaver was that James Siaway had decided to take another wife. He had asked his sister, Molly, who lived in the nearby village of Flumpa, to find him a suitable girl. This Molly had done. All well and acceptable, except James had neglected to inform his wife of his desire to take another wife. Someone—exactly who was one of the matters being discussed in the family pow-wow—had found out and informed James' wife before he had gotten around to doing it himself. The wife was miffed, more at not being consulted than at James taking another wife.

Not many men in Kpaytuo had more than one wife: most couldn't afford two or more wives. Wondering how one maintained conjugal peace in a polygamous relationship, one day when I lived in Kpaytuo I approached my friend, Richard, the village carpenter, who had two wives. He told me he slept with one wife three consecutive nights, the other wife the next three nights. And so on.

Even though the man shared their beds, it was the first—the head wife—who remained the most important wife. She ran the household, allocated the work for the other wife or wives and *all* the children. It was she who mediated squabbles and served as the "big sister" or "aunt" for the second wife, invariably many years her junior.

When I lived in Liberia it was a $140 fine (equivalent to almost $1,000 in today's dollars) if one were found guilty of adultery with a head wife, as $140 was the approximate price of her bride price; but only $10 in 1967 for any other wife. Nevertheless, even $10 was too much for most young tribal men to come up with circa 1967. If found guilty, the lover might choose to work off the debt on the aggrieved husband's farm. Many a fat, old and wily chief encouraged his young wives to consort with unmarried young, strong tribal men, the easier for him to acquire cheap labor for his coffee, cocoa and rice farms.

❖ ❖ ❖

I ate dinner with Sammy Wowah. The celebration of his recuperation was still going on after 30 hours, with no sign of letting up. Sammy apologized for the state of his father's house—unpainted, unfurnished, unscreened, uninsulated, like almost every house in Kpaytuo. Nevertheless, he made me feel like a royal visitor, and I was touched by his effort: his people had prepared enough rice and freshly killed antelope to feed ten. While we ate, many of Sammy's relatives danced through the room, amazed that he had returned after being so close to death. "God has blessed Sammy," more than one person told me. Sammy apologized for their interrupting the privacy of our meal and, I think, felt embarrassed in the mistaken impression I thought such behavior unsophisticated and inappropriate to the occasion of my visit. Had he known me better, he would have realized it is just these expressions of tribal culture I so admire and savor.

After dinner, we went outside, where his people and others of the quarter were dancing, singing, and listening to a tape of tribal music. Moses Karma, one of my ex-students, about age thirty, approached with a few friends. Moses raised his right hand, indicating he wanted the music and dancing to stop so he might speak. He told us how helpful Sammy Wowah had been when he (Moses) had suffered a hernia. Somehow Sammy had persuaded a hospital official to charge Moses less than the normal fee for X-rays and for his subsequent operation. Moses wished he had something special to give as a way of thanking Sammy and of celebrating the fact that he had survived the terrible accident, but he did not because he was experiencing hard times. At least, though, he had a gourd of palm wine. A glass was brought from Sammy's father's house, the palm wine poured into it, with Sammy Wowah having the honor of the first sip; then the glass was refilled and passed around to every male present. After a long day, particularly when the rice was growing and there was no pressing work to be done, village men gathered in a circle under a tree, and there, as the sun began its descent, communally drank palm wine and got slightly crocked. I was often invited to join them, and though I was no great fan of the drink, I usually did, always enjoying the camaraderie and high jinks of the occasion.

I left Sammy Wowah's with the celebration in full swing. Thomas Karngbeae accompanied me the one hundred and fifty yards or so walk back to Tado's. Liberians rarely let me walk about alone at night. They walked with me as they are naturally solicitous and also, I think, to protect me from any witches or spirits hovering about.

Tribal Liberians feared the dark, the ideal time for a spirit to come and "catch you." Most slept with a lighted hurricane lantern inside their rooms or, as in Tado's house, in the hallway. (In the old days, when they all slept in the one room of a hut, fire had provided light and warmth through the night.) The villagers must have thought me especially brave, as I didn't mind walking about the village alone in the night— either when I lived there or during my return visit. Indeed, I enjoyed it. And I preferred sleeping in a dark room. Alas, having been mugged by three young thugs one night in Philadelphia while out for a walk, I'll take my chances any old time with the spirits and witches of Kpaytuo.

Chapter 43

On my last day in Kpaytuo, I wanted to walk in the bush, for who knew when the opportunity might come again. During my Peace Corps years I looked forward to my afternoon hikes with Sammy Dahngbae and his gang—Memba, David and Andrew Karma, and Sammy Gweh. We'd visit their families' farms or watch the women fishing in a stream. Sometimes we'd climb palm trees and then, back on earth, the boys would strip and plunge into a nearby creek that had been dammed up. Whatever we did, Huckleberry Finn would have approved.

I envied the ease with which my young barefooted students, all of them between ages eleven and thirteen, glided through the dense rain forest, while I, in heavy boots lumbered along behind. (Eventually I realized it made more sense to wear sneakers on these excursions.) As we weaved through the forest, one of them inevitably turned to me and said: "See the bird over there, Teacher?" I strained and looked and more often than not failed to see a bird (or any living creature) camouflaged amid the verdure. The boys knew the name in Gio of every animal, insect, plant, shrub and tree we encountered in the forest: more than that, they knew which to avoid and which to hoard, which plants and fruits were edible, and which served as medicine for rashes or stomach aches. And not least, they knew which could kill you. "Teacher, the bush is our ABCs," they used to tell me.

❖   ❖   ❖

On that final day in Kpaytuo of my 1982 trip, I asked Arthur Wonyou to accompany me into the bush. He had been my guide about a month before when we went looking for driver ants, and my former student, then about age thirty-seven, was a font of tribal lore and village gossip. It wasn't long before we were among the various species of palm, mahogany, ebony and camwood trees that make up the great rain forest. Many of the taller trees were festooned with vines and creepers, a tangle of vegetation that twisted into the most grotesque and stirring shapes. A band of lovely white butterflies with gold-tipped wings fluttered about us as we walked.

Arthur pointed to a tree he called the "man tree." Chewing its bark, I was assured, increased a man's sexual potency. With his cutlass Arthur cut a chunk out of the tree. He sucked on the bark and swallowed the juice; while I, curious to test the bark's alleged aphrodisiacal powers, couldn't tolerate the bitter taste and spat my piece out after a few seconds. He then pointed out scores of such "man trees," all of them dead from having the bark chopped away. Interesting, I thought, because when a Liberian couple couldn't conceive, it was always the woman, never the man, believed responsible. We also came across a soft plant that Arthur told me Kpaytuo's citizens used for toilet paper. And then he showed me a tree that he claimed caused gonorrhea if rubbed against. (Note that I said Arthur was a font of tribal lore, not accurate medical information.)

We continued winding our way through the bush. About a mile from Kpaytuo we came upon Old Man Karngbeae and two young men, flailing away at an enormous tree some eight feet in diameter. It would take the three of them at least five hours to fell the monster. It was an impressive sight: three grown men slashing and hacking with vigor for the better part of a day just to remove one tree, a task that with a power tool might have taken them an hour or less.

We walked until we came to virgin forest, by which time I was dragging, so we began the hike back. Suddenly Arthur was yelling and jumping, pounding the ground with his walking stick. Beneath him, bludgeoned to death, lay a scorpion that had stung Arthur when he'd stepped on it. The incident was over in a matter of seconds. Considering that a scorpion's bite is poisonous, though not fatal, Arthur was remarkably blasé. I expected him to collapse at any moment. Then we'd really be in a fix, for I had no idea how to get back to the village to summon help. To my repeated questions as to how he felt, all Arthur would say was that when we returned to the village, he'd ask James Siaway for country medicine to treat the sting.

Never once after it happened did Arthur mention the sting, much less complain about it for the rest of our walk, demonstrating something I had seen confirmed many times: Liberians can bear pain to a degree inconceivable to a Westerner. We reached Kpaytuo hot, tired and dirty. Arthur went to find some country medicine for his wound, while I repaired to Tado's house to clean up and rest for the evening's festivities— a farewell party in my honor.

❖   ❖   ❖

Before the celebration began, I called Tado, Chief Bleeton and Old Man Tuazama aside and told them, as I had previously promised, that I intended to give $2,000 (that's equivalent to almost $5,000 in today's money) to the village for constructing draw-bucket wells—at least one in each quarter. I asked Tado and Chief Bleeton to meet me in a few days in Monrovia, where I'd open a bank account in the town's name. They were the only ones, I explained, who would be allowed to take money from the bank account, and both of them would have to sign before any money could be withdrawn. I wanted Tuazama, a village elder and an important member of the small Christian community in Kpaytuo, to be aware of the gift, and to know the amount of the gift in order to forestall the inevitable talk that I had really donated more than $2,000 for the wells, but that Tado and Chief Bleeton (and who knew who else might be accused) had embezzled the balance. As it was, there was nothing to prevent Tado and Chief Bleeton from "eating" my $2,000 once the account was opened. Nothing, of course, except Tado's integrity, in which I had the ultimate confidence.

Around 8:00 P.M. townsfolk began to arrive at Tado's house, in front of which the program was to be held. Men sat on benches borrowed from the new school, while women and young boys and girls stood bunched together behind the benches. Sammy Marwiah, the principal; Alfred Siaway, the master of ceremonies; Thomas Karngbeae, one of my former students who was himself a teacher; Tado Jackson, and I sat facing the audience of about two hundred. Tuazama opened the program by thanking me for travelling all the way from America to visit Kpaytuo, and, after invoking God's blessings on the proceedings, said a prayer.

Alfred, who assisted Tado in teaching night school in the village, spoke next: "Our respected guest of honor, government officials [there were none], parents, student body, ladies and gentlemen: I am very much enthused to be standing among my friends to introduce the program. Our program consists of selections, native songs, etcetera, etcetera. Your kind and usual cooperation is also needed during the course of the program. Ladies and gentlemen, the program."

Thomas Karngbeae began the ceremony by reading a brief biographical account of my life. This was followed by the schoolgirls singing a Gio song.

Then I was asked to speak. "Chief Bleeton, members of the school board, citizens of Kpaytuo: While Thomas was giving his speech, I kept thinking about what some of my friends told me before my visit. Many of my friends in Philadelphia can say to me, 'You've been gone for fourteen years, maybe the people won't remember you. Fourteen years is a long time. Maybe you'll reach Kpaytuo and the people will say, "Who is this man?"' I laughed when I heard them say that. I said to my friends, 'The people will remember me.' But even I began to doubt it, a little. Of course some of the people here were so-so small boys and girls when I was here. So I didn't expect them to remember me. But I had confidence that the students that I taught and their mothers and fathers and brothers and sisters would remember me.

"Nineteen eighty-one," I continued, "was a bad year for me. My father died. I thank God so far that 1982 is a good year. It can be a good year because I spent part of February, all of March and part of April in Kpaytuo. When I return to America it will seem like a dream to me that I was here. I'm very happy to be back. I hope that I will be able to return again. My home, of course, is in Pennsylvania. But I consider my second home Kpaytuo. Thank you."

Then Sammy Marwiah, the twenty-four-year-old principal, addressed us: "Mr. Robert Cherry, our honorable, distinguished, philanthropic and patriotic guest, my fellow intellectuals, government officials, industrious guests and fellow Kpayturians, and ladies and gentlemen: It is indeed another great opportunity that I have seen to elucidate to the people of Kpaytuo about my entire observation of the program. I will promise you, Mr. Cherry, that your philanthropic deeds show, and will never be eliminated from the minds of the people of Kpaytuo until every grain of sand on the beaches on the earth is recounted. Also, Mr. Cherry, we will carefully and efficiently utilize those materials presented to the school for the purpose for which they have been intended. Mr. Cherry, I do wish you a very safe and harmonious journey. Farewell."

The donation the principal was referring to was $100 in supplies I had given to the school. His overblown rhetoric, unfortunately, was typical of many so-called "educated" tribal Liberians of that time. Nonetheless, it was heartfelt and appreciated.

Next to speak was Tado Jackson, my friend, and during my visit to Kpaytuo, my host: "We Africans enjoy entertaining strangers and can hardly forget about them no matter how far they may go away from us," he began. "Our guest of honor, Mr. Cherry, on behalf of the people of Kpaytuo and the government of Liberia, I will ask you to stand up."

I did as instructed. Addressing me, Tado said: "Truly speaking, I sometimes feel like crying. As a white man and as an American who lives so many miles away from us, with a different culture altogether, to remember us because of your service in our country, is marvelous. And then to spend so much of your money traveling to see us, to go through Monrovia, where you can live in luxury in a hotel, and come to Kpaytuo is wonderful. When I saw you getting down and asking for my ugly little dwelling, I can remember that you have something given to you by God for our interest. I don't think there is anything we can say or do to satisfy you as a reward for what you have undertaken to do for us. However, on behalf of the people, we want to make you a town chief of Kpaytuo. When you go home, before you get down from the plane, we would like for you to get down as an African chief and not as an American. So I'd like someone to come here and change Mr. Cherry to a Liberian."

They brought me a blue and white striped cotton chief's gown, which I put on.

"Thank you, thank you all too much," I said. "Now that I can be chief, I want everyone to bring me one cow." Knowing my sense of humor, the villagers laughed.

Last to speak was Chief Bleeton. "The reason I was so quiet and slow in standing up is I am not too well tonight. However, I will try my best to say a few words. The first thing I want to say is thanks to every-one who is present here tonight. Sometimes there may be two citizens from a whole town who are good ones. And because of their goodness they can cause the whole country to regard that town as a good town. The second one is that I sincerely give you my heartfelt thanks, Mr. Cherry. I am happy that we have somebody now in the United States. Not only to us in Kpaytuo, but there was no one in Liberia who could think that a white man could travel from America, particularly in the interest of Kpaytuo. Even in Saclepea some of my friends were making remarks that the Kpaytuo people are lucky—here they have an Amer-ican man who traveled all the way and went to them and has spent two months with them as a friend. So, we thank you, Mr. Cherry. The way God gave you the feeling for us, I know there is now a family relation-ship between us and it will continue forever. When you go back, I am sending my greetings to the rest of your family. When you go back home, please remember to tell those of your friends who were doubting that we would remember you, tell them that the town chief of Kpaytuo, Michael Bleeton, and all of his people, send their greetings to you."

◆　◆　◆

I had timed my departure so the moon would be full during my last nights in the village, and so it was. After the program, we feasted on rice with goat meat, antelope and chicken and many sauces, including my favorite, cassava leaf. Then the celebration moved down the path to Galonpoo's house, in front of which, barefooted, padding about on the trodden dirt, girls in their late teens or early twenties formed a circle and sang and danced.

After a while the older women took over. Heavier and much less sprightly than they had been in their early twenties, when last I had seen them dance, they moved round and round. Their sometimes pon-derous movements produced good-natured laughter and teasing from the crowd, some of whose members were the grown sons and daughters of the dancers. These "older" women were my contemporaries, and my return to Kpaytuo had reminded them (and me) of our youth, most of it gone. If I were no longer young, neither did I consider myself old at thirty-nine. Not so with my contemporaries among the tribal women, whose lifespan was about fifty-five years or fewer. Whether it was Zoelay Retty, Galonpoo or Pela, they referred to themselves as old, although they were not yet forty. But their hard lives—chopping wood, fetching water, cooking and years of producing children—had already taken their toll. They may have had only a decade or so to live, I realized, and that unnerved me, especially as I expected to live another four, and if I were fortunate, five decades.

While most of her close friends were dancing, Zoelay Retty left the circle and sat down on a bench in front of Tado's house, leaning forward, despondent about my imminent departure—possibly the last time we'd ever see each other. I've always considered Zoelay Retty a cool customer, not so quick to show her emotions. She revealed them then. Between my trips to Ganta and Monrovia and her being ill much of the past three weeks—possibly with malaria—I had not seen much of Zoelay Retty. And there was also my new-found attraction to, and relationship with, Betty Leeleh. But Zoelay Retty and I had a bond forged many years before and I could—and would—never stop caring about her. She said she intended to remain up all night, and if I wanted to see her, she'd be at Garty's house. While she was speaking, I thought about what Arthur Wonyou had told me that afternoon on our bush hike: Zoelay Retty had told him that she wished she'd had a child by me back in 1967, when we were lovers.

The music and dancing stopped around 2:00 A.M. Before going to say goodbye to Zoelay Retty, I strolled through the village. A mist had settled over it. I mused about my trip, soon to be over. I conjured up Monrovia: the honking of car horns, the crowds of friendly and smiling—and, truth be told, argumentative and litigious—people gathered on almost every street corner; and the smell of oranges, peanuts and palm oil; African and Jamaican (reggae) music seemingly blaring everywhere, all the day and most of the night; women in brightly-colored *lappas* selling fruits and vegetables on the sidewalks; and Mandingo men, in flowing white and powder-blue robes gleaming in the intense sunlight, going to or from the mosque. I thought of the Holiday Inn: of Dabo, the diamond and gold merchant whose "office" was in the hotel

291

lobby—a rascal to the end who continued to inquire about the water project and whether I wanted him to find me an African wife; of the young man from Guinea who sat near the hotel's entrance hour after hour selling Juicy Fruit gum by the stick, earning maybe $5 a day; and all the others like him, making "small market" with their biscuits and candy and cigarettes, the latter sold two at a time. The bizarre Mother Dukuly marched through my mind with her brand of, to me, primitive and sometimes fraudulent Christianity. And the equally surreal, but all-too-true newspaper accounts of witchcraft and poison and human sacrifice. Then my thoughts turned to Ben and Sammy Cooper and the fallen Americo-Liberians.

I thought of the teachers, preachers, missionaries, doctors, nurses, hotel employees, restaurant owners, waiters, economists, secretaries, soldiers, policemen and bureaucrats I had come across in these two months. There came to mind the new Peace Corps friends I had made—specifically the Volunteers in Ganta, Scott Lewis and Paul Steinwachs. It was with Paul I had spent those unforgettable hours in the Ganta Leprosy Center. And how could I forget Walter Barron, the former Peace Corps Volunteer who remained in the country and whose Liberian wife and children I'd met. I gratefully remembered the friendship and hospitality of David and Maud Carson, the missionaries in Saclepea. I thought with the utmost respect of their striving against difficult conditions to impose Christian order and bring the Christian ethos to the Liberians. After forty-plus years, they'd be leaving Liberia in a year or two: their time there, in my opinion, well spent. Call theirs a rich life.

I could hear the sound in my head of money buses rumbling on the red, pock-marked dirt road of the interior, discharging passengers in the hamlets, villages and towns of up-country Liberia. I thought of the majestic and awesome rain forest, falling before man's hand; of the poor tribal farmer, bewildered by the changes in a world he little understood; and of the warmth and dignity of the tribal people; and of the encroaching, alien—though welcomed, and mostly beneficial—Western culture.

There came to mind my old love, Zoelay Retty; and my new one, Betty Leeleh. It was unlikely that I would marry either of them, our lives being so different. Still, I treasured my time with each of them.

I had traversed the village by then, and turned to retrace my steps. Kpaytuo stood before me. The moonlight bathed the town in a soft radiance. I thought of all my friends in Kpaytuo—like Sammy, my former houseboy, and Kamah, my one-time cook, and Paul (now Major) Tuazama who—like almost all of my students—had left the village and had gone to Monrovia in search of a job; and the handful of others, students and non-students, like Tado Jackson, Andrew Karma, Edwin Siaway, Galonpoo and her husband, Albert Kpeah, and Arthur Wonyou, who had remained behind. My former students were a transitional generation in Liberia's modern history: they'd lived the early and middle years of their lives under the old tribal ways, but the rest of their lives, and certainly the lives of their children and grandchildren would be shaped and fashioned increasingly by the *kwi* (read modern) world.

Much as Liberia fascinates and seduces, I realized during my trip I could not live or even remain there for more than a couple of months, not least because of its debilitating climate. And though I was exhausted in body, the trip had, ironically, rejuvenated me. It was time to get on with the next phase of my life, which I hoped would include marriage and a family.

After almost being arrested in my Kafkaesque run-in with the police and security officials the week before in Monrovia, I had vowed that never again would I set foot in Liberia. I had uttered the words in the lobby of the Holiday Inn, at the end of my encounter with the security forces. After which Sammy, my one-time houseboy who was in the lobby of the Holiday Inn waiting for me, had turned to me and, looking sad, asked, "For true, Teacher?"

Even as I'd spoken the words, more so as I mulled them over the last night in Kpaytuo, I knew it was not "for true." In spite of the ferocious heat and humidity, the sickness, the stealing, the corruption, and the paranoia, I hoped to visit Liberia again. For that is where my African friends and my African "children" are. That is where Kpaytuo, my African home, is. Also, and forever, a part of my heart.

Epilogue

In 1983, a year after my return visit, the citizens of Kpaytuo constructed six wells with the $2,000 I had given them. And just in time, for that year Liberia, along with much of Africa, suffered through one of the worst droughts of the twentieth century. For the first time in memory, water was sold in many villages of up-country Liberia, and people went from village to village in search of it. Not so in Kpaytuo, where there was plenty of fresh, clean water, available for all.

Afterword

As the events I've described happened so many years ago, I'd like to recount briefly the fate of my closest Liberian friends in the intervening years—and also that of their maddening, beleaguered and resilient country.

After my 1982 trip, I corresponded regularly with Tado Jackson, my kindred spirit and during most of my two-month return visit, my host; with Sammy Dahngbae, my irrepressible ex-houseboy who had joined the Liberian army; and also with Betty Leeleh, my favorite ex-student who, a mature woman of about twenty-eight, had become my lover; with Kamah, my ex-cook; and, among others, with two new friends, David and Maud Carson, the stern but caring missionaries who ran the Saclepea mission and were Tado's mentors and spiritual advisors.

Over the ensuing years the group, as individuals, wrote me more than one hundred letters, almost all of which I have and excerpts from a handful of which follow. I begin with my girlfriend Betty Leeleh, who wrote me in June of 1982, a couple of months after I had returned home. The punctuation and phrasing remain as written in this and all those excerpts that follow:

My dearest Robert,

Lovely greeting is coming to you this day from your friend Betty. How have you been since you left Liberia? I hope life is coming on smoothly with you.

With me everything is so-so here in Ganta. I'm very sorry to write too late, but it was due to the hard study. I am missing you until every day I can dream about you. I wish I was a bird to fly over your home in order to see you. I am anxiously awaiting to read letter from you so I can think too much.

295

In January 1984, I invited Tado, Sammy and Betty to visit me that summer in Philadelphia, my treat. With the bad luck that seemed to follow her, Betty was struck by malaria days before the three of them were to fly to New York, where I was to pick them up. She explained apologetically to me in a letter that she thought it would be embarrassing to visit me while ill. As fate would have it, soon thereafter I became seriously involved with a woman in Philadelphia, and that spelled the end of my romantic relationship with, but never my good wishes for, Betty. More about Betty to come.

Tado and Sammy arrived in June of 1984. During their three-week trip we made a one-day excursion to New York, another to the Amish Country in Lancaster, Pennsylvania. I had made contact with an Amish farmer there and Tado watched him work. Tado was enthralled and learned so much from the farmer. We spent most of their three-week stay in and around Philadelphia, where they saw the city of my birth and met my mother, my friends and other Liberians. They loved every minute of their trip, the first time either of them had been on a plane or out of their country.

Herewith an excerpt from one of Tado's letters, written after the trip, in July 1984:

Dear Robert,

Well brother, we've safely reached home. The trip was pleasant because I was less nervous than before [*their departure and flight*]. We had an hour stop at Dakar [*in Senegal*] and from there we flew and arrived at Robertsfield [*Liberia's international airport*] at 12:30 P.M. I left for the country the next day and of course my people were happy to see me back. In fact my arrival was an exciting occasion. I tell you, Robert, the short trip to America has added much to my prestige. Because our arrival was announced on the radio by some friends from ELWA [*a missionary radio station that broadcast throughout the country*], I am warmly being welcomed everywhere I go.

Robert, I thank you ever so much for all what you did for us in America. It is only the Almighty God who will bless you with a long life, prosperity, and success in all your undertakings.

This one trip to your great country has been the greatest experience in my life. . . . But brother, one thing I do not understand is that even though I'm happy to be back, I'm always feeling homesick for Philadelphia. I just have to force myself to overcome the feeling you know. Of course it is the conditions back here that partially create this lure for America. It is just like returning from Heaven to Hell. But well, what to do! Please do not forget to write me often.

Your brother,

Tado Jackson

And another excerpt from Tado Jackson, written four months after his visit, dated November 5, 1984:

Dear Robert,

This, I'm sure you know, is the happiest season of the year in Liberia. It is rice harvesting time. We began our rice cutting last week. We are also busy in the garden planting bean, cucumber, bitter ball and watermelon. The seeds that you gave me were a great success you know. I'm also expecting about 350 chicks this week from a dealer in the Ivory Coast. My next problem for raising them will be feed. They will require about 20 bags of feed at $21 per bag to bring them to maturity around Christmas time.

I say, brother, do you still remember when I told you that my trip to your great country was as educational as my school years? I've just been reading a book about young people of New York City and as I come across such names as Manhattan, Brooklyn Bridge, Central Park and many others, it seems as if I were [again visiting] in the city itself. As I listen to news and hear the names of remote places such as United Nations, Rockefeller Center, the Empire State building and Kennedy Airport, I feel proud indeed. And last, but not the least, is the memory of your historical hometown, Philadelphia itself, including its many important buildings such as the City Hall, The Franklin Science Museum, St. Peter's Cathedral, and of course the famous and historical Independence Square which will forever ring in my mind.

Please extend my warmest greetings to your mother.

Your African brother,

Tado Jackson

By 1985 Tado wrote that after twelve years he had won the land palaver—against all odds I might add—with a paramount chief. He continued raising rice for his family to eat; and to raise and sell vegetables and sometimes chickens. Almost every year thereafter I sent him bean and pepper seeds, superior to anything he could buy in Liberia. At this time he and his wife Mary had five children, but as he wrote that May his youngest daughter died of measles, age two years and eight months. Thankfully, in September of that year Mary gave birth to twin boys, one of whom Tado named after me—imagine that, a little Bob Cherry crawling around Kpaytuo. As Tado expected the twins to be his last children, he named the other twin after himself. My namesake had a congenital heart problem and died at age one. His twin brother died at two and a half from a childhood illness—a painful reminder that half the babies then born in rural Liberia died by age five. (While mortality rates in Liberia have improved in the last thirty years—so have they in the rest of the developing world; sadly, as of 2015, Liberia's under-age-five mortality rate was among the highest in the world, according to the World Health Organization.)

In late 1985 the missionaries Maud and David Carson left Liberia after more than forty years serving their God and Liberia's rural people. The Carsons first visited his family in Belfast, Northern Ireland, for six months before settling in her native country, Canada; they lived in Edmonton, Alberta. One doesn't "retire" from serving God, so the Carsons conducted a weekly Bible study class for residents of their apartment complex, were involved with a local church, and lamented that the morals of the Canadian people had declined since their earlier visits many decades prior. David also exhorted me, at some point in many letters, to accept Jesus as my savior. I wasn't offended but I am Jewish and proudly will die a Jew. That said, I'm pleased they considered me a friend, as I them.

As for my life, I wrote Tado and Sammy and the Carsons about the changes in it: I had finished the first draft of this book—more about which in the "Acknowledgements"—and had left journalism and was learning about, and then running, my deceased father's salad dressing manufacturing business, which he had left to my sister and me. In an amicable transaction, I had bought her shares. Most significantly, I had begun a relationship with a woman, originally from Europe but living in the Philadelphia area, whom I hoped to marry. Eventually, I fathered a child with her. Sadly, in the years to come we did not make it as a couple, though she and I remain on good terms and I'm in close contact with her and my daughter, both of whom live near me. Tado and Sammy "lived" through it all with me, via letters.

❖   ❖   ❖

In 1989 there began a civil war—actually the first of two civil wars—that spanned fourteen years and tore Liberia apart. The first phase, from 1989–96, primarily was between tribes—President Samuel K. Doe and his Krahn tribesmen fought Charles Taylor and a band of Libyan-trained mercenaries who invaded Liberia from the Ivory Coast. Charles Taylor, supposedly with a tribal and Americo-Liberian ancestry, was supported by Mano and Gio people, who felt persecuted and threatened by Samuel K. Doe and his Krahn tribesmen. The second civil war, 1999–2003, pitted Charles Taylor, triumphant in the first conflict, and his supporters against various rebel factions and warlords.

What were the two wars about? Certainly not exalted constitutional issues. If in the beginning it was grievances and enmities between tribes, the war in time metastasized into a battle between and *among* tribes and self-anointed warlords seeking revenge and power—a deadly contest to determine which corrupt and rapacious faction—of which there were many—could loot the national treasury and rape, plunder, and kill the most Liberians. In the process, the warring parties destroyed the electric grid and water system in Monrovia; closed the government, schools, hospitals and businesses for years on end—even the mighty Firestone Corporation shut its Liberian operations; confiscated diamonds to buy more armaments; and drove foreign-aid organizations and missionaries from the land. And, while at it, some combatants on both sides reportedly indulged in cannibalism and human sacrifice—the latter employed as "medicine" to defeat one's enemies. The fighting featured commanders with *noms de guerre* like General Butt Naked (so-called because he fought in the nude), a General Rambo and *two* General bin Ladens. Many of the combatants were twelve-year-old "boy soldiers" wielding machine guns. Some of the "boy soldiers" and many of their older counterparts were high on marijuana, their leaders on cocaine. It all would have made for a great farce but for its catastrophic consequences.

Until the whirlwind subsided, between 200,000 and 250,000 Liberians perished, most of them civilians, about one out of every fifteen people in that grieving, blood-stained land. And estimates vary, but from a half million to one million Liberians—approximately twenty-five to fifty percent of the population—were displaced. The Liberian Civil War ranks among the deadliest and most destructive in modern Africa's history.

◆　◆　◆

And what of my friends and their relatives during the mayhem—and *their* friends and relatives? They suffered: in the early stages of the first civil war, while soldiers fought in Nimba County, indeed tanks and artillery firing on and from the only road in tiny, peaceful Kpaytuo itself, its citizens hid in the nearby forest. Other Liberians, the counterparts of my Kpaytuo friends, ran when the fighting engulfed *their* part of the country or, in time, Monrovia. Some fled to the bush, tens of thousands more to the Ivory Coast or Sierra Leone, whose borders adjoin Liberia, respectively, on the East and Southwest, where they ended up in overcrowded and squalid refugee camps. The luckiest Liberians, especially during the chaotic and fateful period from 1989 to 2003, made it to America, some legally, others not.

Sammy, my ex-houseboy, who by the time of the civil war had long since left the Liberian Army, was in Monrovia for most of it. I had sent him money to start a dry goods store, which would be one more victim of the war. Tado Jackson watched as Samuel K. Doe's soldiers burned his house, though they spared him and his family. (I helped him rebuild the house, the new one located even farther from the village proper.) Tado eventually sent his children to the West African country of Ghana for safety, where under difficult conditions they continued their education or scratched out a hard life, bereft of parents.

I was able to write Tado intermittently through the central post office in Monrovia. But there were times when the road to Monrovia was impassable or too dangerous to traverse—one rebel faction or another had commandeered or fought over sections of it—so I also wrote to

Tado through his sons, Nerwah and Liberty, who with their sister, Angea, were in Ghana. Tado sometimes traveled ten hours to the Ivory Coast to send me letters or to call. And through some of the war years, when circumstances permitted on their end, I sent Tado and Sammy money in Monrovia or through a missionary in the Ivory Coast—thank God for Western Union.

Not surprisingly, some of my ex-students number among the tens of thousands of war dead. When the fighting reached Monrovia in 1990, my one-time girlfriend, Betty Leeleh, sought sanctuary in a Lutheran church, according to her nephew. She and scores of others were massacred for the crime of being in the wrong place at the wrong time. Betty was around thirty-six years old. Rereading a half dozen of her letters from 1982–85, at which point we lost touch, and listening to the tape of our conversation in a Monrovia hotel during my 1982 visit and working on this manuscript, rekindled dormant memories and emotions that I felt toward her—dear, lovely, bright, sweet Betty, upon whom good fortune rarely shone.

When the fighting was centered in Monrovia, two hundred miles from Kpaytuo, life in the interior of the country resumed some normalcy, although the specter of the conflict, and its consequences, were always present. On September 1, 2000, I received a letter from Tado, parts of which follow:

Dear Brother Robert,

Best greeting from your African brother. I hope you are all right as usual. I received your letter sent through Ghana in Nerwah's care. [*Nerwah is the son Tado had with his first wife, who died shortly after giving birth.*] Oh, how I enjoyed reading it! I think I have read it more than five times. You know reading such a long letter from you was just like listening to you in a conversation. Please do not forget to write another one before this year ends.

I'm happy to learn that you are still active and even undertaking the writing of a book. [*Having sold the salad dressing business, I had begun to write a biography of the basketball great, Wilt Chamberlain.*] I hope your book will be as popular as one of those bestsellers. Thank God for the old Ma, your mother. Isn't it wonderful to hear that she can still move around! [*My mother was eighty-eight at the time.*] Please

301

extend my warmest greeting to her. And your dear daughter. How fast time can fly. When I visited you (sixteen) years ago you've not even met her mother yet. Then to say that she is in high school is just surprising for me. Yes I like the way you described her. I'm sure you are proud father to have a girl who is well behaved, well-educated and respectful in today's world.

You know, Bob, when I read the paragraph about her my mind went straight to my son Liberty, in Ghana. I recently received a letter from him the content of which almost made me cry. You know he is a determined ambitious young man. In that letter he appealed to me for help that will enable him to advance studies.

Well brother, I do highly appreciate all what you're doing for my family. In spite of all your many financial obligations you still find time to assist me with a good amount of money. . . .

I wish to bring something to your attention regarding the last $500 you sent for the clinic [*in Kpaytuo*]. When I reported the money most of the people especially the young people suggested that we use the money to build a palaver house as a town hall for the town. But I told them no because that was not the purpose for which you sent it. So it became quite an issue in the town. However because many of the older folks all were with me and realize the need of medical care for the district, we spent it on the clinic as intended.

For myself, I am feeling very fine this year. I love my family life you know. The new house you help to build for me is contributing to my health and happiness in recent time you know. . . .The Bible verse below has become my philosophy in life: 1 Thessalonians 4:11 says "This should be your ambition: to live a quiet life, minding your own business and doing your own work."

Mary [*his wife*] is fine. Yes not only that she a devoted Christian wife, but is also very hard-working. I'm really proud of her. I will not forget to mention something about my five children. Despite the problems the Civil War has created for young people, all five of them are serious in life. Most of our young people here have lost interest in learning. They only believe in sex and having children. But for my children I'm proud of them.

Again I want to remind you to please send me a large-size picture of you that I can use to decorate my sitting room with. I think the best person to send it will be Rebecca's mother anytime she is coming.

Your brother,
Tado Jackson

302

In April, 2002, Tado wrote:

Hi Robert

Though I've not been too well from the gas problem for some time, I thank God that I'm feeling much better now. With the exception of Leeko, the boy next to Liberty, all of our children are away from home. We have seven other children living with us presently some of them are grandchildren. Among them is a girl who lost her parents during the war. We picked her up about eight years ago and now she regards us as her dear parents. We love her so.

In August of 2003, the Liberian Civil Wars finally ended, thanks to the accumulated interventions over a number of years by a military force from African countries, pressures from the United States, a rescue operation by U. S. Marines, a U. N. peacekeeping force and the efforts of many courageous women in Liberia, sick of the devastation and murder. The women demanded the warring parties put down their arms and meet in Accra, Ghana, and not leave until they agreed on a transition to peaceful civil government. Miraculously, the last of at least eight ceasefire agreements and negotiations worked and has held. Charles Taylor, the president of Liberia and the most infamous, though hardly the only instigator of the civil wars, had left for exile in Nigeria and would eventually be tried by an international court and sentenced to fifty years in prison for war crimes and crimes against humanity. He is presently in a prison in England. And Liberians dispersed in refugee camps or in other circumstances in nearby countries returned to Liberia, including Tado's children. Count them as relatively fortunate, for the war left a legacy of tens of thousands of parentless, homeless and uneducated children. In 2005 Liberia elected a woman, Ellen Johnson Sirleaf, president—a first for any African country. She was reelected in 2011.

❖　❖　❖

The war over, Liberia began to rebuild, thanks to foreign aid. By 2005 Tado called me for the first time on his new cell phone; and in April of 2007, using his son's email account, he wrote me an email from Monrovia, to which he would bring his produce to market or visit family and friends. Herewith excerpts from some emails:

Dear Robert,

Best greetings from your African brother, Tado Jackson. Yes, for long there has been no communication between us. I miss you so much you know. How are you coming in life? I hope you are fine and how is your dear mother? Yes brother, thanks so much for the care you are giving to her. How is your teaching job? [*Having published my biography of Wilt Chamberlain and while overseeing the health care of my mother, who was in her mid-nineties, I taught business writing and public speaking part-time at Drexel University.*] This job seems to be keeping you busy, isn't it and how is your dear daughter? I'm sure she is almost a woman now.

As you know Bob, for the past 40 years my relationship with you has been a great blessing to my life so when I stop hearing from you for such a long time, it makes me almost sick. Since we may not easily meet in person again, at least communicating with you is always a blessing to my heart. It used to cost me hundreds of [*Liberian*] dollars to travel to either Ivory Coast or Monrovia in order to communicate with you. But now I can easily do it from Saclepea or even Kpaytuo right on my farm. So brother, I want to hear your friendly voice again. My cell phone number is 06-909-400.

Presently, I am in Monrovia visiting my son and his family. Also I came to seek solution to a problem I'm experiencing—some kind of dimness in my eyesight that need medical attention. I can hardly see a distance now. It is even difficult for me to read small prints nowadays. So pray with me that it does not become serious.

Over the next months Tado and I spoke often on his cell phone. He was so proud of it, while it never failed to amaze me that he could call me on a cell phone from the interior. I suspected his eye problem was glaucoma, for he mentioned his eye pressure was bad; but the dimness could have been from cataracts; or both.

On October 5, 2007, he sent me an email from his son's account:

Dear Robert,

I'm back in Monrovia for my operation since the dimness of my eyes is growing worse. I feel that I need an operation, so please pray with me for successful result.

From my intensive and prolonged hard work, I've developed the second physical health problem—that is a very painful backache. I've suffered from this new problem for the past three or four months. I can hardly walk straight now because of the back pains.

Well, brother, my wife Mary and I are doing fine and very busy with our farm works. Since we are expecting a vehicle [*a used pick-up truck*] for the farm, we want to plant enough pineapple that will keep it busy when it is bought. But Bob, old age seems to be slowing down my speed and strength of working nowadays. My wife is getting more busy each year than me now. Yes, she is very energetic and industrious wife. I'm really proud of her you know. By God's help we hope to fulfill our dream of shipping carloads of pineapple from the farm starting next year.

Your friend, Tado Jackson.

Tado called me from Monrovia a few days before his scheduled eye surgery. It was to be performed on the Mercy Ship, the largest non-governmental hospital ship in the world and part of an international charity that provides free health care to the citizens of poor African nations.

Eager to know how the surgery went, I heard nothing from him for a week. And then on a Tuesday afternoon, around 4:00 P.M., my phone rang. It was Tado's son, Nerwah, who told me Tado had died earlier that day in Monrovia from kidney failure. I burst out crying. The date was October 16, 2007. Though Tado was around seventy-two years old, he had the curiosity and thirst for learning of a child; the zest for life of a twenty-year-old; and within his five foot five inch frame beat a heart as courageous as Africa's mightiest lion. He loved his God, his family and was an example to his countrymen and women of how to work and live. A special friend for forty-one years, I miss him terribly.

❧   ❧   ❧

Then there is the other Liberian, after Tado, I have been closest to and in touch with the most, Sammy Dahngbae, my "son." Of course, as I noted earlier in the book, he is not my biological son but because he worked for me when I was a Peace Corps Volunteer lo those many years ago, and as I have helped him regularly since, he and his family, and the villagers, consider me his "father."

Sammy formally married in 2003 because in his words, "the church he and his woman attended threatened to throw them out if they were not married in a church." That marriage was short-lived, for within two years he was living with another woman. It was that woman, he told me in the summer of 2016, he was going to marry in a traditional (read tribal) wedding. He asked if I'd help him by sending money (which I did) so he might buy his fiancé's family "country cloth" (I think he meant traditional gowns) for the wedding and to pay for their transportation from the interior to Monrovia, where the wedding was to be held, and for food and drinks. He had been with his fiancé for eleven years. She's in her early forties while he—whom I employed and taught as a thirteen-year-old—is sixty-three, a grandfather many times over. He and his fiancé earn a living manufacturing hard soap, one of whose ingredients is palm oil. He sells the soap to dry good stores and Liberians use it to clean their clothes. Sammy and I talk twice a year, during which I ask him about Kpaytuo and Monrovia and my ex-students and friends.

In retrospect, I wish I had brought Sammy and Tado to the United States again—this time to stay, especially after the civil war began. But I was busy with, and at times overwhelmed by, my responsibilities to my family—my sister's illness—she was diagnosed at age fifty-seven with early onset Alzheimer's disease—and my mother's aging, with the attendant problems therefrom, absorbed much of my emotional energy, to say nothing of, in my mother's case, my time. And there was my daughter and her mother to look after and to support. Still, I wish I had tried to bring Tado and Sammy to America.

❖　❖　❖

Since the lifespan of the average Liberian is about fifty-five (compared to the late seventies for residents of the developed world), many of my ex-students and Kpaytuo friends are gone. Gratefully, a score of my Liberian friends are still around, but like the author of these words getting on in years: the teenage boys and girls I taught in 1966–67 are grandfathers and grandmothers in their mid-to-late sixties.

Paul Tuazama, who was a major in the police force at the time of my 1982 return visit, is circa 2017 chief of security at Liberia's Temple of Justice. He is also a candidate for the Liberian Congress, hoping to represent Nimba County. He is still handsome and dashing, as I see from his photo on social media. I'm also in touch with one of Betty Leeleh's daughters, who aspires to be a nurse. I sent her a photograph of her mother at about age twenty-eight, probably the first time the daughter has ever seen a photograph of her mother at that age—maybe at any age. Galonpoo and Albert Kpeah divorced, according to Sammy; she is a traditional midwife, while he works in Kpaytuo's clinic. For years, I thought Zoelay Retty Sonkarly, my first girlfriend in Kpaytuo, was dead, courtesy of information from Sammy. I mentioned her recently to Liberty, Tado's son, who thought she was still alive. He checked with his mother and she confirmed that Zoelay Retty is alive. Renting a motor bike, Liberty tracked Zoelay Retty down to a village on the border between Ivory Coast and Liberia, where she fled for her life during the war and never returned to Kpaytuo. Two of her children weren't as fortunate; they were killed. She is old and poor, so shriveled by age and hardship that I didn't recognize her—at first—from the photographs that Liberty emailed me.

Sammy Cooper, the wealthy Americo-Liberian who owned the sawmill in Kpaytuo, left Liberia for a much safer London in the early 1990s. There in 2003 he died, age eighty-three. His son, Benedict, better known as "Ben," whom I saw in Monrovia in 1982, died there in 2010. He was in his mid-sixties. John Cooper died of cancer in New York, where he lived ever since leaving Liberia in 1981. And Oscar Cooper, one of Sammy Cooper's children, is running for the presidency of Liberia in 2017.

Paul Steinwachs was the then twenty-three-year-old Peace Corps Volunteer who guided me around the Ganta Leprosy Center that unforgettable day in 1982. Paul, who told me that he hoped to become a doctor after his Peace Corps service, is a pediatrician in Georgia and, according to the many social media postings, adored by his many patients. He has been married for all these years to the woman who was his American girlfriend when he and I met.

Dr. Margaret Chambers, the medical missionary nun who ran the Ganta Leprosy Center, continued working in Ganta until the mayhem from the Civil War forced her to leave in 1989. She continued her work with the Medical Missionaries of Mary, an international religious congregation of Catholic women, based in Ireland. She died in Drogheda, Ireland, in 2001, age seventy-nine. Theresa Hicks, the nurse and lay missionary whom I met along with Dr. Chambers during my stay in Ganta, is still active in the Society of African Missionaries. Theresa left Liberia in 1992 and like anyone who experienced the Civil War has and knows many others with harrowing tales to recount. Thanks to the Internet, I found her in Tenafly, New Jersey, where at age sixty-seven she recruits lay missionaries and priesthood candidates for the Society. She has invited me to visit her and her compadres, many of whom served in Liberia.

David and Maud Carson ran the Saclepea Mission for decades and then, in 1985, settled in Canada, her native country, but some years later returned to Northern Ireland, land of his birth, to care for his sick twin brother. There David died, age ninety, in 2001; Maud, age ninety-five, in 2008. They are buried in Belfast and if I'm ever in Ireland, I will visit them to pay my respect. Liberians, some of whom live in the United States and others in Europe, all of them educated, mentored and inspired by the Carsons, have formed an organization that continues the legacy of the Inland Mission in Liberia.

If Liberians hadn't already suffered enough tumult, hardship, sorrow and death from fourteen years of civil war, there struck in March 2014 a plague of the Ebola virus. But the people, including my above-mentioned friends, are resilient and have survived even that; and today, with no new cases reported, the virus seems to be contained.

I am in contact with two of Tado Jackson's children, his son, Liberty, and his daughter, Angea. During the Ebola crisis I sent Liberty money to be used on behalf of the citizens of Kpaytuo; and he sent me, via emails from an Internet café in Monrovia, photographs of the supplies—latex gloves and drums of disinfectant, metal buckets and surgical masks—that the town bought with the money. Since the wells Kpaytuo's citizens constructed with my help in 1982 are long gone, and 2015 was dryer than normal, I also sent Liberty money with which he is overseeing the construction of two wells—one for the citizens of the town and one on the family farm. Occasionally when we talk on the telephone, Liberty puts his mother (Tado's widow) on and Mary and I exchange greetings in Gio, with Liberty then translating what I say to her and she to me. I had contemplated visiting Liberia in 2015 but with the Ebola crisis then raging, I decided against it. Now that the Ebola crisis is over, I'd still like to visit Kpaytuo, though at age seventy-three, and given the country's climate and still-difficult traveling and living conditions, I don't know if that is a prudent move.

◆　　◆　　◆

I have always thought that Liberians are among the most attractive and photogenic people. I rest my case with Exhibits A, B and C, the three girls whose photographs grace the left side of the book's cover. From the top down, they are Rebecca Bormentar, Mary Pratt, (then the one male, Arthur Wonyou), and Kamah Fendahn. I don't know the women in the blue *lappas* who so joyously adorn the right side of the cover. They, and many thousands of other visitors from around the country, had come to Monrovia in January 1968, celebrating President Tubman's election to an eighth term. Much of Monrovia had shut down, for everyone was either watching or taking part in the celebration when I, soon to depart for America and home, snapped the picture.

The second photograph from the top is Mary Pratt, then about seventeen, who would have gotten my vote for the cutest girl in Kpaytuo circa 1967—and there were many candidates. Always more modern than her contemporaries in Kpaytuo, Mary spent most of her adult life in Monrovia, where she raised a family and worked for the Ministry of Finance and where, in her Monrovia home, I visited her one evening during my 1982 visit. Mary died of natural causes in 1986 and is buried in Kpaytuo. The bottom photo is Kamah, my one-time cook, wearing blue lipstick and white makeup—girls will be girls, and thank heaven for them, as the song says. Dear Kamah succumbed to illness in the early 1990s, far too young. I write about Arthur Wonyou, the male on

309

the cover, early and late in the book. He worked at the Kpaytuo clinic and then ran a drug store. He is presently about seventy, showing signs of age, and also heartbroken over losing three children. But Rebecca, the girl whose lovely image occupies the top spot, with her dazzling smile and sparkling eyes, is fine, if many decades older than her cover photo. Rebecca taught school in the interior for many years. Now in her early sixties, she owns a convenience store in Monrovia, has three children and three grandchildren. She calls me every couple of months just to say hello, often late at night her time, and plans to visit Philadelphia soon, her first visit to America. I talk to and occasionally see Rebecca's older brother, Kyende, who lives in Philadelphia. He also owns a convenience store and whenever I visit his Philadelphia home his Liberian-born wife makes sure my favorite Liberian dish, cassava leaf gravy over rice and meat, is ready to serve.

◆　◆　◆

Of course Liberia has changed since 1982, when last I visited the country, but not as much as one would imagine; and much of the change is on the surface: yes, many Liberians have smartphones and access to computers; and watch, even create, YouTube videos. However, the roads in the interior are still unpaved, and while Liberians are healthier and thus live longer, many villages—including Kpaytuo—still lack electricity and clean water, too many infants still die from malaria and acute and persistent diarrhea and some tribal people still seek out medicine men to bewitch an enemy, win a lover or make their fortune. And Liberians are still sweet-natured, if at times exasperating or argumentative.

I hope that I have done justice to the memory of Tado Jackson and Zoelay Retty, Sammy Dahngbae and Betty Leeleh; and to my other friends from Kpaytuo, living and dead, and to Liberia and Liberians. I thank you, dear reader, for accompanying me on part of my African journey by reading this book, which has been fifty years in the making—a truthful account of one of the great adventures of my life.

Acknowledgements

In April 1982, after returning from my two-month visit to Liberia, I spent the next two and a half years researching and writing this book. My friend and colleague Merle White was its first editor. Then came my nephew, Andrew Greenberg, whose airfare on our trip to London I paid for as a thank you for reading it. Bob Nordlie, a Ph.D. in English and a neighbor in Tempe, Arizona, when I lived there, also read most of the book; as did my Peace Corps buddy, Bill Fickling.

After some months of trying, I told my agent in 1985 to stop sending the manuscript to publishers, for I wanted to get on with my life. (I did and that included falling in love, taking over my deceased father's salad dressing business, doubling the work force while improving the bottom line and then selling the business, traveling the world, overseeing the health care of my mother for a decade and writing two books.)

Meanwhile, this manuscript lay in a cardboard box on top of a bookcase in a spare bedroom in my home, undisturbed and unread. In the summer of 2015, I opened the box and for the first time in thirty years read the manuscript. Damn, I said to myself, this is good and ought to be published and read. (I'll admit that maybe I was prejudiced in the matter.)

While there are many things I can't do as well today as thirty-two years ago, I know more about writing and how to tell a story. So I reread the journal I kept as a Peace Corps Volunteer, the stacks of letters I sent to my parents and sister during my Peace Corps service—which they saved and gave to me—and then, the big find, in a dust-covered carton, under a tarpaulin in my attic, long believing that it had been lost when I moved from apartment to apartment and then from house to house, I found and read the 200-page journal I typed, and the notebooks I filled and the carbon copies of letters I wrote, during my 1982 visit to Liberia—and on which I relied, more than any source, to write the original manuscript.

This is essentially the manuscript I wrote thirty-two years ago, but every page—nay, almost every paragraph—has been revised. And in late 2016 into 2017, wishing to bring the story up to date and as I gathered the information, I wrote the Afterword.

On this go-round, the editors have been Mallory Leonard, who worked with me on *Cherry Delight*, a memoir of my family; and Chuck Kelly, a dear friend and colleague from our days at *The Arizona Republic*. A special thanks to Mallory, who suggested the main title. And special thanks to Chuck, an award-winning investigative reporter and an author in his own right. Both write well, know grammar better than I and, like their counterparts before them, both improved the book.

This time, unlike 1984, I sent the *entire* manuscript to Bill Fickling, the only person, other than myself, who read the manuscript *and* who had been a Liberian Peace Corps Volunteer. Bill saved me from many "Liberian errors" and with his almost photographic memory and breadth and depth of knowledge worthy of any contestant on *Jeopardy*— a show, by the way, to which he was addicted—he added incidents and insights to the book. I quote him throughout and treasure the memory of the fifty-year friendship with Bill, my closest friend, who died unexpectedly in October 2016.

Many other people who had worked or lived or live in Liberia or had the requisite medical or technical knowledge read excerpts from the manuscript or, in days before the Internet, responded via letter to my queries. They helped me make sure I got my facts correct, which is the aspect of my writing that I am most proud of. To that end, I thank David Carson, Tado Jackson and Sister Dr. Margaret Chambers, all deceased. I also thank Scott Lewis, Paul Steinwachs, Theresa Hicks, Sammy Dahngbae, Liberty and Angea Tarlo (Tado Jackson's son and daughter, respectively); Joel L. Bleah, Daada Luogan, Oscar Cooper, Paul D. Tuazama Sr., Kyende Bormentar, Dana Barbieri, Andy Patilla, Pete Lester, Dr. Steve Robinson, Dr. Paul Getty and Dr. Austin Murray.

Cheryl Mirkin has been a delight to work with. She designed the marvelous cover and terrific interior of the book. Cheryl is a gifted professional who knows everything there is to know about designing and publishing a book.

312

When I have a computer or technological question or problem, my cousin, Nealla Morton, is always available to fix things—in person, via the Internet or over the telephone. As if she doesn't have a family and job. Thanks once more, Sweetie.

The above are not just people who helped me improve the book: many of those who are gone were friends, while many of those alive are friends. I have broken bread with them. (Make that enjoyed Chinese or Italian food.) And may we continue to do so for many years to come.

— Robert Cherry
Wynnewood, Pennsylvania
June, 2017

I'm at my desk in Kpaytuo circa 1967, writing home about Liberia. (Fifty years later, I'm still writing about Liberia, though now for an audience larger than my family—I hope.)

About the Author

After his Peace Corps service, Robert Cherry became, in turn, a journalist, businessman and author. He has been a general assignment reporter or editor at four newspapers, including *The Arizona Republic*, and his freelance work has appeared in *The New York Times* and *The Jerusalem Post*, among other publications. He is the author of *Wilt: Larger Than Life*, a biography of Wilt Chamberlain, and *Cherry Delight: A Family Memoir*. He lives in Wynnewood, Pennsylvania and Pompano Beach, Florida. (*Photo by Eli Nachmani*)

robertcherry2@aol.com
www.robertcherry.org